THE ULTRA SPY

THE ULTRA SPY

THE AUTOBIOGRAPHY OF WINSTON CHURCHILL'S PERSONAL LIAISON WITH BLETCHLEY PARK

F.W. WINTERBOTHAM

FRONTLINE
BOOKS

THE ULTRA SPY
The Autobiography of Winston Churchill's Personal Liaison with Bletchley Park

First published in Great Britain in 2025 by
Frontline Books
An imprint of Pen & Sword Books Ltd
Yorkshire – Philadelphia

ISBN 9781036135348

A CIP catalogue record for this book is available from the British Library.

Typeset by Lapiz Digital
Printed and bound in the UK by CPI Group (UK) Ltd, Croydon, CR0 4YY.

FSC www.fsc.org
MIX
Paper | Supporting responsible forestry
FSC® C013604

The Publisher's authorised representative in the EU for product safety is Authorised Rep Compliance Ltd., Ground Floor, 71 Lower Baggot Street, Dublin D02 P593, Ireland.
www.arccompliance.com

For a complete list of Pen & Sword titles please contact

PEN & SWORD BOOKS LIMITED
47 Church Street, Barnsley, South Yorkshire, S70 2AS, England
E-mail: enquiries@pen-and-sword.co.uk
Website: www.pen-and-sword.co.uk
or
PEN AND SWORD BOOKS
1950 Lawrence Road, Havertown, PA 19083, USA
E-mail: uspen-and-sword@casematepublishers.com
Website: www.penandswordbooks.com

CONTENTS

Chapter 1

FIRST CHANCE

There have been many changes during the past ninety years. I should like to give some idea of what it was like to have been born the son of a fairly prosperous solicitor in a country town in the west of England during the last years of the old Queen's reign. My father had followed his father and grandfather in the business of law, and I was obviously destined to carry on the family tradition. My father, a large, kindly man, had not married until he was nearly forty, so by the time I knew him he was almost middle-aged, with a somewhat reddish moustache and twinkling blue eyes. His life was his daily work at his office, which eased off a little only when he was nearly eighty. He died aged eighty-four.

My mother was more ambitious, the daughter of a fairly wealthy family whose ancestry went back to King Edward I in the Middle Ages. Her charm and ability were undoubtedly the source of the many friends that made up our life in those halcyon days before the First World War. It was my mother who ran the family and gave all the orders. Tall and dark, she was considered a great beauty, inheriting her looks both from her parents and from the ancestral family of the Vernons, of which the famous Dorothy Vernon was a great beauty of her own time.

We lived in a rambling old family house, surrounded by our own fields, on the side of a hill just outside the town of Stroud. There was of course only horse transport in those days, and we had a strong cob and a smart dog-cart ably driven by my mother. There was also a tub-cart, mainly for my sister and myself, which was driven by Mr Brush, the groom, who was also the gardener; and there was an open cart to carry the luggage to and from the station when necessary.

On my fourth birthday I was given a beautiful new prayer book, covered in dark-blue velvet, with the head of Queen Victoria on the front in silver. It was now that I joined my sister, who was three years older than myself and had beautiful golden hair, and my mother and father on their Sunday walk to church. On the way back we always had to call in at the house of one of my father's cousins who was a manager of the Capital and Counties Bank at Stroud. He and his wife lived in an old house above the bank. Uncle Edward and Aunt Emily, as we called them, had also been to church, he in a frock coat and a top hat and she all in black with a Victorian bonnet. My mother and father were dutifully offered a small glass of sherry in the shaded drawing room, where the pale mauve coverings of the chairs and sofa were carefully guarded against the sunlight. It was all very dim and proper, as were all Victorian Sundays. I felt I had been badly let down when I was told some while later that Queen Victoria had died.

We had the usual Victorian nursery presided over by a nanny. There were of course my sister's doll's house, a good rocking-horse and a polyphone which played tunes off the revolving metal discs. Sadly, Nanny left us when I was four and a half years old, to follow the nanny tradition of marrying a policeman.

My mother used to take us out for drives in the dog-cart. She was an expert driver and would reach a cracking pace, with old Jock the deerhound following close behind. She took us to the meets of the Berkeley Hunt or up the Stroud valley, but more often we went up the steep Butter Row Hill, where we had to walk on to Minchinhampton Common, that great expanse of free land that later became our playground.

My mother had been educated in France and was determined that we should learn to speak French as fluently as she did herself. So, when our nanny left she engaged a French *bonne* (nursemaid) to look after us. The poor girl spoke no English, and I am afraid we gave her a rotten time. There were two *bonnes* before Mother finally decided to get us an English governess. We called her Trunny, and she remained with us for many years after my sister and I had started school. I think the chief change in our lives when she arrived was that we had to join her when she indulged her passion for walking. I suppose she found it the best way to keep us occupied when we were not doing our lessons. We went for long walks over the green fields around us and sometimes we would go along the Gloucester Road, which entailed walking down a small lane past the brewery, where the hissing steam and the glorious smell of beer were great attractions. A little further on we saw the brewer's drays being loaded up with their barrels of beer, and two enormous horses impatiently waiting to take them around to the public houses. Since this was long before the motorcar we were allowed to bowl our wooden hoops along the footpath and to follow them even if the hoops ran off into the road, since most of the traffic was slow and horse-drawn.

Trunny was also allowed to take us shopping in the town. We used to pass the livery stables, where we hired a cab if we were taken out to parties. The inside of those horse cabs always smelt of musty leather, eau de Cologne, cigars – or all three. They were also cold, so we had to take large woollen rugs to keep our legs warm as the old horse clip-clopped along the road to one of the houses of our friends and back again in the evening. We used to pass a Mr Bishop, the fishmonger, in his blue apron and straw hat. He always had masses of Dover sole, turbot, cod, mackerel and, hanging above, the large yellow smoked haddock, almost eighteen inches long and a foot wide, full of great flakes of white meat. Mr Bishop used to hose them down with water every now and again to keep them fresh.

It was a great treat to go to the barber, because after snipping away at one's hair he would produce a large rotary brush which he attached to a rubber belt from the pulley in the ceiling. This strange contraption mechanically brushed one's hair in all directions. It was a marvellously exhilarating experience, but I believe it was later thought to be dangerous to the operator, so it was scrapped. From the barber we would go across the street to the grocer, whose bags of dried peas and beans and rice and brown sugar, with their wooden scoops for filling the cone-shaped paper bags so deftly made by the grocer from a sheet of brown paper. Then on the way back we would go to an old loft which had been turned into a workshop by Mr Wood, a rather quiet little man, but an excellent woodworker. He would show us the different types of wood which he used to repair the antique furniture which he bought at sales for my mother. He loved his work and would explain to us how old furniture is like an old friend – it goes on from one generation to another, it is warm and smooth, and it can ever evoke memories of home and times gone by. Mr Wood was quite right, and his antiques are with my family today.

My mother, bless her, always believed that good health came first, and she was convinced that in summer the air of Stroud, which lay in the valley at the western foot of the Cotswold Hills, was not fresh enough, so she rented a small house on the top of Minchinhampton Common which was reached from Stroud by a long steep hill called the Butter Row. It was probably the best-remembered road in my youth, because when we drove up it in the tub-cart we always had to get out and walk most of the way. Here in the summer, we had our first ponies, which we learned to ride all over the Common. There was no one to teach us to ride, so we would take the ponies with their bridles on to the Common and ride them bareback. The Common was a glorious open area on the edge of the Cotswold Hills. I never knew its actual size but to us children it seemed endless. The old mounds and ditches around the edges indicate it must have been some sort of ancient Roman fort. There was a golf course, a reservoir and two long straight Roman roads which bisected the Common and met at Tom Long's Post, where the old gibbet once stood. As we grew up this was our vast playground. The shallow turf was always short and dry and kept grazed by the commoners' cattle. In the summer it was a mass of wildflowers – harebells and gentians, wild thymes, cowslips and orchids.

It was here too that my grandfather Graham, who used to come and stay with us and tell me his stories of his travels in the Pacific, taught me how to make and fly a box kite out of a few straight sticks and *The Times* newspaper. He was a cycling enthusiast and had learned to ride on one of the old penny-farthings, and he insisted on giving me my first bicycle too. And it was on Minchinhampton Common that I first started to play golf; I won my first golf prize for putting in 1904 when I was seven. When I began to play a little more seriously my mother presented me with a steel-headed mashie which had been made by the famous Benny Sayers, the professional at North Berwick.

Minchinhampton Common was where we saw our first motorcars. They used to come up to practise on the long, straight roads, which had been made out of the soft yellow Cotswold stone, so that one could see them coming some miles off. It gave us the greatest excitement, when we saw a cloud of dust in the distance, to rush to the gates of our little house and watch the motorcars go by. It was a little time later that my mother took me over to meet some friends in Bibury, where the husband had himself bought a single-cylinder motorcar which seated two in front and two in a little compartment behind with small round seats. It was in this that I had my first ride in a motorcar. We were going quietly along a straight road when in the distance we saw a farmer coming our way in his horse and cart. It was all too much for the horse, which reared up and turned the cart over into a nearby ditch. We had a great job rescuing the unfortunate farmer and his horse and carriage, but he was most polite and told our friend that he could never have wished to be run over by a nicer gentleman.

When I was about eight years old and my sister was eleven, my mother thought it high time that we went to an even more bracing climate for our holidays. This was to be Felixstowe on the east coast. We knew another family of three girls who went up there with their parents, so we were not alone. I still remember those cold mornings when we were all shooed into the sea. In the evenings we used to walk up the pebbly beach and pick up pieces of real amber and cornelians. I was collecting them, of course, for the prettiest of the three girls, but come Christmas time I found that most of the good pieces were put on the end of long hat pins and sent as Christmas presents to our aunts.

It was about this time that a new instrument, the telephone, was installed in our house in Stroud. I never knew how much it cost to make a telephone call, but my mother used to say it was much cheaper to use the red penny stamp with King Edward VII's head on it. Nevertheless, the telephone made a great difference to our lives and meant that we could keep in touch with our young friends more easily. In consequence there were more parties and tennis, and cricket matches to go to.

So many exciting things happened in 1907. I went to my first school at St Andrews, Eastbourne. When I set off from Stroud station my father came to see me off and gave me the traditional tip of five shillings, and my mother bought me a daily paper. This proclaimed the most exciting news: the Wright Brothers had actually flown a heavier-than-air machine in America. I was met by an aunt in London and after lunch we took a growler, as a horse-drawn cab was called, to Victoria station to join the swarm of boys in the Pullman cars on the train to Eastbourne. Among my luggage was a square, wooden tuckbox, full of goodies and jams. Unfortunately, all of it had to be handed over to the matron of the school and doled out as she thought fit.

St Andrews was a marvellous place. It was just outside the town and its playing fields stretched up to the Downs, but it was near enough to the sea for us to go bathing in the summertime. It was run by the then well-known headmaster E.L. Brown and his two brothers plus six or seven young masters. The school was so popular that E.L.B., as he was called, would never take more than ninety-eight boys, because (so he said) if he once passed the hundred he would not know where to stop. I enjoyed every moment of my years at St Andrews, where we not only played cricket and football but fives and squash racquets and where the punishment for any minor offence was to dig up a given number of plantains in the playing fields instead of the old-fashioned penalty of writing out so many hundred lines about what you must not do.

There was a cold plunge-bath into which we all had to dive every morning and where Sergeant Jefferies taught us to swim. Diving was easy to learn; you stood on the edge of the baths and Sergeant Jefferies took hold of your ankles and tossed you over his head. At half-term in the summer one's parents came down and there were strawberry teas in the hayfields next to the cricket grounds. My mother and sister stayed at the Grand Hotel, where I first listened to Degroot and his Palm Court Orchestra, who became such a popular feature of the radio when I first made my own set with earphones some years later.

That same year my parents bought their first family motorcar, a shining red Clement Talbot with beautifully curved coachwork and a hood that came over the front windscreen and was held by two long straps on the front mudguards. It had two enormous brass headlamps which one filled with carbide and a drip feed of water to produce the gas; the rear light was an ordinary oil lamp. The brass horn was operated by squeezing a rubber bulb. There were no self-starters for many years to come – one just wound the handle at the front of the vehicle. But it all worked, from the throttle on the steering wheel to the long brass handbrake.

That summer too, the old home in Stroud was sold and we moved to a magnificent mansion, called Moor Court, on the western edge of Minchinhampton Common. It was a paradise for the young. There were large gardens, and one looked out of the windows of the great rooms across the Severn Valley to the Welsh Hills some forty miles away. Down below the house sheltered from the wind were wonderful greenhouses, a long peach house, which also grew nectarines and figs, and more heated greenhouses which grew grapes as well as the flowers for the large conservatory which was attached to the house. Just outside the front gates leading on to the Common was the golf course, and without disturbing the golfers I could get a good deal of practice on a green close by among the dunes. The Common was of course an ideal place for riding our ponies.

As in the old house, there was no electric light or central heating. The great rooms had large fireplaces which took much of the time of the tweeny (between-maid) to keep in order and light. The lighting was mainly gas and lamps. In the front of the house was a portico under which carriages could load or unload in the dry, and above the portico were two bedrooms, the lower one of which was mine. Just outside my window a flycatcher used to build her nest and in a yew tree close by a golden-crested wren made her home. There was a rookery too within the grounds, and we now had our own Jersey cattle for milk and cream. For Sunday lunch my father would carve a large sirloin of beef with a tender undercut and after the dining room had been served it went down to the servants' hall. George the garden boy had to look after the mowing, which was done by a fat cob. In the Lodge by the gates lived Mr Dean, who acted as both chauffeur and groom. Alas, as my father grew older, the walk up the steep path from the little station in the valley got too much for him and when in 1919 I came home from being a prisoner of war in Germany, I found that the big house had been sold and the family were now installed in a charming Cotswold house closer to my father's office.

At the age of fourteen I duly took my entrance exams for Charterhouse. The school had originally been founded in London in 1611, but at the end of the nineteenth century it had been moved to a wonderful site on the Surrey Hills above the town of Godalming. There were some 600 boys in the ten houses, and the school had splendid grounds for all the usual games together with squash and real racquet courts, and large baths as well as the River Wey to bathe in. My first year there, 1911, was the tercentenary of the school's foundation, and the headmaster was also retiring. I think we had a half-holiday every week of the term.

It was also during this first term that all schools were given a week's exeat for the Coronation of King George V and his queen. I went to London to stay with my uncle Lindsey, who had obtained for us splendid seats in the stands which lined both sides of the Mall from Buckingham Palace to Admiralty Arch in order to see the Empire Procession on the first day; we also had seats opposite Westminster Abbey for the Coronation on the second day.

As we sat waiting for the procession, we admired the brilliant scarlet uniforms of the Foot Guards lining the route and listened to their bands playing. Then came the Life Guards, white plumes from their silver helmets flying in the breeze, their drawn swords glinting in the sunshine. After them came the open landau with the King and Queen, drawn by six beautiful horses, with postillions and outriders. The King was dressed in his admiral's uniform, with gold epaulettes and cocked hat; Queen Mary was all in white, wearing a magnificent hat and cascades of royal jewels. On either side of the carriage rode the two great heroes of the time: Lord Roberts of Kandahar on a rather excitable chestnut, and the more sedate Lord Kitchener of Khartoum riding a well-mannered black, white plume from their field marshall's cocked hats dancing as they rode. Immediately behind the royal carriage rode the crowned heads of Europe and the princes of India, the colour and the brilliance of uniforms and turbans raising tremendous cheers from the crowds. I remember particularly seeing the Kaiser riding an enormous horse, a golden eagle on top of his helmet and beside him the Tsar of Russia in a dazzling white uniform. Never have so many crowned heads, before or since, ridden together.

They were followed by the Indian Cavalry as a mark of honour, the pennants flying on their lances, and all the troops of the dominions and colonies – Canadian Mounties with their scarlet coats and splendid black horses, mounted troops from Australia and New Zealand and South Africa.

The procession up the Mall must have lasted an hour and, as the cheering of the crowds and the music of the bands died down, we were to learn that this Empire Procession wound its way right to the East End of London and back again to Buckingham Palace on a different route so that all London would see it.

The next day came the Coronation itself, and from our seats opposite the great doors of Westminster Abbey we watched once again the cavalcade of the Household Cavalry escorting the King and Queen, now dressed in their ermine robes and riding in the great Irish glass and gold coach drawn by six greys, the postillions this time wearing gold-braided uniforms. We stayed in our seats, during the ceremony in the Abbey until, with a great roar from the crowd, the King and Queen came out of the Abbey doors wearing their magnificent crowns. They stood for a while acknowledging the cheering before they set off once more for the Palace.

It was not long after the Coronation celebrations that there was to be a royal review of the British fleet, the lifeline of the Empire, and I was lucky enough to get an invitation from my uncle Owen to go and spend a week on his yacht at Cowes to see the review. There were three lines of ships stretching from Spithead to The Needles, and the day before the review we were able to sail up and down the Solent between the lines of ships, and we could see the sailors on board making ready for the following day. I suppose there has never been such a collection of ships of the Royal Navy as were assembled at that time. There were the great battleships like Dreadnought with their vast sixteen-inch guns, then came the battle cruisers followed by the ordinary cruisers and the destroyers, and, last but not least, the submarines and the fleet auxiliaries. I cannot remember the number of ships present but the lines at anchor seemed endless. On the following day the King in full admiral's uniform stood on the bridge of the royal yacht as it made its slow progress up and down the lines he could see the crews in their white summer uniforms lining the rails of the ships. The royal salute of guns was deafening and the spectacle on that hot summer's day was one of the most memorable of my young life.

Chapter 2

SECOND CHANCE

It all really started when I somehow contracted measles, closely followed by the German variety, at Charterhouse in 1913. The fact that even at fourteen I was already over six feet tall had had some ill effect on my heart and the doctors proposed a long sea voyage. I opted for round the world.

There were probably several reasons for this. Firstly, there had been my grandfather's wonderful tales of his own travels as a young man in New Zealand and the Pacific islands. Then, as a result of his stories, I had avidly collected dominion and colonial stamps. Finally, I had been thrilled by the celebrations at the Coronation of King George V and Queen Mary. I was brought up in the days when the British Empire covered half the world. Now I wanted to see it.

My school agreed that I should take a six months' exeat so long as I studied for my Cambridge exams. But by far the best education and preparation for the very demanding life I was to lead in the war-torn and changing years of the twentieth century were the experiences I had in the various countries I visited in 1913.

It was late September of 1913 when I said goodbye to my parents and joined the boat train in London bound for Liverpool. Small groups of Canadians who had been on holiday in England were greeting each other, and among them I noticed a tall, white-haired man whom I was later to get to know as Mr Pemberton, the principal real-estate dealer in Vancouver. Young men were clustering round his attractive daughter. My cabin trunk and suitcase were stowed away, and I tried to settle down for what was the most exciting journey I had ever embarked on.

I was sixteen, but since I was already six foot tall I could pass as several years older. As the boat train drew along the quay at Liverpool I got my first view of the White Star liner *Laurentic*. She was 15,000 tons, a great ship for those days, and was propelled by vast reciprocating engines, which I was lucky enough to be taken to see by the Chief Engineer, at whose table I was placed in the saloon. These engines had not yet been replaced by the turbine.

I had taken with me such books as I should need for my studies, and a rowing machine to try and keep myself fit on the various sea voyages I would be making. I was allowed to set it up on the boat deck and it was here that I made friends with a Canadian boy about my own age who had been in England with his father, a well-known Montreal jeweller. I let the boy have a go at the machine; the father was grateful and later took me under his wing and gave me a marvellous description of all that I should see in Canada, explaining how different it would be from my life in the English countryside. His pride in Canada was fully justified, but I was none the less unprepared for waking one morning off the coast of Newfoundland to find that the temperature had dropped with a thud and that we were steaming among giant icebergs. We had reduced speed considerably and were giving these great ice islands a wide berth, but as we passed them the temperature fell well below freezing. Everyone was thankful when we entered the great St Lawrence river and drew alongside the wharf at Quebec. Later I stood in front of the Frontenac Hotel, where Montcalm had tried in vain to hold Quebec for France.

When we got to Montreal my friends' excitement was infectious. I shall never forget the first time I heard the clang, clang, clang of the great bells mounted on top of the railway engines, those vast black monsters with their searchlights and cow-catchers which pulled the heavy grain trains from the prairies and the long sleeper trains across the continent and over the Rockies to Vancouver. I was shown with pride the great corn stores and, above all, in the distance the yellow streetcars, or trams, which had only just been introduced in the city.

It was autumn and the golden colour of the maple trees covering Mount Royal was unforgettable. I took a horse-drawn open cab and we clip-clopped our way up the winding road to the top of the Mount and looked down at the lovely old Victorian buildings of Montreal. I then planned my journey across Canada with the help of the Canadian Pacific Railway, seated in their palatial offices. The CPR was not only the backbone but the great developer of Canada. I decided to go to Toronto to see the Niagara Falls, and then to catch a boat across the Great Lakes, before rejoining the railway, which would take me on my journey west.

I had been warned by Mr Pemberton aboard the *Laurentic* about the great boom in real estate, that it would be taken for granted that I, as an Englishman, had come to Canada to buy land and that there were crooks who were selling land they did not own. It was therefore important to establish the legal title before purchase. He was so thoughtful that I forebore to tell him that I was not a real-estate buyer. Nevertheless, the morning after I arrived at my hotel in Toronto I was rung up by a man with an English accent who claimed to come from Gloucestershire and declared that of course I would know his friend the Duke of Beaufort – would I like to buy a choice plot of land? I went down to breakfast and the bellhop in the lift had an equally promising bargain to offer me.

The Niagara Falls were indescribable. Like everything else in Canada, they were vast. The walk along the platform attached to the rocks, actually behind the falling water, was breathtaking. To see this unbelievable mass of solid water, hurtling downward only a few feet in front of one, was like a trip to the Underworld. I crossed the bridge on to the United States side of the Falls just to record my first visit to that country before making my way to the port whence the boat would take me on my journey west. Alas, there had been a violent storm on the lake and the boat had not been able to come back east. There was no accommodation, just a few houses and offices and the ever-present white pegs showing some area of real estate for sale. But the *Imperial Limited* the great CPR train that runs east to Vancouver, was alerted, and all the passengers had to tramp about four miles – carrying their suitcases – up a small railway track to the little town of London on the main line, where the train would stop for us. I had never been so glad when I heard the clang, clang of the bell in the far distance. It was getting dark as the headlight came round the last bend and very soon we were able to climb up into the warmth of the long green coaches, which doubled as sleepers at night. We were welcomed aboard by the smiling, coloured car attendants in their spotless white jackets. How good dinner tasted that night! I found no difficulty in falling asleep in my upper berth.

I woke to find the train at a standstill and made my way to the washroom where I discovered that we were alongside the shore of Lake Superior. We were told that the storm which had prevented my boat from coming back from the west had washed out part of the line ahead of us and we were likely to be stuck there for the rest of the day until the line had been made good. It was night again before we moved on. Next morning we were once again at a standstill. This time there had been a head-on collision with a repair train further up the line. The CPR certainly had problems. Luckily I had no special date, except with the ship which was to take me across the Pacific from Vancouver Island. I was due to leave the train at Golden, on the other side of the

Rockies, to stay for a few days with a young friend who had emigrated and taken up a freeholding close to the Columbia river. It took all that day to clear the line, but at last we set off and, as we started to cross the great prairies of Central Canada, the vastness of everything astonished me. No longer the small green fields of England, with villages and woodlands; here was mile upon mile of flat, open land, as yet only partly cultivated, which could feed a continent with corn. We stopped for a while at Regina, where the CPR had a large depot with grain trucks about three times the size of those we used in England, their big black engines waiting to haul the wheat to Montreal. Farmers were bringing in their golden harvest in their horse-drawn wagons to fill the grain silos from which in turn the wheat would be automatically loaded into the trucks. The railway ran along the northern side of the town, which consisted mainly of official buildings and houses for the workers, but at the far end of the one main street were the barracks and offices of the Canadian Mounted Police, now becoming well known for their exploits all over Canada.

The clang of the engine's bell told us it was time to climb back up into the train. Most of the passengers had been stretching their legs on the platform, which was at ground level, but I had gone to the observation platform at the end of the train. There I had found Mr Pemberton's daughter standing alone, tall and straight, looking out with pride at her heritage.

I talked later to a passenger, himself a farmer, who told me why Canadian wheat was so popular with the millers in Europe. He explained that it was sown in the autumn when the ground was already too cold for it to germinate; then the winter snow kept it free from frost until it thawed in the spring, giving water and warmth to the seed. Growth was then rapid and by harvest the grain was full and hard and dry, ready to travel anywhere in the world.

The long haul across the prairies seemed endless until we came to the foothills of the Rockies and Calgary, where they were more interested in cattle and cowboys than in grain. I had been told by the CPR of a small place called Banff at the foot of the mountains where there was a thermal swimming pool and an hotel. The idea was to have a break from the railway coaches and to get some idea of the mountains that now had to be climbed. There were only two other visitors to this solitary, wooden hotel, but the swim in the natural warm water was just what I needed. Of course, there had to be an attractive Canadian girl who came and swam with me, and later served me and one other guest with dinner.

I boarded the next train going west the following day to make the memorable crossing of the Rocky Mountains. Surely this must rank as one of the greatest feats of railway engineering. As the two great engines hauled the train up the winding corkscrew track, one could look up from the observation platform and see the head of the train already on a curving line above one. In places there were snow sheds covering the track to keep the line clear where drifts were known to have blocked the rails. It seemed a gigantic effort to get the train to the top of the Kicking Horse Pass, where a notice proclaimed, 'The Summit'. The run down the western side to the Columbia river must have required strong and reliable brakes. At Golden, the small station by the bridge over the river, there were two or three houses and a general store, and it was there that I got down, hoping to meet John Chalmers and spend a few days in his log cabin, three miles down the river on the wooded slopes. I was not surprised after all the delays to find that he was not there. However, the kindly storekeeper got a message through to him and after some hours he arrived with his horse and open buggy.

After loading my luggage and some stores, we set off. It was cold now, for the first snows had just begun, and the horse's hooves rang on the frosty road. Before long, we turned up a dirt track to the cabin. I was in for a pleasant surprise: his two sisters had come out to see how he was getting on and he had acquired a partner, Pete, a splendid Norwegian who was helping him to clear the timber off the holding. Pete had two strong horses which drew the felled trees out into the open where I was given the job of cutting off the branches. Pete and John wielded their glistening axes and the ring of the steel as they struck the trees echoed through the forest. The two sisters did the cooking, and I was pleased to hear that sometimes partridges could be shot. An old bear had come down the mountain to her cave in the hillside above the cabin, so all doors had to be locked at night when the creature used to forage among the empty tins in the trash can.

The temperature had dropped to thirteen below zero as John drove me down the frozen dirt track and alongside the river, its green glacial waters now swirling in its haste to get south. The train was on time, and I knew that the next day I should be looking out on the green lands of British Columbia. The car attendant took some delight in pointing out to me the asylum on a nearby hill, with the remark that it was where they put the English. I asked him whether the view of the railway from the asylum was equally good. He looked after me well after that. I was learning fast.

Vancouver was obviously growing rapidly and had all the atmosphere of a boom town. Among the Victorian buildings, now being surrounded by new homes, stood one big high-rise block of some nine or ten storeys. The Pemberton Building was painted white with green window frames and stood out in the old town for all to see. I called round to see the great man and he told me with some excitement how the CPR had decided to build a new branch line from Calgary up to Edmonton way north of Vancouver and with their usual sagacity had put up for sale alternate lots on either side of the proposed line. They were selling like hot cakes and must have paid for a large part of the construction of the line. Land around the small town of Edmonton was also going sky high – it was a sort of fever. There had been a young man with a charming voice who used to come and sing at some of my mother's parties. He had emigrated to Vancouver, so I looked him up. He at once co-opted me to help him to fence a plot of real estate which he had bought just outside the town. It had to be done quickly before a new owner of an adjoining plot had pushed his fence a yard or two too far. Meanwhile, Mr Pemberton kindly put me up for his club, where I was able to stay in comfort.

I moved on after a few days by boat to Victoria on Vancouver Island. It was almost like coming back to England: the harbour was full of small yachts, and behind lay green fields and woodlands and typical English houses. Here again I had an introduction to a delightful family and was shown how carefully their island was being preserved for its residents. I watched a golf match between the English professional, Ted Ray, and the local champion. It was hard to believe I was so far from home.

My friend offered to run me down to the harbour in his big Cadillac, which would, he said, make it easier to get someone to carry my heavy suitcase aboard. The new CPR liner *Empress of Asia* came slowly into the bay; the large entry doors on her starboard side opened and, as she came alongside the long timber pier, the bright lights shimmered across the water, while a Philippine band played its fascinating music. The effect was magical. This band also played for us every evening at dinner time. There were not many passengers to go aboard – most had done so at Vancouver – so we sailed again before nightfall. I found my trunk had been duly stowed in my cabin and a Chinese steward was waiting to unpack such clothes as I should need on the ocean. I was to sit at the doctor's table and from him I learned that the few Canadian passengers were mostly Canadian missionaries and their families going out to China.

The ship was due to take the shorter northern course to Japan, coming close to the Aleutian Islands. The ocean here was anything but pacific and we had a rough ride for the first few days. There were a number of children belonging to the missionary families and the great game was to rush from one side of the ship to the other counting the number of whales we could see sending up their great spouts of water. The doctor told me that despite the few passengers in the first class, below there were hundreds of Chinese going back to China for the New Year, or, in the case of the very old, going back to die in their beloved land; many of these never made it and Doc was kept busy embalming them – apparently quite a lucrative sideline. Despite the weather, the *Empress*, with her new, straight, sharp bow, was going to reach Yokohama on time.

Chapter 3

FAR EAST

As we steamed a more south-westerly course towards Japan we left the whales behind, but now we were joined by a large school of porpoises, those wise mammals of the ocean who are believed, by seamen, to be the incarnation of drowned sailors. They evidently were not used to the extra speed of the *Empress of Asia* and from time to time had to make a mad rush to keep up with us. We came slowly into Yokohama Bay, and I had my first view of the great god-mountain of Japan, Fujiama, a vast grey volcano now extinct. The sun was setting and the white snow mantle which hangs like a necklace around the summit had turned into a golden crown – an elegant welcome to Nippon. A fleet of sampans also welcomed us as they fussed around the ship. The usual medical customs and routines were soon dealt with, and I was then greeted by a smiling Mr Suzuki bowing three times. Standing about five feet two inches tall and wearing a smartly tailored brown suit, he had a small black moustache above an almost perpetual smile. He explained that he was a government-appointed guide – I had asked for one in advance – and that he would show me anything I wanted to see in Japan. He also wore a Homburg hat turned up in front, which was soon turned down to match my own. In order that I should not forget his name he told me that it was the equivalent of Mr Smith in England.

The efficient CPR had agreed to forward my cabin trunk and my rowing machine to the Japanese Line Offices in Shanghai, where I should be boarding the *Kumano Maru* for the voyage to Sydney. Now for the first time I was to explore the lifestyle of a truly oriental country, and the doctor on the *Empress* had told me, 'If you can't be good, be careful.'

Mr Suzuki and I took a sampan for ourselves and our baggage to the shore amid a hive of activity mostly of rather short but evidently strong men dressed in short blue overalls on the backs of which there were letters in white circles showing which firm or business they worked for. This was also to be my introduction to the rickshaw, that excellent mode of transport in the Far East. Ranged in a line, they looked like a row of some strange animals at prayer, their black hoods covering them from the weather, their slender shafts laid flat on the ground like the arms of a praying insect. In front of them sat the rickshaw boys with their large round waterproof hats, all eager to take one at a gentle trot to one's destination. Mr Suzuki uttered a few clicks of the tongue, and we were away to a splendid European hotel.

In 1913 Yokohama had not, of course, yet succumbed to the high-rise block. The hotel was a two-storey stone building, as were most of the houses in the city, but in the outskirts they appeared mostly to be made of timber and paper with tiled roofs. I enjoyed a European meal while Mr Suzuki went off, no doubt to get his supper of rice and fish. We had arranged to meet later to discuss plans for the three weeks I had planned to spend in this old country. It eventually boiled down to whether I was primarily interested in temples or girls. I suggested a suitable mixture of both, plus some trips into the countryside to see how the Japanese lived. At length, smiling and bowing, Mr Suzuki bade me goodnight. I asked him to forget the bowing, but he insisted that he should do so here in public otherwise the government might think he was being impolite.

In the event he proved to be a wonderful guide and organised the personal side of Japanese life which I wanted to see. I thought it best to get the temples over as soon as possible and we arranged to start the following day.

I have seen temples of various religions in many parts of the world, but Niko is different. Here a great park has been fashioned in much the same way as one would make a miniature garden with little hills and valleys, lakes and rivers, and everywhere beautiful trees. Small roads connect the various temples and half-moon-shaped red-lacquer bridges cross the streams; in a shallow lake stands a toree, that fabulous gateway to be seen all over Japan, its two pillars carrying a splendid carved cornice arising at each end like curved wings, compelling you to admire their reflection in the still waters. Among all this are the temples, their bright red, lacquered walls gleaming in the sun, topped with ornate tiled roofs.

There are two types of temple, one for the followers of Buddha, the other for the Shinto religion of worship of one's ancestors. In the Buddhist temple the bronze image of the god himself sits cross-legged on his cushioned throne, his well-filled tummy matching the serenity of his face. Parts of his bronze body shine where the faithful have rubbed him in the hope that their own pains in that part of the body may be relieved. From time to time a gong may sound, but stillness is the essence of the shrine and only outside on the stone steps, flanked by carved stone lanterns, does the clatter of the wooden sandals of the women and children disturb the peace. The Shinto shrines are much the same, perhaps a little more gilt and candles, with the sound of little bells as the worshippers try to attract the attention of their venerable ancestors. Here, for a few yen, one can drink saki or rice wine out of a little saucer just to help the ancestors along in the next world, and for a few more yen one can take the ornate little saucer away.

A charming, rather elderly American couple had come with us to Niko and that evening in the hotel they were trying desperately to record in their diaries all they had seen. I suggested they should copy out much of the excellent guidebook that Mr Suzuki had given me. They found they had missed the famous carving of the three monkeys, one covering its head, another its eyes and the third its mouth – the original of think no evil, see no evil and speak no evil.

Next day there was to be a tour by rickshaw into the countryside away from Yokohama. Every square foot of land that was able to grow something in this land of mountains and volcanic soil was used. In 1913 Japan had little industry or cash to import food, vegetables and rice had to be won from the barren soil, while fish was supplied from the vast industry around the islands' shores. In the villages of timber, thatch and paper houses, life was obviously hard. Women and children always wore rather drab kimonos, with high wooden sandals which at least kept their feet above the open drains which ran along the side of the road. The relief was to come that evening when Mr Suzuki had planned a visit to the red-light area of Yokohama.

It is, I think, difficult for a European to visualise the exotic and picturesque way in which the sale of sex was presented in 1913 in Japan. When we arrived in the red-light area in our rickshaws the milling crowds forced us to abandon our transport, so we asked our drivers to meet us at the other end of the street in an hour or more. On either side of the wide street, a quarter of a mile or more in length, were houses with their shop fronts open to the street. There were no windows only tall brass pillars highly polished and sometimes twisted like barley sugar, about nine to ten inches apart; these turned the whole street into a series of gilded cages, in which the girls either sat on cushion stools or walked quietly about their stage smoking delicate little pipes, a tiny bowl at the end of a stem ten inches long. Each house had its own colour scheme with brilliant kimonos and contrasting obis, those big silk bows worn at the back of the waist. The wooden sandals and exotic coiffures, with waves of black hair piled high above their beautifully made-up faces and bright red lips, made them look taller than they really were. It was far more like a beauty-cum-fashion show than a sex market. I was standing in front of a gilded cage, watching seven or eight lovely girls in deep red silk kimonos and bright blue contrasting obis, when to my surprise one girl came over to where I was standing, put a delicate hand through the bars and tapped me on the shoulder with her little pipe. With a half-giggle, half-smile she said quietly in English, 'Mister, I love you.' I looked up at her delicate features and wondered how she managed the exotic hairdo, or whether it came off in one piece. I never did find out.

A rather disappointed Mr Suzuki came back with me to the hotel. The next day we would make an expedition to a hot lake and a comfortable hotel up in the hills, where there was a natural hot-water swimming pool and both European and Japanese food.

It was one of those bright autumn mornings with the promise of a nip in the air. Another American couple from our hotel were to accompany us on the trip, and as we assembled in our four rickshaws the charming American wife laughed gaily when a number of children greeted her with the word 'Ohio' which in Japanese means 'Good morning.' We soon discovered that she and her rather portly husband came from Ohio in the United States.

It was to be an uphill journey, so each rickshaw had to have a puller and a pusher to get up the hilly road. At times Mr Suzuki's pusher had to go to the aid of the American husband as he was a bit overweight for his single pusher. Luckily there were little thatched tea houses along the route, only a few miles apart, where we sat out on the verandah and drank green tea out of little bowls. These stops also gave welcome rests to the rickshaw boys. At one large tea house we were given sandwiches and sweetmeats for our luncheon. At last, a somewhat exhausted party of travellers arrived at the modern European hotel.

It was in a lovely setting in the hills, the mist already rising from a hot lake as the evening air began to cool. There was also one of those high thin waterfalls which look like an endless light silk scarf dropping some three hundred feet from the rocks above. This particular one was famous for its suicides. I decided to go and have a bathe in the natural hot-water baths before dinner. These were housed in a wooden building not far from the hotel. In deference to the European clients, the baths had been divided by a wooden screen which came down within a foot or so of the clear blue water. I was alone and wasted little time in getting out of my clothes – bathing costumes were not worn in Japan. The hot thermal water was wonderfully relaxing. I had not been in long before I heard someone enter the ladies' department, followed soon after by a splash. Without any sign of embarrassment, a girl floated under the partition and gave me a sweet smile as she stood up. We both laughed and she began splashing me. I caught her hands and whirled her about in the water. The evening was drawing in, and soon a bright light came on and lit up her slender body in the clear blue water. She held my hands and, as I smelt the sweet scent of mimosa in her hair, something more than laughter came into her black eyes. But I never knew her name.

The journey back down hill was a little more frightening than the previous day: our pushers had now become pullers helping to steady the rickshaws. The same tea houses supplied refreshment and the couple from Ohio were delightfully enthusiastic.

It was a more peaceful day when on the morrow we again went out into the country and lunched in a tea house on the edge of a large lake in which Fujiama was reflected. Small fishing boats were dotted around, and the hillsides were covered with magnificent Scotch pines.

My guide thought it was about time I had a real slap-up Japanese dinner in a restaurant in Yokohama which allowed one to sit up at table. Waitresses in white silk kimonos embroidered in the green of their obi fluttered around us. The saki was excellent, and for the first and last time I tasted the principal dish for which the restaurant was famous – raw salmon trout. I manfully got through most of it watched by most of the staff and encouraged by Mr Suzuki. We left amid much bowing, and he now suggested that we spend the rest of the evening at the Geisha. I readily agreed – anything to take my mind off the raw fish. He sorted out the clamouring rickshaw boys again with his now familiar clicks.

One had of course heard plenty of stories about the Geisha girls, but in the event the performance on stage was not breathtaking – colourful, yes, rather like a respectable music-hall show. On one side of the stage sat six girls in blue silk kimonos decorated with the ever-present cherry-blossom motif. They played some rather tricky music on their instruments, which seemed about halfway between banjos and guitars. It was called a samuseng and the twang it made was rather like Mr Suzuki's commands to the rickshaw boys. On the other side of the stage more girls sang in a rather low pitch to match the music, sitting cross-legged on a wooden platform some three feet above the stage. It all looked highly dangerous, but the platform was moved intact off the stage with the singing girls still on it. The programme was also suitably interspersed with troupes of dancing girls in various brilliant-coloured silks. The dances were traditional – no high kicks. I am quite sure that the performance was much admired by the Japanese, but Mr Suzuki was a little bored. I too was glad to get to bed. We had just about done Yokohama, and I felt there was much more of the real Japan to be seen.

Mr Suzuki had suggested I should now learn how a Japanese gentleman would live in a real Japanese hotel. There was, he said, an excellent one near the sea close to Kamakura, a town which claims to have the largest statue of Buddha in the world. We had to make a short journey in a train from Yokohama on the line that ran up to Tokyo. I stood in the corridor in order to see the country as we went by. There was an elderly man in a European frockcoat also in the corridor and I was surprised to find that, as we slowed down to pass through the stations on the route, crowds of citizens would cheer our train. It was only when Mr Suzuki overcame his own shyness and asked me to come back into the carriage that I learned I had been standing next to the Emperor's uncle, who had been up to Yokohama for some function. I did not know at the time that it was highly impolite, if not lèse-majesté, to look at the Emperor or his relations. The elderly man smiled at me as I was led back into the compartment.

After an inspection of the great Buddha, inside which was a shrine where the faithful could worship, our rickshaws were pulled and pushed up a winding hill road to a real, totally Japanese hotel nestling against the side of a hill. It was constructed entirely of wood and paper with wide verandahs running right around it giving access to all the rooms. At ground level there was a freshwater pool full of carp and goldfish, while in an annexe close by was the ever delightful hot-springs bath. Way below on the seashore were endless fishing boats and enormous basketwork containers in which fish could be kept in the seawater until they were needed. As the bicycle bells on our rickshaws heralded our approach, the whole staff of the hotel came out to meet us – the word had evidently been received that an English guest would be arriving. Some of them knelt to replace our shoes with soft slippers, so that the beautifully polished floors of the hotel should not be damaged. I noticed that the staff included a number of girls dressed in pale blue silk kimonos embroidered with green dragons and completed with bright green obis; these girls seemed to have an infectious giggle, whether from nerves or from the sight of me in my Western clothes I never discovered. Mr Suzuki was as efficient as ever. We were led to a lovely room overlooking the sea. The size of the rooms was measured by the number of mats covering the floor, each mat being about six feet by four; a six-mat room was for a single person, but as an honoured guest I had a ten-mat room. The Area Hotel was doing me proud. In the centre of each room was a low table about nine inches high around which one sat cross-legged to eat one's meals. The table had a brass box let into its middle in which burned a charcoal fire and on this one cooked one's meals on a little grid or boiled a kettle for tea. The fire also kept the room warm, though luckily the air was not so cold down by the sea as the twenty degrees of frost we had had up in the hills near Yokohama.

There did not seem to be many other guests in the hotel. I suppose there were only about a dozen guest rooms in all, and anyway it was really a summer resort. At first I felt I should be a bit lonely so I persuaded Mr Suzuki to have his meals with me – he could, I explained, have raw fish if he wanted to. It was early evening before I had settled in and found where the mattresses were hidden behind panels in the wall. The pillows were a little hard – in fact they were filled with sawdust. There was, I was pleased to discover, a nice clean, dark-blue kimono for me to wear in the hotel. It had been a tiring day and so I decided to find the hot baths and get into my kimono before supper. The hot blue water, reputed to be full of health-giving salts, was as before thoroughly relaxing. When I returned to my room I was politely rebuked by Mr Suzuki for not asking a girl to accompany me. I was told it was her job to look after me and undress me and dry me after my swim. I promised to remedy this in the future, and Mr Suzuki agreed it might take a little while to get into the Japanese habits.

Some girls appeared with a red-lacquer plaque which turned out to be a menu, but as it was all in Japanese Mr Suzuki read it out to me. I was told that there were some lovely fruits and sweetmeats to end up with, that the sea food was plentiful and fresh from the sea below me, and that I could cook the prawns or little lobsters on the charcoal fire. We had our own waitresses to look after our meals and there would be two or three personal maids to attend to our every want. No wonder the Japanese gentlemen came to stay here. I began to wish we had come here first of all, now that I had only a few days left before boarding the CPR ship at Tokyo which was to take me on to Shanghai.

I rather felt the need of an easy chair but compromised with a couple of cushions against the cupboard door – one could not lean against the paper walls. It was not long after the girls had cleared up our supper that Mr Suzuki suggested I should go to bed after our long day. He was looking at me a bit sideways – it was only later that I understood why: there was the sound of footsteps outside and at a word from Mr Suzuki the three girls in their blue kimonos came in, pulled out the mattresses and then lined up against the back wall. It was obvious they were having difficulties in keeping their attractive faces straight. Mr Suzuki rose and before leaving explained that it was a custom of

Japan that I, as a guest, should choose which girl I wished to put me to bed and then remain with me for the night. He went on to say that it would be considered impolite not to do so. Who was I to argue with the customs of the country? One of the three girls, a little taller than the others, had a wonderful grin and laughing black eyes – somehow she seemed to know that I would choose her. The others left quietly with some evidently traditional phrases of encouragement and good luck. My number one blue girl came over and bowed, a mischievous twinkle in those oriental eyes. Luckily I had discarded most of my European clothes after my swim.

She must have rolled quietly off her mattress early in the morning for when I finally surfaced she was bathed and dressed, wearing a plain dark-blue kimono instead of the pale-blue silk. She was busy cleaning the room and she suggested I go for a hot bath while she finished. I asked her if she would order some eggs for breakfast, and so later I was able to cook scrambled eggs on toast.

Mr Suzuki came to see us after breakfast. I had just finished telling my number one girl that I was going to call her Cherry, short for cherry blossom, because it reminded me of her lovely complexion. I simply could not pronounce her real name, despite some help from Mr Suzuki. She was so happy and somehow seemed to make it all so perfectly natural. I think she knew I had fallen in love with her. Mr Suzuki too seemed quite delighted. He wanted to make the arrangements for moving on to Kyoto that afternoon, though there were still several days before my ship sailed. I told him I was staying put in this idyllic spot for another two days – he could forget about Kyoto with its old paper-and-wood royal palace, and I would take his word for it that by clever carpentry all the passages creaked as one walked along them, so as to give those guarding the Emperor due warning of anyone's approach. I invited him to take the day off, and Cherry and I would look after ourselves. Later I saw him in a pair of old trousers, with his shirt hanging out in Japanese style, walking briskly towards the village.

I was explaining to Cherry that I was going to remain longer than expected when I noticed a clear strip appearing on the paper panel dividing our room from next door. I had heard male voices there and now I spotted the traditional trick of wetting one's finger and sliding it down the paper panel so that one could see what went on next door; I began to wonder what would happen next. Very soon the panel leading out on to the verandah was opened and a young man bowed and asked in English if he could come in. He was taller than the average Japanese and his good-looking youthful face was longer and had a more aristocratic look than the round ones of his countrymen. He was wearing a dark silk kimono over his trousers. Cherry excused herself as I invited my visitor to sit down on a cushion. I did not know what the etiquette was for entertaining a stranger, but I should not have worried – Cherry came back with some tea and cakes, then bowed herself out again.

Renji Kondo introduced himself. He was almost my own age, and he told me he was on holiday with a tutor after taking his university exams. He explained that his father was owner of a shipping line and he, Renji, was preparing himself to join the firm, and already spoke English and French. This was just what I had been hoping to meet: a well-educated young Japanese who could speak some English. I told him that I was going round the world; he was envious and wished that he could do the same. The Japanese, he said, saw too little of the tall, fair, blue-eyed English. There was not a flicker of an eyelash, but I noticed how he had looked at Cherry when she came in, and he may well have had a look through the gap in the paper earlier on. I was anxious to learn from him the views of a young Japanese on the subject of Japan's economy, its way of life and his hopes for the future. He was thoughtful for a few minutes as we drank our tea and then he began to tell me in his rather faltering English about his hopes for Japan, about the difficulty of getting major industries going, and about the general poverty of the people.

Eventually, the young man rose and bowed, and thanked me for my patience, while I thanked him for talking to me so freely and told him that I had booked a passage on one of his father's ships, the *Kumano Maru*, for the passage from Shanghai to Sydney, Australia. He promised to see that I had the best attention on board.

I was writing a few notes when Cherry returned. We had arranged to go down the hill to town and maybe go to the beach. It was some distance, but we both enjoyed the outdoors and the exercise. I found a little silversmith and bought for Cherry a little silver bracelet. When I slipped it over her dainty hand she almost wept with delight, but with a finger to her lips let it be known that it would be impolite to thank me properly in front of the silversmith.

We passed those idyllic days walking in the gardens, feeding the carp in the pools and ourselves bathing in the hot springs. And then came the hardest part of all.

Cherry was in our room waiting for me. She bowed to me, her cherry lips trembling, and she did not lift her eyes. I picked her up in my arms and held her close to me, my face buried in her sweet-scented hair. Two large tears started to roll down her cheeks, but as I stilled her lips with my own I felt the tension in her body relax. Then I put her down gently on to a cushion. She did not look up as I left the room. I did not like myself one little bit: I had come to Japan as a schoolboy, and there I had come of age; now I began to wonder what my newfound self-confidence had to do with love and hurting other people. My God, how much I had learned in the three weeks I had spent on this ancient island. I went down now to say goodbye to the smiling, bowing staff. Politeness forced me to smile back, despite the dull ache in my heart. I knew now that I should remember Cherry for the rest of my life and despite the oft repeated music of Puccini, I prayed that my butterfly would be happily married and perhaps give one of her children an English name.

I duly saw the imperial palace at a polite distance in Tokyo and was dazzled by a great show of flowers in the park nearby, chrysanthemums of every size and colour. When I finally said goodbye to Mr Suzuki, he bowed six times – he was worth every one of them. I promised him I would write a letter of appreciation to his government. He was delighted.

The *Empress of Japan* was rather a scruffy little ship compared with the large one in which I had crossed the Pacific. She was only 6000 tons, and my tiny cabin was on the non-sunny side of the ship and close to the evil-smelling galley. It was also extremely hot, but the heating could not be turned off. I was a little caustic with the Purser who was complaining that he had not been transferred to the new *Empress of Asia*. My fellow passengers were two boisterous teams of American baseball players and their wives. I was glad it was only a short trip down to Shanghai, yet I forgot all about my discomforts on the following morning when we steamed down the great inland sea of Japan.

The calm waters were protected on either side by the bandy legs of southern Japan. Thousands of little islands were covered with deep green pines, and they were still visible when we steamed into Japan's naval base at Nagasaki in order to coal. Canvases were hung along the decks to stop the coal dust getting into the cabins, a huge barge of coal drew alongside and the wide doors on the side of the ship just below my cabin were thrown open. Then two long planks from the barge to the ship were hoisted at about an angle of forty degrees and the scene began to resemble a maddened beehive. Coolies wearing only loin cloths scuttled up one plank clutching baskets of coal on their heads, tipped their load into the hold of the ship, then ran down the other plank. Their empty baskets were promptly refilled in the barge. This mad rush, accompanied by grunts from the coolies and the clatter of the coal, went on all night. I had managed to persuade the Purser to give me a cabin on the other side of the ship for the night – he could hardly refuse. Next day the ship had to be washed down by the whole ship's company before we could restart our journey. One felt the only consolation for the wives of the tough coal carriers would be that they would have only a loin cloth to wash – as well as their husbands of course. The easier world of oil and turbines had not yet come.

The short trip from Nagasaki to Shanghai with the baseballers was great fun, and when I got to Hong Kong I watched one of their games. Shanghai was the principal trading door to China, and the main Western countries each had their own enclave in the town and also their own go-downs on the quay. It was here that I saw for the first time some of the Chinese dock workers still wearing their pigtails. At Shanghai the giant Yellow River – actually a brownish colour, full of the rich earth of China – stained the ocean for miles out to sea. I had been recommended to take a rickshaw drive down the Bubbling Wells road out of Shanghai. Here the more prosperous European merchants and bankers had their lovely houses and gardens. A little further on I came to a Chinese theatre which I had been told to visit. Apparently women were not allowed on the stage so female parts were taken by men. All the characters were dressed in brilliant mediaeval Chinese robes. The play had already been going on for two days and was likely to continue for some time yet. As I did not understand any of their speech or posturing I left after a short while.

That same evening, I went on board the Nippon Yusha Kaisha ship, the *Kumano Maru*. I was greeted with a delightful welcome, due no doubt to my young friend Kondo. It was a friendly little ship, but when we had sailed out into the ocean, we were caught in the tail of a typhoon. The Japanese had engaged British captains for their passenger ships in order to attract European customers to the line. Now the Captain and I were the only two people in the saloon for meals; plates refused to stay on the table despite the three-inch-high fiddles, those wooden hurdles which fitted round the tables in rough weather to stop everything sliding on to the floor. Luckily by this time I had got my sea legs and up on deck I felt the challenge that mariners of old had had to face on their sailing ships in days gone by. There were only about ten people in the First Class, but down below, the ship was full of Japanese and Chinese passengers bound for Hong Kong or Manila, or perhaps for the Japanese pearling fleet which operated off Thursday Island at the northernmost tip of Australia. I fear that it soon became obvious that the Captain was a bit too fond of the hard stuff, but the Japanese officers were highly professional. One of our passengers was a young

Austrian who was a salesman for a new fly repellant called Flit; I think he must have made a fortune in Australia. In the storm it was the only time I have seen flying fish soar from the top of one wave to another over the ship itself.

Hong Kong was so very British. There was the usual excellent club, where I was put up for the night I spent on the island. Here again I took a ride in an old open cab with an even older horse to the top of the peak. I managed to eat a pomelo, a sort of giant sweet grapefruit, as I looked out over the spectacular view and watched the coming and going of the junks around the island. As I returned I saw there was a parade of British troops on the broad open space between the town and the sea. I learned that the British Governor was welcoming the French Governor of Indo-China. The inspection of the troops had just been completed when quite suddenly a Chinese funeral procession appeared. It started to cross the square, the coffin, borne on a long pole between two strong men, preceded by outrunners and followed by wailing mourners. There were a few sharp words of command and the whole funeral procession broke into a fast trot, the coffin swinging wildly from side to side and the mourners doing their best to keep up with the procession and wail at the same time. At last, they passed from view, order was restored, and the official welcome continued.

Next day the weather was calm as we steamed out among the many great square-sailed junks, but despite the big eyes painted on either side of their bows it was difficult to navigate – sometimes we had only a few yards to spare. The Captain had found a hard-up English girl among the passengers on the lower deck, who had been a governess to a family on the island. He graciously carried her off to his cabin and she joined our small party.

Our next stop was at Manila, the capital of the Philippines, which had for so long been an outpost of the Spanish Empire but was now an American colony. To me the South Pacific islands have a magnetic attraction all their own, a built-in atmosphere of romance, pirates and palm trees. We had not gone very far before we were to experience a monumental tropical thunderstorm. The great black clouds seemed to gather together in a vast circle around the ship, then the show began. The banging and rumbling was almost deafening at times, and as dusk fell the whole sky for miles around was lit up with continuous lightning. Passengers were ordered inside, and I confess the whole thing was rather frightening. Next came the rain. There is no need to describe a tropical rainstorm – it comes in sheets, not drops. The Captain recommended whisky all round.

As we steamed south the following day – there was no need to swab the decks that morning – we played at island-spotting in between the tense moments of deck quoits: the first to see the top of a coconut tree on the horizon, which eventually emerged as an island, scored a point. Our Austrian friend complained that there were no flies on the ship on which to show us the efficiency of his new fly destroyer, the Captain continued to be not quite sober, the governess asked to come and join us, life was tranquil and warm, I put off my studies and did not even unpack my rowing machine. At our ship's concert I was asked to sing 'My Little Grey Home in the West'. There was a tall, slim Chinese girl on the deck below, who used to blow me a kiss as she came out each morning to hang up her washing in the stern of the ship. The Japanese passengers began to make a huge rice cake for Christmas or the New Year. It was another world.

I was thankful the Japanese did not go in for the ancient British rites of mock shaving and ducking a first-timer crossing the Equator. The little ship did us proud at Christmas; a real Christmas dinner with champagne, turkey, plum pudding and ice cream, the Captain's young lady sitting rather timorously on his right at the top of the table. I doubt that anyone could have realised that it was to be the last celebration of peace on earth for many of us for a long time.

Chapter 4

AUSTRALASIA

As we made our way south between endless small islands, past the Celebes and round the western end of New Guinea, the Chief Officer told me about the treacherous shallows in these areas. Fortunately, the *Kumano Maru* was small and especially suited to these waters, but it must have been a nightmare for the Navigator. Some people say it was here that the mermaid myth was started by the ancient mariners. I was told that there were very large fish which suckled their young from their breasts like humans and that they were said to sun themselves on the sands and rocks in these warm waters. We passed through the Torres Straits to Thursday Island, and in a calm lagoon a Japanese pearling fleet was riding at anchor. On shore there was a little white church which had been constructed from the timber of a large sailing schooner wrecked there some years before. The small settlement had one or two ships displaying every sort of adornment that could be made from mother of pearl, so readily available from the pearling ships. I took the Captain's lady ashore – she seemed happy to be free and on land again. I made her take off her glasses and rumpled up her hair, then stood back and admired her. We had a good laugh, I think the first she had had for some time, then I bought her a mother-of-pearl brooch. It was a happy change of scene for both of us.

It did not take long for the Japanese passengers to go ashore or for the crew to unload the cargo for the pearl fishers, and we took on board some fresh pawpaws for ourselves. It was hot, too hot presumably, because no sooner had we started again on our voyage south than another sort of tropical storm began to develop. This time giant twisters swirling black water spouts started forming out to sea; it was quite uncanny to see the great black clouds pulling these water spouts up towards them, as if by some strange magnetism, and then sending down a helping hand to meet them, after which they started racing towards us on their way to the shore. Navigation became a 'stop and go' to avoid these dangerous pinnacles of swirling, twisting water, each about a hundred feet tall. I counted about six of them coming our way at the same time. The Captain warned us that if we ran into one we might well be swamped. But eventually we left this extraordinary storm behind and sailed, now unhindered and sheltered by the Great Barrier Reef, down the yellow sandy coast of Queensland to Townsville. The Great Barrier Reef is that great wall of coral, built up over thousands of years by the little live polyps, which protects the whole east coast of Australia against the tides and ravages of the Pacific Ocean. It also provides a wide, clear and calm passage for shipping between itself and the shore.

The calm waters inside the Reef were more comfortable and at last we began to enjoy some of the Australian sunshine and also get used to the eucalyptus or gum trees. There were a few small islands inside the reef with an occasional wooden hut and a boat alongside and I had my first sight of Australian Aborigines at Townsville. There had been some at Thursday Island, but I had not been able to see them. There were green pastures as we turned into the Brisbane river. But, though our ship was small, we could go no further, and we had to tie up at Pinkenbar, some distance downriver from Brisbane. Unfortunately, there was a rabbit tannery on the north shore opposite to us, and the smell was terrible. I was advised by Jimmy King, an Australian fellow passenger, to stay the night in Brisbane.

A small railway connected our landing stage with Brisbane, and it also served the homesteads of the farmers, who kept livestock including horses on the fertile, flat fields, where for centuries good earth had been washed down from the hills behind the town. It was delightfully informal, stopping if anyone wanted to get on or off, and little girls acted as ticket collectors. The homesteads were raised on pillars about three or four feet high. I thought at first that this was to keep them dry if the river flooded their meadows, but later I found that all the homes around the town were built the same way so as to have an air cooling beneath the floor. They were all constructed to the same design, the red-painted corrugated iron roof extending some six feet out over a verandah which ran right round the house. In Brisbane there was one main street, Queen Street with a bridge over the river at the top end. Shops and offices on either side of the sandy street had the same sort of roofs which stretched over the pavements. The street surface was ideal for the horses, which were the only means of transport. I booked a room at the hotel near the bridge before walking around to see something of the principal town of Queensland, which was largely populated by Australian Irish – one could hardly miss the blue-eyed girls with their long black eyelashes beneath a wealth of dark hair.

I had the usual six o'clock supper with tea and was preparing for an early night. I could not have been more misguided: it was New Year's Eve 1913. Half the male population of Brisbane must have gathered around the bar or outside and tonight they were going to celebrate. About 10.00 p.m. when the celebration was at its height, the Salvation Army band arrived and struck up just below my bedroom window. They were admirable: they played solidly, drums and tambourines included, until about 2.00 a.m. next morning, they helped the over-inebriated to their homes, they sang hymns and calmed down the argumentative drunks – in fact, they kept the peace.

For breakfast I enjoyed steak and eggs washed down with tea. I was soon to learn that tea in the daytime was the national drink, not only for breakfast but for dinner, tea, supper and night-cap. As I walked to catch the little train back to the ship, I passed barrows on the streets selling small pineapples at around sixpence each and I was told that trials were being carried out to grow sugar cane, while on the green hills of the Darling Downs, rolling away to the west, cattle and sheep stations were doing well. I had no doubt that Queensland was going places.

We left Pinkenbar and its rabbit factory as quickly as possible. One of the officers told me he had caught enough fish overnight to feed all the Japanese passengers left on the ship. A number of newly wed couples had come on board our ship and were going down to Sydney for their honeymoons. I experienced for the first time the Australian custom whereby, when drinks time came round in the evening, all the men gathered at one end of the saloon leaving the women at the other. The black looks I got when I talked to one of the brides did not, however, deter me from ignoring what seemed to me a rather strange practice. I did manage to talk to some of the young men and learned of their exciting plans for Brisbane. As we approached Sydney, the sea took on a strong swell now that the reef was much further from the shore, and the surf was breaking on the sandy beaches which were sheltered on the land side by high dunes covered with scrub. All this gives way rather suddenly to a rocky headland and unless one is prepared to turn sharply to starboard one can easily miss the gap in the Sydney Heads which leads you into one of the most wonderful harbours in the world. Just as suddenly we saw the city of Sydney on the southern side; the harbour itself stretched away to the east as far as the eye could see. It was of course, mid-summer there, in January 1914.

There was a card waiting for me at the Sydney club from Oliphant Shaw, the owner of the sheep station for which I was destined, informing me of the date when I was to meet him in Adelaide. This allowed me a few days in Sydney before I went on to New Zealand. I took a little ferry boat from Rose Bay across the harbour to the north side. There was a little foot pier to take us ashore and a pathway over the scrub-covered dunes to a long sandy beach called Manly. There were very few people about and I decided to have a swim, but the surf was so powerful that I did not go in very far. I dried myself in the sun.

My next adventure was to take another small ferry up to the far western end of the harbour to the little town of Paramatta, with its sandy street and awnings from the shops to keep the pavements cool. Evidently it did a good trade with the farmers and saved them the long drive into Sydney. I came back to Sydney itself on a little railway and enjoyed the comfort of the club that night. It was lovely to see the girls in their pretty cotton dresses and the men in short sleeves. The next day I booked a berth with the New Zealand Shipping Company to sail to Auckland. As a child I had always longed to go and see New Zealand after my grandfather had told me how, in the middle of the nineteenth century, he had gone out to New Zealand under sail. He had also had a wonderful time on the island of Fiji, where he had a love affair with a Fijian princess, who later was to marry the King of Fiji himself. Years after this he gave my mother the princess's colourful wedding invitation, with an envelope pinned to its back containing her wedding dress minus the grass skirt. This caused considerable embarrassment to a Victorian lady, who had it framed and hung up where only the tallest could see it. Back in New Zealand he met the girl he was eventually to marry, my grandmother. Her father owned a small farm outside Auckland, Remuera, now the most fashionable suburb of Auckland city.

I had been told that the trip across the sea from Sydney to Auckland was always rough, and it certainly was. On top of that, I found that all the cabins were for six people, so that night it did not take me long to go up on deck where I found a chair and put it alongside an attractive girl who had made the same decision as I had. We got the Steward to bring two large rugs, and she slept the night with her head on my shoulder. Early the following morning we discovered that the boat was full of Australian-Scots on their way to the Highland Games in Auckland, where many Scottish families had settled. We were awakened to the sound of pipes, which mingled uneasily with the screech of the seagulls following the boat for scraps. When we eventually docked at Auckland my newfound friend Claudia asked me to go ashore with her and meet her parents. But I had noticed a cluster of young New Zealanders waiting to welcome her and I did not want to spoil the party. She insisted on kissing me goodbye in full view of all her admirers. I went ashore later by myself.

Remuera lived up to the description my grandfather had given me, except that now the green slopes of the hill were covered with splendid houses and only the very top was not built on, the reason being that it was an old volcanic crater now grassed over. The view from here, and indeed from the houses, was magnificent, looking right over Auckland harbour and the sea.

My mother told me that my grandfather was reputed to have made three fortunes and to have lost two of them. To me he was possibly the most inspiring person I have ever known. Alas I never knew my grandmother, for she died before I was born. All three of their sons went to Russia where they farmed a large area in the Ukraine and bred the finest black horses, which were bought for the Tsar's bodyguard. In addition, they built up a large business importing British agricultural machinery into imperial Russia. My grandparents' youngest daughter married my father. The youngest son, my Uncle Owen, came back to England and bought a beautiful sixty-ton yacht which had belonged to one of the English princesses. Ill health forced him to spend half the year in the West Indies, returning to England in the summer when I used to spend long holidays with him while he was based at Cowes. With a crew of six it was almost luxurious. His elder brothers had to flee for their lives during the 1917 Revolution, leaving everything behind them.

There was a railway line from Auckland to the famous thermal area at Rotarua, which had to be seen to be believed, the great geiser blowing boiling water high into the air at regular intervals. All round were what were called the Boiling Porridge Pots, their foul-smelling sulphurous mud bubbling away. Close by a hot stream emerged to run parallel to a cold trout stream, so that standing in one place you could catch a trout and with a turn of the wrist drop it into the other stream to cook. The whole place was covered with a layer of a pale pink powdery substance which I was told was eagerly sought after because it made the most beautiful face-powder. One could not spend too long on that area because the soles of one's shoes grew too hot. It was at Rotarua that I first met the Maoris, a lovely people, and in the hotel that evening a number of girls danced the Pui dance for us, twirling what looked like little snowballs on the end of short strings. We were also given an exhibition by the young men of the Maori Haita, which consists of making terrible faces combined with ferocious movements and shouting designed to frighten their enemies – it certainly had that effect on me. Next day I hired a boat with a Maori fisherman and went to catch trout on Lake Rotarua. I caught the only ten-pound trout in my whole life and everyone in the hotel enjoyed it enormously for supper. As the railway ended at Rotarua I had to travel some miles south-west to the headwaters of the Wanganui river – what better way than an open coach and four horses? It was a wild country, sandy in places with small scrub trees. We passed close by a large lime-green lake which, I was to hear some time later, had suddenly disappeared. There was a good inn at the halfway mark of our journey, where we were to spend the night. The passengers were warned not to walk about in the scrubland around the inn for fear of falling into a bubbling mudhole.

During the second half of that journey the country was more rocky. Eventually we came to our destination where the Young river was flowing below us in a deep ravine. The two-day journey down the river in the most amazingly strong small boat was notable not only for the lovely scenery, often between steep cliffs on either side, but for the profusion of different shades of green in the foliage – including, of course, the great tree ferns, their pale green standing out like enormous stars in a dark sky. The river itself was full of enormous rocks, which were only avoided by a very strong boatman in the bows who did his best with a long pole to guide the boat between them. Even so, our progress down this rapid river was a bumpy one and I was to hear from the Captain that the English-built boat, which somehow had withstood all the bumping, had an especially strong double bottom; it was, however, necessary to hold tight on to the stanchions around the open stern where we were sitting. We were accompanied by an ancient Maori woman smoking a clay pipe who begged anybody smoking for some tobacco. One of the passengers was the new young Bishop of Auckland who kindly supplied her. First, she looked at it, then she smelled it, put her pipe in her pocket and proceeded to chew the tobacco. Fortunately, she was right in the stern.

In the afternoon we came to calmer waters and rather flatter country and here at a spot called Pipariki, at a very nice wooden hotel, we were given a good dinner and stayed the night. However, before our meal that evening, the Bishop and I walked across a meadow to the river, the tree ferns glistening in the light of the setting sun. We came upon a pool in which two Maori girls were bathing. They waved when they saw us to inveigle us in to have a swim – the question of bathing costumes did not arise. The Bishop turned to me and said, 'Go in, if you like, but it might cost me my job if I came too.' I was much too frightened to go it alone.

Next morning, a beautiful summer's day in New Zealand, the flowers and the trees suddenly induced my friend to burst out singing, 'Oh all ye trees and flowers of the earth, praise ye the Lord'. We had a lovely English breakfast of eggs and bacon. The second half of this river journey was calmer, passing through the flatter land of the west side of New Zealand's North Island, until we arrived at the town of Wanganui, which was also the rail head. Here I caught a train to Wellington – 'Windy Wellington', the capital of New Zealand, where umbrellas are seldom used because they turn inside out.

Along the quay stood the green ships of the New Zealand Shipping Company, like the one in which I had travelled from Sydney to Auckland, and I spent the rest of my day looking at Parliament House, which was a large wooden affair, and window gazing in the well-stocked shops. After spending the night in another comfortable hotel, whose furniture was upholstered in green plush, I once again boarded a ship which took me to the South Island, to the port of Wanganui on the east coast, from where I took a train inland to Canterbury. It was exactly like coming into an English town, with willow trees bordering the River Avon, and a cricket match, the players in their whites on a beautifully kept green ground which formed part of a lovely park. The hotel was entirely English, and I had dinner with an old soldier who had come out to New Zealand at the time of the Maori war. He explained 'I never seemed to get around to going home.'

Canterbury is of course the centre of the great sheep-producing Canterbury Plains where the lamb we eat in England comes from. I had learned from the Scots coming over on the boat from Sydney that a large proportion of the population of Auckland was Scottish; Canterbury, on the other hand, was very English. Now I was due to go south again to Dunedin. It seemed reasonable that the further south we went the colder the climate became, since New Zealand is upside down to England on the other side of the world. The country becomes much more rugged with snowcapped mountains in the distance. We crept very slowly up the twisting river to Dunedin on that Sunday morning and to my surprise there seemed to be nobody about, either on the quay or in the town which spread back to the hills. 'What else would you expect,' someone exclaimed when I remarked on the silence, 'since this is the Sabbath?' Dunedin and the country behind was totally Scottish.

Comfort was not a conspicuous feature of this hotel, and the food was frugal. But on the Monday everything came to life. I had been urged to go up into the highlands. This was a delightful journey, for in New Zealand before the First World War the main railway did not go very far. We had to change into a smaller-gauge train which wound its way up to the edge of a beautiful loch. Here the small party to which I had attached myself was given a splendid lunch in the little wooden building which served as a station. From here our journey was to be across the loch in a small motorboat. The scenery was magnificent, added to which there was on the other side a fine hotel. This time the plush upholstery was red, and the food was marvellous – mainly trout from the loch and lamb from the highland farms. I made friends with some people in our party and discovered that their son had just started at Charterhouse; of course, I was able to set their minds at rest by telling them what a happy school Charterhouse was. The whole scenery of these highlands was enhanced by the backcloth of the great range of snowcapped mountains on the western side of South Island.

My last port of call was Invercargill, right on the southern end of New Zealand, its fame coming from the ever-hopeful heroes who set off from there to the South Pole. I was taking a different route across the Roaring Forties, north-westerly to Tasmania. This enchanting island used to be famous for its whaling station; now it is more famous, I think, for its apples. There I climbed to the top of a very high hill, from where I could enjoy the most wonderful view of Hobart and its big harbour busy with ferry boats.

As I stood there, the ship which was to take me back to Melbourne came in. To my surprise it was full, and on enquiry I found that most of the passengers had come on a return trip in order to gamble. The sea was far from calm, and I now realised what the yachtsmen had to put up with during the now famous Sydney to Hobart race. We entered the Melbourne river and steamed slowly between the muddy banks up to the quay.

Before I was born, my father's elder brother, Uncle Percy, had decided not to go into the family firm and had set off for Australia. In those days it was such a long journey that he fell in love with one of the girls on board and married her. They had settled down in Melbourne, where he started up a real-estate business. I knew that he had a young family, but I did not know what to expect. He met me off the boat and took me along to his house on the outskirts of the city in one of those beautiful open-sided trams, which I found were still running in the Second World War. I was welcomed by his wife, but I was still uncertain what sort of reception the cousin from England was going to get from the three children of about my own age. I already felt at home with Uncle Percy because his voice was exactly like my father's. We went in and I was met by three grinning faces, and we all fell into each other's arms. Nothing could have been nicer for me. The following day

I felt even more at home when we caught a little train out into the country to pick blackberries, which were as big as large cherries. We took a picnic and with the exception of the blue of the gum trees in the distance we might have been in England. My cousins were two boys and a girl, all of whom were destined to carve out fine careers for themselves. Little did I know that many years later my own daughter, Pamela, would marry Keith, the son of the eldest boy, by then a highly successful doctor in Brisbane. My cousin Freda is one of the principal secretaries of the Melbourne Courts of Justice; the younger boy became a successful lawyer, thus coming back to the family tradition.

I could not spend very long in Melbourne because I was due to meet Oliphant Shaw in Adelaide, the owner of a vast sheep station in the outback of New South Wales. He was a friend of my family in England, where he now lived, but he still spent some time every year on the station. It was a long overnight train journey from Melbourne to Adelaide, but fortunately the only other occupant of my carriage was a pretty girl. We stopped about midnight at a station which refreshed us with sandwiches and tea but found that we now had to share our carriage with an elderly couple who obviously took us to be married. They suggested we cuddle up on one side of the carriage, but the seats were not very wide, and it seemed sensible that she should curl up on the seat with her blonde head cushioned on my coat in my lap, so we both got some sleep.

I duly met Oliphant Shaw at his hotel. I thanked him for putting me up temporarily for the Melbourne Club, of which he was a member. There I had seen the famous postage stamp stuck on the ceiling by some athletic combination of members and also the wonderful portrait of a nude girl which hung over the bar. Now all that was behind us as we set off to catch the train which would take us halfway to Broken Hill. At midnight we had to change trains at the South Australia and New South Wales border as the railway gauges were different. I had found that I was not the only visitor to the sheep station: with us was now an old friend of Mr Shaw, a canon of the Church.

Broken Hill was at one time a very profitable silver mine, but now large mountains of spoil, from which the silver had been extracted, were being processed to extract zinc. It was midday before we arrived at this outpost of industry where the railway stopped – it had originally been built to serve this mine. In the courtyard of the little station, where Mr Shaw was warmly welcomed by his old friend the station-master, two large open American Overlands were waiting for us and it was here that I first met Mr Tapp, the manager of the sheep station. Everything about Mr Tapp was large – his smiling, round, sunburned face, his hands (which entirely enveloped my own) and the joy with which he greeted the owner and ourselves. The distance from Broken Hill to Yancannia was about 180 miles, the road was hard red sand a mile wide, and on either side the flat, almost desert, country, sometimes covered with low scrub, seemed to go on for ever. There were rest houses, which also acted as pubs, about thirty miles apart; they also served the horse-drawn mail coach which ran once a week from Broken Hill up to Wilcannia, where there were some opal mines north of the sheep station. We stopped the night at a sheep station belonging to friends of Oliphant.

The next day our journey was not to be so smooth. During the night there had been terrific thunderstorms somewhere north of us and, as we set off to cross one of the dry creeks which often crossed the road, a six-foot-high wall of water came thundering down. We had to wait several hours until the water subsided and then we had to revet the creek; fortunately, there were a number of small gum trees in this area and the wise Mr Tapp had brought saws and shovels as routine. We set to, cutting down some trees and laying them lengthwise in the wet sandy bottom of the creek. The canon was splendid: he rolled up his trousers and stood on the bank telling us all what to do. Then we had to slope the banks on either side before we could get the cars across. All now went well, and it was exciting taking shots at the big red kangaroos travelling some distance from the cars in single file, each giving the others plenty of room for their enormous leaps. They are the greatest menace to the sheep farmers, because they pay little attention to his long wire fences, knocking them down and letting the sheep wander for miles. This was my first sight of Australian wildlife, and to me it was the sight of a lifetime.

But our troubles were not yet over, for now, in the distance ahead of us, a great reddish cloud was moving towards us. Mr Tapp stopped the cars, and we were given scarves which we dipped in water and tied round our faces; then we pulled our hats down. It was a blinding sandstorm whipped up by a vicious wind and we had to drive through this for about five miles before we got out of it. I can see old Mr Tapp now, crouched over the wheel, determined to get through as soon as he could.

At last, bloody but unbowed, we arrived at the owner's house and his great sheep station. It was a comfortable six-bedroomed bungalow built at the edge of a milk-chocolate-coloured lake, part of an underground river which flowed beneath the station, coming up from time to time to the surface to form billabongs. The whole station with its ten-square-mile paddocks amounted to over two million acres.

Mrs Tapp was waiting for us and had cooked a marvellous supper of roast chicken. During the night I was woken by thunder, and then came the sound which every Australian sheep farmer longs to hear – rain on the corrugated iron roof. Next morning there were smiles all round, except for the canon, who complained of a sleepless night.

The house was about half a mile from the station buildings and as I was getting ready to walk over to them I saw outside a lovely horse and buggy waiting for us. Mr Shaw was a first-class driver but since the rain had formed miniature lakes on the hard sand it was difficult for him to keep the horse going because it wanted to stop and drink. The whole station was well organised and self-supporting. I had a look at the great stockyards with their timber surrounds, which were used for cattle and sheep and horses; at the shearing shed with its holding pens, where some thirty sheep could be shorn at once when the highly skilled teams of shearers came round; and at the wool-washing shed with its great tanks where the melted-down fat from slaughtered bullocks mixed with soda provided the soap which extracted the heavy grease from the fleeces before they were put out in the sun to dry. There was a machine for pressing the fleeces into square canvas bales so as to allow precise size and weight for the camels, each of which carried two bales on their long trek back to Broken Hill. They were owned and operated by Arabs, who had brought their families with them to Australia. I was induced to take a ride on one of these beasts – it certainly gave me some exercise. The female camels were allowed to take a lighter load than the males and if they had a calf at foot they were often turned loose and picked up again when the young were old enough. One bale either side of the big males was looped over a sort of pommel on the camel's harness. There were enormous, covered barns which housed the horses' fodder – oats cut green and dried as hay.

I was shown the wooden quarters which housed the white jackaroos; the Aboriginals lived in canvas tents. When Mr Shaw took me to see them we found one Aboriginal wife with her head roughly bandaged. She explained that her husband had hit her over the head – we never discovered why. In the next tent was a very old Aboriginal man whittling away at boomerangs: long, heavy, slightly curved ones which were used against animals, and lighter, fully curved ones for knocking birds out of trees. They were marvellous implements, and I was given one of each sort to take home with me.

The Aboriginals were very good horsemen, and they seemed to have some sixth sense both for the weather and for where one would find a sheep in the huge paddocks. In another corner of the station buildings lived an extremely good old saddler. There seemed to be nothing in leather that he could not make: the horses' bridles out of kangaroo hide, with elaborate anti-fly fringes, or any other of the equipment that was needed, to say nothing of the repairing of the English-style saddles, which seemed to suit the extraordinary loping pace peculiar to the Australian trained horse, giving a comfortable ride for long distances. He had also made a stock whip with a handle of perhaps eighteen inches and a plaited thong of kangaroo hide some fifteen feet long, which, before the advent of camel trains, used to be used on the old-fashioned wagons drawn by teams of horses. He taught me how to use the stock whip without touching the animals and, much to his delight, I bought it from him.

Close by was a store which supplied the requirements of the station in general, and here I was presented by Mr Shaw with a badge of the jackaroo – a billy-can. I was to be allowed to go out with the boundary riders the next day to mend a fence some fifteen miles away, broken by the roos (as they called the kangaroos). We had also to see whether any sheep had got out. The land at Yancannia could in a normal season support one sheep for every ten acres, which means a lot of sheep on a station of that size. Since I was going to ride a horse belonging to one of the jackaroos, Mr Shaw thought I had better try it out that evening. All went well. On the way back to the house he showed me an old tree stump by the edge of the lake. On it were carved the words 'Burke and Wills dig five feet'. This referred to the famous attempt by two men to cross Australia from south to north back in the nineteenth century; no doubt this food cache was put there in the hope that they would pass by this lake. As the sun was setting there was a faint colouring of green on the red sand. The following day we were up bright and early. I looked out of my bedroom window and saw a miracle. Grass seed, long dormant in the sandy soil, had been made warm by the summer sun and when the rain came it sprouted as if in a hothouse. As far as one could see the ground was covered in green grass. My companions were waiting up at the station with my horse. The leader was John, one of the white jackaroos, and there were two Aboriginals with a couple of dogs. It was estimated that we should have to spend only one night away unless some of the sheep had got out.

Once away from the station we settled down and loped along for about an hour and then stopped for a while – the horses, of course, being mad keen to get at the new grass. We were soon on our way again and finally passed through the gate of the paddock where we had to repair the fence. There was wire available for the purpose near the fence, so we picked it up. It looked as though the sheep had not found the gap – at any rate, the Aboriginals could find no trace of them escaping. The next job was to find the sheep and count them. They were not too far away, evidently enjoying the young grass. The dogs rounded them up, cleverly letting them escape between the two Aboriginals on the one side and myself and John on the other. It must take years of practice to count sheep at that speed. Apparently they were all there and a satisfied John said we would now make for the water and fix ourselves up for the night. The billabong was about five miles on, surrounded by groups of gum trees. John explained to me that normally if one is out for two or more nights one catches a sheep and, having killed it and skinned it, has it for food, hanging it up between meals in a fly-proof bag on one of the branches of a gum tree. This time, for only one night, we took our grub with us. If one killed a sheep, one hung the skin over the paddock fence to prove that it was jackaroos who had killed it and not a dingo. The horses were unsaddled and shackled between their forelegs and turned loose on the new grass; they were easily caught the next morning. We rolled ourselves in our blankets and went to sleep after watching a wonderful sunset across the flatlands of the outback. It was a strange thought that I could ride probably a hundred miles without seeing a human being.

Back at the station the rain seemed to have brought everything to life; not only the grass and the low scrub, known as the teatree, which covered large areas, but now the tall trees round the lake were alive with the chatter of galas, those lovely grey parrot-like birds with pale-pink breasts, and of little green parakeets. Evidently they had found food to their liking round the station. The mail coach had been through while I had been away, and Oliphant had received an urgent request to ship some forty young horses to India. This in itself was unusual, and he was a bit alarmed because although he kept a number of good Australian mares and had bred from a thoroughbred stallion, he was only used to selling a dozen or so polo ponies to India. There was also a good sale for young horses in Australia and Yancannia needed replacements as well. I do not know just how many horses there were on the station, nor had I had the chance to go and see them, but counting mares, foals and young stock there must have been some four hundred. Oliphant was rightly proud of the young stock he bred – from my own short experience they were lovely rides. Now the four-year-olds had to be rounded up and brought to the station and corralled in one of the yards. They were not really wild as they had been used to hand feeding on the open hay in the dry times, nor was the breaking in as rough as some people believe. There were one or two Aboriginals who were splendid at the job. The youngsters were handled carefully; rugs and then sacks of grain were placed on their backs and eventually a saddle and bridle. Only when they were fairly quiet was I employed with others to ride them about for a while.

I had had a letter from home by the same mail. There had been an incident with the Germans and there was some disquiet about their intentions. I was advised not to delay my return too long. This, with the sudden demand for horses by India, decided Oliphant that he too ought to think about getting back home. The canon was delighted. He liked neither the heat nor the flies nor the screech of the magnificent white cockatoo, with his brilliant yellow crest, which lived in the house. Meanwhile the whole station began working to get the consignment of young horses ready. The Aboriginals all came along to watch Joe, one of the best Aboriginal horsemen, backing them. Sheep and wool were for the moment forgotten.

For me it was a most marvellous experience to have so many different horses between my knees and to judge their different temperaments even if I was not allowed to let them out of a walk. Little did I then realise that within months I should, as a teenage cavalry officer, be given the job of fitting a hundred Bristol boys, whose sole knowledge of riding was on delivery bicycles, on to a hundred Canadian horses supposedly broken and backed like the ones at Yancannia. I think it was because of my experience at Yancannia that I was detailed to do this. Unfortunately, instead of the lovely well-bred Australian horses, the Canadian ones were short-necked, tough, rough-coated animals, most of which had but one object in view: to get one off their backs. Nevertheless, by using the Yancannia technique I managed to turn out a pretty efficient squadron of cavalry.

The days passed all too quickly, I was beginning to find it a wrench to leave these horses and not to have the opportunity to go out again into the bush and experience the exquisite loneliness. Before we left I went with Oliphant and Mr Tapp some twenty-five miles to see his northern neighbour who had, apparently, put down a bore-hole and achieved a big gusher. Oliphant wanted to make sure it would not deplete his own underground water supply. As we approached the Yancannia border I was surprised to see a large lake spreading away to the west; not only were gum trees growing all round it, but the tops of trees were showing above the water. I remarked that surely the rains had not caused this; Oliphant smiled, for I was looking at my first mirage. No wonder men had gone mad trying to reach water, only to find it receding as they approached it. The gusher, it transpired, was not coming from Oliphant's supply. It was strange to see a fountain of water some ten feet high gushing out of the sand in the moonlight. We spent the night here sleeping on the verandah of Oliphant's friend and after the traditional breakfast of steak and eggs and tea, we set out for home. Inside Yancannia we saw a rabbit. Rabbits were kept down as much as possible in order to conserve the grass for the sheep. Oliphant stopped the car, gave me a stick and told me to knock the creature on the head. However, it disappeared down a hole and, as I knelt down to see how far in it was, a large iguana, one of those enormous lizards, put his flat head out, his forked tongue scenting food – me! I made it back to the car in double-quick time.

Tragedy had not yet struck my young life, though within the year the First World War would bring it to all of us. Somehow a telegram from India had finally got through to Yancannia. It had taken three days, and it told my host the devastating news that his eldest son, who was serving with his regiment in India, had been badly mauled by a tiger while out shooting. I knew his son was the apple of his eye. Now the tough bushman went into action; we were to leave the next day for Adelaide; Mr Tapp would come with us and make all the arrangements for the shipping of the horses at Adelaide. It was estimated that they could be got away in another week.

The moon was still high in the sky when we left for Broken Hill, the great green Overland car was having a few final checks as we arrived at the station in the buggy, a second buggy bringing up our bags. Everybody seemed to be there to see us off and to shake the owner by the hand. It was just daylight as Mr Tapp put his large foot on the throttle and with a roar we started on our homeward journey. Later that day we met the mail coach coming up from Broken Hill. There was a letter for Mr Shaw: his son had died. As he read the letter the steel seemed to snap. He walked quietly away into the scrub – it was a moment when he wanted to be alone. Alas, the canon thought he could help but he could not. I shall ever remember that lone figure in the middle of nowhere, his head bowed in grief.

Chapter 5

YEOMANRY

Mr Tapp had never been as far afield as Adelaide before. It was dusk before we arrived and found rooms in the hotel. Then we checked that there was accommodation on the P & O liner, SS *Medina*, which was due to sail in three days' time.

As he looked out of the hotel windows the next morning, Mr Tapp was surprised to find a vast mirage beyond the roofs of the town, nor was he convinced that it was the sea until we had taken him down to paddle in it. Fortunately, Oliphant Shaw had some friends in Adelaide, a charming widow who was able to help him in his distress. She had a lovely fair-haired, blue-eyed daughter, who helped me to pass the time. We shared picnics out at the old whaling station by the sea, where she told me about life in Adelaide, so different to the outback. Her family had an interest in some vineyards not very far from Adelaide. The wine was certainly good.

The sea was blue, the sun was hot. I almost felt I was going home too soon.

Little did I know then how much my life would be linked with Australia, nor how many times I would come back again, nor that three of my children would one day become happy and prosperous citizens of that wonderful land. As I write the numbers of my greatgrandchildren are hard to keep up with.

The Great Australian Bight lived up to its bad reputation. It was rough and not until we left Fremantle did we get into the calm, brilliantly blue waters of the Indian Ocean. I had not done a stroke of work since I had arrived in Japan, now I really had to get down to five weeks of concentrated slogging. It was fortunate that there was little diversion to take my mind away from my books. There was no one of my own age on board, but luckily my table companions were a delightful family, well-known sheep people who were bringing their eldest boy back to public school in England. The father knew Oliphant Shaw well and I was able to talk to them on their own ground. The boy was much intrigued by my studies, wondering, I suppose, what he himself would be up against before long.

The *Medina* was due to stop over for a couple of days at Colombo in Ceylon. Once again I was to find the tropical magic I had first experienced at Manila, only now the Union Jack hung limply in the heat instead of the Stars and Stripes.

I ate the traditional lunch of curried prawns at the Galleface Hotel, where the tall coconut palm trees bend out over the sea as if seeking extra moisture. Then came the steady climb on a small railway up to Kandy, past the tea and coffee plantations, and the scent of the pepper and nutmeg trees in the Peredrinia Gardens, where, years later, I was to spend some time at Lord Mountbatten's headquarters in the Second World War.

In the river, the elephants were getting a wash and brush-up before donning their magnificent apparel and joining in a noisy procession later in the afternoon. In the dusk, I went for a ride around the lake in a rickshaw, soundless but for the pad of the coolie's bare feet, past the little white temple, the resting place of one of Buddha's teeth. There was moonlight on the lake, and the smell of spice, of pepper and nutmeg trees, and the sweet scent of frangipani, the fireflies darting all around one. Yes, it was magical.

Back home, I returned to Charterhouse for the summer of 1914 and went to Cambridge to take my exams. I somehow managed to steer Caesar and Xenophon through their Latin and Greek campaigns and was accepted by Trinity College, where I duly sat and ate an inaugural dinner in the great hall. It was to be my first and last dinner in that great building, for after five years of war, I eventually went up to Christ Church, Oxford. With my exams behind me, I settled down to enjoy that fine summer of 1914. I captained my house at cricket and enjoyed tennis at the headmaster's house. Frank Fletcher, the Headmaster, liked a good hard game and then, among the blue delphiniums of their garden, tea was poured from a silver teapot into bone-china cups by his delightful wife.

At the end of term, I went to the Officers' Training Corps camp. There were about half a dozen other public-school contingents with us, but on the third day we were awakened to a rather unprofessional rendition of reveille. All the professional soldiers who ran the camp and cooked for us had silently slipped away. We had to do our cooking and chores until a day later when we were issued with railway warrants to our homes.

Excitement was now running high. I had to change at Gloucester station. I was in uniform and a hero; beer was pressed upon me. A woman asked me to hold her child while she went to 'spend a penny'. Without a thought of the old cliché, I took the baby. I was still holding it when my train came in; I passed the buck. It was 4 August 1914 and the Kaiser's war had begun.

If I was asked for my memories of Charterhouse, I would recall the making of toast for tea in front of the fire on a winter's evening until I was old enough to get a fag to make it for me, making half a century when leading my house to victory at cricket, the roaring sidelines when playing football for the school, bathing in the River Wey in the summer and the smell in my study when sausages were frying for supper. Perhaps above all, I recall the sound of 600 voices letting go when singing the Russian national anthem in the Old Chapel on Sunday and the tenor voices of the choir singing 'Nunc Dimittis' at evensong.

Luckily not every generation walks out of the security of school into the middle of a world war. In the spring of 1915 when the First World War was barely half a year old, such was the excitement and novelty of this world upheaval, which was supposed to have been over in six months, that the race was on among teenagers like myself to get into it before it ended.

How strange was the illusion that although one's friends might get 'knocked off', there was no way in which one was going to get killed oneself. How little we knew what we were in for. Early in 1915 there was little choice for a seventeen-year-old. Either one joined the infantry or, if one was lucky and as mad about horses as I was, there was a chance of joining the cavalry. The regular cavalry regiments in France proved a disaster in the face of trench warfare and the power of the German machine-gun fire, but the county yeomanry regiments including the Royal Gloucestershire Hussars Yeomanry were doing a splendid job in the sands of the Middle East, keeping the Turks away from the Suez Canal. Early in 1915 I heard that a second-line regiment was to be formed both to back up the regiment in Egypt and to act as a complete unit if necessary. I applied to join, and at seventeen I became the youngest subaltern in the regiment.

In the days of Queen Elizabeth I, the yeomen of England had stood to arms to repel the Spanish Armada. In the South African War, they had distinguished themselves at a time when farmers and landowners supplied their own horses. Now, as then, discipline was given and taken as between countrymen who had known and respected each other from boyhood.

I was to find that I had been brought up among the families of most of the other officers. What more could I have asked for!

I was given a fortnight's leave to obtain my uniform, a long, pointed sword and a villainous-looking revolver. I also found time during my leave to visit my old school and say farewell to the Headmaster and many of my friends still waiting to join up. For many, it was the last time we ever saw each other. Of the ten others who played football with me for Charterhouse in the autumn of 1914, only two were to survive the war.

On my train journey back from Surrey to London I passed Brooklands race-track and was wildly astonished to see someone flying a little monoplane upside down. I was to learn that a Frenchman was doing a bit of stunt flying upside down for the first time. It never occurred to me that I might try flying myself sometime in the future.

On my return to London, I had also met a schoolfriend who had just joined up in the London Scottish. With him was his young sister, who had enormous brown eyes and a wide smile – my first girlfriend. She was to write to me each week that I was in France and later when I was a prisoner of war. I never quite knew what happened after the war, but I was sure it was all my fault. Somehow she was so very young, and I had aged beyond my youthful years. She knows well my deep love for all the joy and spirit she gave me during those years in a prison camp.

I joined the regiment as it came to camp in Cirencester Park on a lovely spring day in April 1915. My first job was to go to the remount depot at Gloucester, to choose a charger for myself and another for my soldier-batman. On the strength of my having been in command of a section of the Officers' Training Corps at Charterhouse, I was given command of 'A' Troop, 'C' Squadron of the Royal Gloucestershire Hussars Yeomanry. Now, instead of the noise of a handbell rung outside my cubicle at school, I was awakened by the music of the cavalry trumpeters playing the reveille. Having dressed and had a quick shave, I would walk over to the horse lines where my troop sergeant had already got my troopers down to the job of morning stables. After the horses had been groomed, watered and fed, there would be an inspection to see that all their hooves were in good order and the shoes tight, that there were no sores from the ropes which held one hind leg to a peg and that their halters were securely tied by the halter-rope to a long thick hawser which was fixed on the ground in front of them. It gave them plenty of room to lie down but kept them in line. Only when I had inspected the whole troop were the troopers dismissed and sent off to get their own breakfast. It was a routine that one would never forget. I taught it to the children of one of the first pony clubs which I and a friend started up near Cheltenham in the early 1930s.

During those halcyon days of summer 1915, so large was Cirencester Park that one could take one's troop to a quiet corner and train both horses and men in the real work of the cavalry, which in our case included the job of mounted infantry as well.

It was fascinating to see how the horses gradually learned what they had to do. There were the lazy moments when the whole troop would dismount and give the horses a nibble at the grass. The clink of the bits and stirrup irons in the shade of the great trees and the smell of the sun on the horse's shining coats added up to everything I could have hoped for.

Most of the officers had their own cars and lived close enough to be able to go home for Sunday lunch after church parade. They were exceptionally good to me, and I seldom lacked an invitation to one of the family houses. I bought a splendid black Sunbeam motorcycle with a long bright exhaust pipe so that I too could get home when I had the chance. I also lent it to my young soldier-batman to get to his home in Cirencester. Ernest Tanner was a splendid young man; he would never let me go on parade without every bit of my equipment, including my boots, gleaming. After the war he was commissioned, and he spent a full and successful life in the Army.

Our training also included long route marches around the Cotswolds which I knew so well. But by September the regiment was deemed good enough to go on active service. We were not needed immediately, so we were sent off to Hunstanton in Norfolk, supposedly to guard against a German invasion. We boxed our horses in open cattle trucks at Cirencester station and the whole regiment set off for Norfolk. It was a long, tiring journey, especially for the horses. A working party had been sent ahead some days earlier to get our camp ready so that by the time the horses had been fed, watered and rugged up and the men had been given a splendid supper to cheer them up, everybody was ready to hit the hay. We very soon found that we were now to be kept busy digging trenches around the coastline.

Several officers had rented houses in the district. Fred Cripps, who was Brigade Staff Captain, and his wife Connie made me almost one of their family. Major Charlie Scott, who in peacetime was Master of the North Cotswold hounds, had five couples of hounds sent up and we had a drag hunt once a week over the Norfolk countryside. Luckily the farmers joined in and enjoyed it.

Hubert Ponsonby, our Adjutant, soon tried to get me to help him in his job. I felt I could sit in a chair in an office at any time, but now I had a horse and a troop to look after, so I politely declined. Nevertheless, I was soon to be given one of the most fascinating jobs in the regiment. Evidently, someone had appreciated our training efficiency. Now the regiment was to have a fourth squadron made up of young recruits from Bristol. With some surprise I was given command of the new squadron and its training, and I was allowed to add another pip to my uniform. The Colonel told me to borrow such staff as I needed from the other squadrons. Scottie, who was an ex-cavalry officer brought out of retirement to help train the regiment, lent me his excellent sergeant-major, also an ex-regular soldier, and I was lucky to get four good troop-sergeants from the rest of the regiment. Several new officers had also recently arrived and I at once co-opted as my number two Martin Hartigan, a splendid horseman, who later was to become a well-known racehorse trainer.

Will Muir, who was one of the officers in the regiment, bless him, thought that as a result of my promotion and my command of a squadron I should have a motorcar instead of my motorbike, so he virtually gave me a splendid two-seater Studebaker, simple and efficient. It had three gears and a spare wheel which bolted on to an offending punctured one. It also had a hood which could be put up in bad weather. It did all of twenty-five miles to a gallon of petrol, which cost a shilling. Will and his wife Clara also took a house in Norfolk.

Up to that time I thought I knew a little about riding and horsemastership despite the fact that in the days before the pony clubs one was largely self-taught. Nevertheless, my six months as a leader of a troop had taught me so much more that it came as a considerable shock to learn that I really knew very little when I began to read that excellent manual called *Cavalry Training*. The book gave me in precise detail how I was to teach about a hundred young men of around eighteen to ride and to train themselves and their horses to become efficient cavalrymen. Hitherto they had hardly ever seen a horse close up, except those who had been delivering milk or other commodities with a pony in Bristol. The majority of the enthusiastic Bristolians had ridden nothing but bicycles. The remounts which arrived by rail turned out to be short, thickset Canadian horses which had been backed once in their native land, and then put on a ship to England. Luckily, in order to cope with the rough, cold east-coast weather, stabling, built largely of old railway sleepers, had been erected on the sand dunes; at least they were warm and dry. Anyway, the horses' coats were so thick, they were well protected.

It was a difficult job fitting each boy to a suitable horse; I did it purely on size and weight. I then began the job of getting them used to each other. For a whole week, morning and afternoon, I made them take their horses out on long walks – on foot – over the sand dunes. They were each taught how to groom, water, feed and generally get to know which end of the horse went first and, incidentally, to know each other. It was surprising to see the way the boys started to care for their charges. Luckily, the horses had all been newly shod before disembarking but fitting them out with saddles and bridles was not easy; they did not seem to fit anywhere. However, at the end of the week every boy was keen to get on his charger. It was an odd sort of parade among the soft sand dunes as each lad was carefully helped aboard. There were kicks and squeals, and in some cases they were just bucked straight off again, which meant that either Hartigan or I had to mount the horses ourselves and rough ride these tough little horses into submission. Neither of us escaped without a few bruises.

After a few days, all four troops of twenty-four boys were able to ride, or at least to sit in the saddle. Now they rode their mounts about the dunes instead of walking them: there was a sense of triumph and joy among those raw recruits.

I started up a number of riding schools on the sands, each one in the charge of a troop-sergeant, and I myself, following every word of *Cavalry Training*, supervised the whole outfit and had the boys in the saddle one hour on and half an hour off all morning, followed by stable duty and, in the afternoon, lectures on the duties of a cavalryman and a soldier. Nothing was too much trouble for Hartigan, including giving individual riding lessons to the new officers. His language was marvellous, and his broad Irish accent brought more smiles than tears to the faces of the youths he was teaching. I well remember him galloping after one of the young officers whose horse had run away with him along the sands, catching him and giving him a little lecture: 'Did you think now you were in the band beating a drum with your legs?' The whole exercise was one of the most rewarding of my life, especially when I sat upon my charger alongside the Colonel at a regimental review and my squadron rode by at the canter in better line than all the rest of the old hands – their heads high, and even the little Canadian horses realising the sense of the occasion.

During the whole of that winter of 1915/16 at Hunstanton, Connie and Fred Cripps looked after me like a son. Their daughter Freda, a lively teenager, was a joyful companion and I almost felt that I was one of that delightful family. The two boys, Joe and Phil, who were still at school, came down for the holidays and I put them in with my riding school. Phil was to become a well-known contestant in point-to-points, and he and his brother both rode well to hounds. I kept up with the family all their lives after the war. It was always a warm welcome that I received at Ampney, where Sir Fred looked after not only the county of Gloucestershire but all his broad acres as well.

Somehow the tunes of the songs of those early days seem to stay with one. If I was ever asked to give a choice on a desert island, I feel the songs would be those nostalgic memories of the First World War, probably each reminding me of a girlfriend: that haunting melody 'They'll Never Believe Me', 'The Broken Doll', 'If You Were the Only Girl in the World' (just about the only song anyone ever sang from that wonderful show *The Bing Boys*) and, remembering the Americans, 'The Roses Round the Door Made Me Love Mother More Back Home in Tennessee'. There was another popular music-hall song of the time, 'Who Are You With Tonight?' which I heard sung by a middle-aged soubrette from the stage of the Ipswich theatre.

In midsummer of 1916 the whole brigade came together for the first time in Holkham Park, that fabulous home of the earls of Leicester, the fathers of British agriculture as we know it today. The Leicester family themselves were quite wonderful to us – many were the parties in the great house where the girls made us welcome. I never quite knew whether the Earl himself really appreciated three regiments of cavalry training and exercising over his estates. Never had I seen so much game. Wherever one went, one had to be careful not to let the horses tread on the pheasants, partridges, hares and wild duck from the nearby marshes, so thick on the ground were these lovely creatures.

At Holkham I was to meet, for the first time, the officers of the Warwick and Worcester Yeomanry and the ebullient Lord Willoughby de Brooke, Colonel of the Warwicks, well-endowed with a voice which befitted his mastership of the Warwickshire hounds. There is a story that when he was making a speech in the House of Lords he was interrupted by a member of the Opposition and offered in consequence to telephone to Edinburgh to make certain that he was correct. The voice came back: 'Why telephone?'

Colonel Wiggin, Colonel of the Worcestershire Yeomanry, possessed a rather quieter voice as perhaps befitted the Master of the Devon and Somerset staghounds. Most of the officers were hunting people. They were a boisterous lot, which was a good thing in view of the fact that we had to try and keep up the spirits of the regiments at a time when we did not know what was going to happen to us.

There was one thrilling moment when the whole brigade was reviewed by the GOC (General Officer Commanding). It was to prove the climax of our hopes and fears. With bands playing, the regiments rode past in line, first at the walk and then at the canter. Next, from the restless stillness, came the trumpeters sounding the charge. The horses' blood was already up as, with swords drawn, the regiment thundered across that imaginary battlefield, then turned and thundered back 'over the bodies'. This was the only cavalry charge I ever took part in.

The summer of 1916 was wearing on; we were wondering where we should go next. Then the blow fell. Cavalry were no longer needed; the brigade would be disbanded into bicycle regiments. Bicycles! Gloom spread to near panic. It affected us all. Bicycles, we knew, were just a step down towards the infantry. Soon there was a call for volunteers for infantry regiments. They were not taken up. Never have I seen hundreds of tough, grown men unashamedly crying as when we loaded our precious horses once more into cattle trucks at the town of Wells in Norfolk. Our horses were our friends and companions, and I think we had all got to love them during the previous eighteen months. Neighing to their masters, they were now going goodness knows where. It was difficult to keep the men from going wild that night in camp.

We were sent off almost immediately to Tunbridge Wells in Kent, where we were issued terrible bicycles. For many of the old officers like Scottie who weighed a good fifteen stone, it was the end of the dusty road we now had to travel. Language and tempers became raw but were almost lost in the deep mud on the top of Wrotham Hill, where we were sent to get used to our new mounts. Then back to the east coast near Felixstowe – at least I was on ground I had known in the holidays when we were children. We tried to play polo on bicycles; I fell off and sprained my ankle and retired to the Felix Hotel on crutches.

The hotel was still full of guests despite the almost nightly Zeppelin airship raids, and there were quite a few lovely girls and old ladies about, who looked after the 'wounded hero'. There was also a young Flying Corps pilot on leave. We got talking; he had been promoted to major. Major Small confided in me that he was on a very secret job of air co-operation with a new secret weapon called the 'tank'. He enthusiastically suggested I leave the bicycles behind and go flying.

Crumpled, burned-out Zeppelins, looking like dead dinosaurs, were beginning to litter the Suffolk countryside. The corpses of those poor devils who had jumped into that sandy soil had to be dug out for burial – they had gone down four or five feet by themselves.

It was a bit eerie on those dark nights up on the east coast to hear the throbbing of the engines coming one's way with a powerful searchlight slung hundreds of feet below, scanning the ground for targets. Fortunately, there was an anti-aircraft battery just to the north of our camp, so the airships used to make for that and leave our camp alone.

The Colonel was not amused when I asked for leave to apply to fly. Several other officers were already transferring to the infantry regiments, and the second line of the Royal Gloucestershire Hussars appeared to be folding up. Troop transfers were now being selected, not volunteered for; it was a sad time. Fred Cripps helped me fight my battle, and by October I got my orders to report to the War Office in London for an interview. Luckily the young officer who interviewed me had himself been a former cavalry officer. All he really wanted to know was whether I had good hands with a horse and how I should recognise the pole star. Having passed both examinations, I was accepted and told I could take a week's leave before reporting to Queen's College, Oxford, for a course on the theory of flight, how an aeroplane engine was made, and how to strip and reassemble the rotary engine. Finally, with the others of my course, I was taken out to Port Meadow, the university polo ground in peacetime, where we were given our initial flight in a vast, rather obsolescent machine called a Maurice Farman, nicknamed a 'Rumpety', in which the passenger sat on one strut and held on to two more. It was one of the most thrilling moments of my life.

Chapter 6

ROYAL FLYING CORPS

It was a cold, snowy evening just before Christmas of 1916 when I set off for Netheravon on Salisbury Plain in my old Studebaker, the headlights, small enough already, covered in brown paper with a few half-inch holes in them so that I could just see the nearside of the road. I had said goodbye to my family at home and assured them that I was going to take great care in every respect of the flying business. I had also stopped to say farewell to the Cripps family, who had returned to Cirencester. Freda and I had become good friends during my period with the Gloucester Yeomanry, but I realised that, unless the war was stopped fairly soon, the field of competition for her affections would be so wide that only friendship would probably remain.

Both the boys, Joe and Phil, were home from Eton preparing for their Christmas, and Connie was wondering if she would get her husband back also. I had learned that, soon after I left the yeomanry, Fred Cripps had also asked for a transfer to a more active job in France, and it was a toss-up whether he would go before Christmas.

I eventually arrived at Netheravon about midnight, just in time to get settled into a cold, green wooden hut with about five other aspiring pilots. We were all tired and with the help of our warm 'British' greatcoats and all the blankets available, we finally got to sleep.

It was a little disconcerting to find, when we were led out on the aerodrome for our first dual flight training, that we were to start on the old 'Rumpety' that I had first flown in at Oxford. However, the pupil pilot's seat was made a little more comfortable than the struts we had had to sit on then. The only trouble was that one was so close to the engines behind one's back that it was patently obvious that if one did fly into the ground the engines would make mincemeat out of one. My instructor and I clambered up into this vast contraption of canvas, wood and wires, which was pushed forward by a propeller at the back and lumbered across the aerodrome until we gradually became airborne.

Actually, the very size of the machine gave one some confidence; one felt that even if one crashed there would be enough woodwork around for protection. I was lucky to get the feel of the joystick and the controls fairly quickly. The cavalry officer who selected me was right: if one had a light hand for a horse's rein, one could easily manage an aeroplane.

As soon as one had done a few solos on the Rumpety, one was taken on dual training on the Avro 504, that excellent machine with a Gnome-Rhone engine in front – though it had a habit of cutting out without much notice. The Avro was a stable biplane made of wood and canvas, and it was much lighter on the controls than the old Farman. During my solo flights on the Avro, I had to make three forced landings from engine failure, but it was all good practice; there were plenty of fields near Salisbury Plain and one could really put the Avro down on a very small bit of country, although it was mostly snow-covered that bitter winter of 1916/17. The salvage parties were kept pretty busy getting the Avro engines working again, but there was surprisingly little damage to aircraft or to the pilots, so easy were these machines to land almost anywhere.

While we were still at Netheravon, none of us knew what sort of pilots we were going to make, whether we should finally end up in one of those slow reconnaissance machines or whether we should make it as a fighter pilot. We therefore had to do all sorts of training to become proficient in both morse code and map-reading. There was always the chance that one would be downgraded to a simple observer if one failed to fly an aeroplane well by oneself. I had felt that as a fighter pilot one would at least be solely responsible for one's own survival and not be dependent on someone else.

Out of the six of us who arrived that evening, only four survived to go on to Upavon for the advanced training course. We had an old gramophone in the hut and reserved that haunting song, 'When You Come to the End of a Perfect Day', as a lament for any of our friends who had not survived their first solos. I think one of the saddest was big Bill Sutherland, a large, red-haired Australian, who was just finishing his final solo when a young pilot crashed into him in mid-air. He was the last one for our record.

My instructors were evidently quite pleased with me because I very soon qualified on an Avro and transferred to the advanced flying school at Upavon, where I was put on to a 1½ Strutter Sopwith two-seater. This was a fairly new type of aircraft, and I was only given one dual flight with an instructor before being sent off on my own. It really was a lovely plane to fly except that the bottom wings were so wide that one could not see exactly what one was landing on or taking off from. Thus, it was that, doing 'circuits and bumps' on my second day, I failed to see an old man with a large carthorse and a cartful of stones lumbering slowly across the aerodrome filling the potholes in the road. He should not, of course, have been there at all. As I took off on my second circuit, I felt a jolt to port wing. I managed to hold on to the joystick and keep going, but the aircraft began to spin round like a top, and then folded quietly on to the ground. I was left standing in the middle of the wreckage to await the wrath of my instructor. The old carter was highly annoyed because I had made his horse's nose bleed. Apparently, it had reared up on its hind legs when the aeroplane came near; otherwise, I should have missed him.

The loss of this beautiful Sopwith aeroplane had greatly distressed my instructor, and I wondered whether it was going to make any difference to my flying prospects. In fact, it was a pretty lucky escape. I had not got a scratch, but the aeroplane was a complete wreck. I think my instructor was rather impressed with the way I had escaped, and the next day he put me on to the little single-seater Sopwith Pup. This aeroplane, with a radial engine, was absolute heaven to fly. It was very small and wrapped around one like a glove. One could almost bank and turn by leaning to one side or the other. I had been warned that it was wise to get rid of the euphoria of flying before you met another airman with a gun.

A few days later I finally earned the instructor's praise when a sudden fog came down over the plain. I was still some miles away learning to fly across country. I flew towards where I thought the aerodrome would be until I saw a church tower and a tall tree emerge out of the fog, so up I went and turned back into the evening sunshine. I spotted a church, a rectory and a nice green field nearby, the only trouble being that most of the fields had rather tall trees around them. But I calculated I could get in and possibly out; the little Pup obeyed every move I made, and I landed safely.

As I switched off the engine and climbed out of the aircraft, the vicar came running out of the vicarage to see that I was all right. Slapping me on the back, he said, 'Splendid, young man. Now you can come and have a good dinner and a comfortable bed.' I was able to phone the aerodrome, and my instructor seemed thankful that both the plane and I were safe. Early next morning a van came out with some extra petrol and a mechanic just to check over the machine; the instructor also came out in his car. It was going to be a close thing to get the aircraft out of this little field, but I measured a gap between two large elm trees at the far end and reckoned, with five feet on either side, that I could make it. I was told later that my exploit in getting down and away without any trouble had assured me a place as a single-seater 'scout' pilot, as we were then called.

The appalling weather of that winter had made training very slow. There were days when one simply could not get into the air at all. So, it was not until the end of March that I passed as a scout pilot and was sent off to Turnberry in Scotland to be taught two days of battle training with a camera gun. From Turnberry I was posted to No. 29 Scout Squadron in France.

And so it was to be active service at last. I drove the old Studebaker back to my home in Gloucestershire and stowed it at the back of the garage, wondering when I should next get behind the wheel. How full of hope and excitement were those bustling groups of RFC pilots at Victoria station. On the other hand, the infantry, going back to the front after leave, were much more sober; they knew what it was all about. My father and mother had come up to London to see me off. They knew so much better than I that it might well be the last meeting – it so very nearly was.

It was early April 1917, almost two years to the day that I had so blithely joined the Gloucestershire Hussars. After all the frustrations of the cavalry and ideas about quick-ending wars, I was now changing the saddle I loved so much for the bucket seat in a little wood and canvas aeroplane, a joystick instead of reins. I was on my own now; it was going to be me against the Hun, as we called the Germans. At least I could throw a Sopwith Pup around the sky.

The Crossley tender, the workhorse of the Royal Flying Corps, picked up the pilots at Boulogne. The next stop was Isel Le Hameau, a vast flat aerodrome just west of Arras. There were in fact four squadrons on the aerodrome, two scout squadrons and two bomber squadrons. I was the only person to be dropped off at No. 29 and no one took very much notice of the arrival of the new pilot, so heavy was the turnover at that time. Pilots were arriving and disappearing every day. A big push was starting up on the Western Front and the average life of a scout pilot was about three weeks. Early next morning I was hailed by my new Commanding Officer, Major de Crepigny, now, at twenty-one, a veteran of the Royal Flying Corps. He asked me if I had ever flown a Nieuport Scout before. I had seen these unfamiliar aircraft on the aerodrome as soon as daylight had come; they looked even smaller than the Sopwith.

The CO told me to take one up, and to be careful of the tight swing to the left on take-off. I squeezed myself into the little cockpit, made certain that I had got instruments that worked, and revved up the engine. Almost immediately I started swinging to the left; however, the violent right rudder kept me straight until I was in the air. The Nieuport had a 90 h.p. radial engine which gave a speed of about ninety miles an hour. This could be upped a little if one got into trouble. The aircraft was stiff on the controls compared with the Pup. She climbed well but had a single Lewis gun fixed to the top wing. Back in England we had already been taught about the machine guns which were synchronised to fire through the propellers. By 1917 all other scouts' aircraft, including the German ones, had reliable machine guns fixed on to the top of their engines and operated by an oil-pump synchroniser, which ensured that the bullets did not hit the propellers. This system evidently worked wonderfully. I had come across the Lewis gun in the yeomanry and I knew its habit of jamming, especially if it got cold.

The year before, when most of the scout aeroplanes had flown about the same speed, the Nieuport could be manoeuvred beneath the tail of an opponent and aimed upwards to hit it from behind, but the extra speed of the newer German fighter planes made this a difficult trick.

No. 29 Squadron was due to be re-equipped with Sopwith Camels later in the summer. Nevertheless, here I was in a splendid squadron with a fire-eater of a CO and I very soon got used to my little aircraft.

Our main job was to patrol over the front line to prevent any German scout pilots from interfering with our reconnaissance aircraft, which used to fly up and down spotting our artillery shells and correcting their aim. We also had to try to stop any German aircraft coming over our lines and spotting our own artillery positions.

Another of our jobs was to escort bomber and photo-reconnaissance aircraft on those more hazardous operations across the German lines, when the Germans could choose the time and place to attack to their best advantage. It was not until the British new SE5 Scout fighter aircraft came to the Western Front in July 1917 that these fast and reliable aircraft started freelance raids over German air space and literally put the wind up the German fighters. A young pilot called Ball was the leader of No. 56 Squadron. He used to bring his aircraft up to our forward aerodrome at dawn, most of his pilots still wearing pyjamas; then they would go out for a sortie in the hope of catching a German scout squadron in the air.

The approach of 56 Squadron was superb. They practised and perfected a squadron roll in which all the aircraft rolled in the air before going into the attack; this alone, I think, must have given some of the German pilots the jitters. I would have loved to fly one of those

Rolls-Royce-engined biplanes with their two guns and splendid speed and manoeuvrability. They were in 1917 what the Spitfire was to the RAF in 1940. It was a timely boost to the morale of the British squadrons who were being badly harassed by what was known as the Richthofen circus, a brilliant team of German pilots led by the famous Red Baron himself, Richthofen.

Next to us on one end of the big aerodrome on the Arras front was No. 60 Squadron, also equipped with Nieuports. Since many of the pilots had been at Upavon with some of us in 29 Squadron, it was a happy family. The bright light of No. 60 Squadron was called Bishop, a boisterous young Canadian whose favourite sport was to capture a couple of the tame ducks from the nearby farmyard, give them each a stiff brandy and throw them up on to the ridge of one of the huts. Whichever stayed there longest, won. It was Bishop who asked me one day if he could join my flight, a dawn patrol, on the following morning. I was delighted, but I did not know he was using my flight as a cover for the daring exploit which earned him the Victoria Cross.

When we were well over enemy lines, he peeled off as I turned westward again. I saw him going down steeply towards the large German aerodrome of Cambrai. He told me later that he had completely surprised the occupants. He shot up a number of aircraft on the ground, including any enemy pilot who tried to take off. Apparently he was so mixed up with the German aircraft that no one dared to shoot at him. After the war Bishop was to become the Chief of the Canadian Air Staff. Our usual dawn patrols were timed to take off so that we arrived over the lines just before sunrise, which in June was early anyway. The only trouble was that at that time the sun was straight in one's eyes, giving any German aircraft that might be about a distinct advantage.

Aside from bullets in the air, I had a narrow escape on the ground just after the Canadian victory at Vimy Ridge. Apparently the German reconnaissance aircraft were coming low up to the ridge and then zooming up over it trying desperately to spot our camouflaged artillery positions; so, the Royal Artillery rang us up and asked us to come out and discuss how best to stop this. Unfortunately, no sooner had our small party arrived than the Germans started shelling the area. A small piece of shrapnel whizzed across in front of my face, missing my steel helmet but nicking my nose.

I also had an unfortunate ground accident about a month after I had arrived at the squadron. The CO was keen on keeping us fit. I sometimes used to borrow a horse from a nearby army unit and have a good ride. We also played badminton in the orchard near our huts. My ankle, weakened from my bicycle-polo days, went over in the rough ground. I was proclaimed unfit to fly and sent off to the nearest casualty-clearing station. It was one of the most distressing nights I have ever spent. I was to recall the words of Major Small when he was persuading me that I ought to join the Flying Corps, 'If anything happens to you, old chap, it happens quick.'

My accident coincided with the beginning of a fairly large push up the front. Casualties were coming into the tent thick and fast; the crowded beds held quietly dying men. Next to me was a friend from No. 60 Squadron who had been terribly broken up when the lower wing of his Nieuport ripped off as he dived steeply near our aerodrome. The poor lad did not survive the night. Next morning we were told that everybody had to be evacuated down to St Omer. The nurses told me that the casualties had become so bad that we should all probably be going straight through to England. I just could not go back to 'Blighty' on the strength of a turned ankle, so I managed to get my CO on the phone and begged him to send transport to bring me back to my squadron. After I had spent an anxious morning, an order came through to return me to the pilot pool at St Omer. It took several days before my CO could get me back on his strength, but at least it gave my ankle time to repair. The pilot pool was full of exuberant young pilots just out from England, all determined to get their DSOs as quickly as possible; they wanted to know what it was really like up at the front. I did not disillusion them. As evening fell they went happily to town. I was aching for a good night's rest. On the following morning one of them told me that every red light had been full up; 'Omer' was a busy nightspot.

I rejoined the squadron and had the lower wings of my little aircraft thoroughly tested. I had missed those evening games in the mess hut trying to synchronise two old gramophones with two records of that popular song of the moment, 'Every Little Girl Can Teach Me Something New'.

On a day when no flying was possible, the CO sent a bunch of us in the old Crossley tender down to Amiens. One member of my flight had been there before and together we went straight to the old Coq d'Or restaurant in the cathedral square where we ordered the most sumptuous meal available at that time and two lovelies to go with it.

Then I strolled across to the great cathedral and said a silent prayer. A gentle nun approached me with her blessing and gave me a very small circular metal token, a replica of the lovely round stained-glass window depicting the weeping angel of Amiens. I wore it on my identity-disc chain. The rain was clearing when we arrived back late that night at the aerodrome. I would get just two hours' sleep before

I was knocked up for dawn patrol, but I had won a blue silk garter which would now decorate my compass.

In June, after three months on the Arras front, I was given my three weeks' leave. 'Simmy' Simpson, my Flight Commander of 'C' Flight, was also due to go home. He had managed to complete his full tour of six months. Few did. He told me that he had recommended me to take over the flight when I got back. I made a note to buy some extra pips and braid for my uniform which I could sew on if I were to become a captain.

There was a small hotel called the Washington at the Berkeley Square end of Curzon Street, where the family usually stayed when in London, and where I went the evening I arrived back. Like every other hotel, as I learned, it was full up, but the good proprietor fixed up a bed for me in the bathroom. After I had had a long and luxurious bath, it was filled with cushions and a mattress put on top. Close to the hotel was a splendid men's hairdresser. The next morning, I had a marvellous time having a haircut, shampoo and a shave, and I then felt fit to meet the world. I phoned my girl's parents and arranged to come back to London from Gloucestershire for the last few days of my leave, and then I took the midday train from Paddington to Stroud.

Somehow the welcome from my family, together with the quiet of the Cotswold house, the peace and lovely laziness of it all, was able to banish the whole atmosphere of the Western Front in a matter of days – banished, too, the thoughts of going back. The sadness over my dear sister's loss of her fiancée was forgotten for a while as we closed in to enjoy being together at a time when every day brought tragedy to some of those we knew. I rode my sister's hunter round the countryside; I stroked the bonnet of my old Studebaker, which now stood at the back of the garage; and my sister and I visited a few of our friends, but, alas, most of them were overseas and many we should never see again.

I think my leave in the summer of 1917 brought home to me more than at any other time the dreadful slaughter of the best and brightest of the young men of Britain in that war. A whole generation would be nearly wiped out, leaving the mothers and girls to mourn and perhaps never marry, and in 1917 some of the bloodiest battles were still to be fought. The tank, the secret weapon which had first fired my imagination to join the Flying Corps, and which was supposed to win the war, had to be used prematurely to save the morale of the French Army. They had taken such a ghastly hammering at Verdun that the whole army was ready to revolt. British tanks had to be put into action and, although too soon and too few, they saved the day, but did not win the war.

Fortunately, when I joined the Gloucestershire Hussars in 1915, I had been persuaded also to join that elite institution, the Cavalry Club, which looked out over Green Park from its splendid position in Piccadilly. When I was a raw subaltern I was almost too frightened to go there, as it seemed to be full of generals from the War Office. But now I had a little more confidence, and it was a godsend to be able to have a bedroom there, and to give one's friends an excellent meal in those times of shortages.

It was a hectic week in London with my girl and her family. We had of course to see *The Bing Boys* with George Robey and Vi Lorraine singing 'If You Were the Only Girl in the World'. Then there were little restaurants, and dancing and champagne and some taxi rides around London. There was one night when we were supposed to go to see *Chu-Chin-Chow*, but as a mark of respect to Sir Herbert Tree, the great Shakespearean actor who had recently died, the show was cancelled at the last minute. I always felt that I must have been the only person who never saw it. Too soon came the inevitable return to France. My girl came to see me off. How tensely artificial were those farewells at Victoria station, families and lovers desperately trying to be brave and cheerful. She was only sixteen and looked so very, very young as the train finally drew out. There were tears at the last moment.

There was a surprise for me at Boulogne. The driver of the squadron car which had come down to meet me told me that the squadron had moved. I had been looking forward to a room to myself in one of the Nissen huts and had even bought curtain material to decorate the place. Now all that would be useless; apparently the squadron was under canvas in a little field not far behind the lines at Poperinge in Belgium. I did not question the driver further, but after we were some miles out of Boulogne, I noticed that he was getting dozy over the wheel. We stopped the car, and I suggested that I drive for a while. He was grateful.

Round a sharp bend in the road, we came to a level-crossing with the chain gates hanging down against us. I suppose I had been going a bit too fast, but we just dented one of those gates before I was able to pull up. The train was due at any minute, and the gate-keeper came out and in voluble French asked me to pull in because I would not be allowed to go on until I had paid for a new gate. After the train passed by, several other military cars started sounding their horns. The old gate-keeper having no option but to open the gates to let them through,

I wasted no time and left him shouting and waving his fists. Anyway, I am certain he could have put the whole thing right with a hammer.

I did not know the road after we got into Belgium, so the driver took over again, and it was late by the time we arrived.

The aerodrome was both short and narrow, aircraft having to take off and land one by one. Even that was tricky with a field of maize on one side, an orchard at the bottom, and a stream on the other side. Also, we were within range of the German high-velocity guns, and surprisingly, although we used to hear some of these shells whistling over our heads, they never seemed to find our exact location.

I took over my flight. One or two new boys had arrived while I had been away, but the CO seemed glad enough to see me back. He explained that we had been brought up north because an enormous push was in preparation. The Germans could hardly have failed to notice this also – every road in the district seemed crammed with troops, guns and tanks. I was soon to learn that the Germans themselves had brought up all their best fighter squadrons in order to stop the Allies from finding out their strength and positions on the other side.

Poperinge was a hot spot. Close to our aerodrome, too, were some of our own observation balloons, which seemed to be an easy target for the German fighters sneaking in at low level. One of the popular well-known young actors in London, Basil Hallam, was killed this way, close to us. The CO used to stand on the aerodrome and curse, but of course it was too late to go up by the time the enemy aircraft had shot down a balloon and escaped again.

It was a very different matter with the German balloons, which were their principal method of observation and artillery spotting. Somehow, they had developed a winch which pulled the balloon down at a tremendous speed once an enemy aircraft was spotted heading in that direction. Each balloon position was circled by a battery of what we called 'flaming onions', a continuous stream of balls of fire shot up around the site. To try and shoot down a German balloon was a very hazardous business; unfortunately, our own balloons had no such protection.

On Friday, 13 July 1917, I was sitting in the mess tent enjoying my bacon and eggs and a cup of coffee after I had taken my flight out on dawn patrol. It had been a misty morning and was evidently not bright enough to induce any German fighters to come up and try and catch us with the sun in our eyes, but it looked as if it would be one of those hot July days. My breakfast was interrupted by the CO who looked a bit agitated. He told me that the Army had demanded an urgent photographic reconnaissance opposite our front, and that I was to take my flight up again at ten o'clock to escort the photographic aircraft over the German lines.

The Royal Flying Corps was of course subject to orders from the Army Command, who seemed blithely unmindful of the tremendous losses of highly trained pilots and valuable aircraft which the air photography entailed, and which the Germans were anxious we should not carry out. I told the CO that my own aircraft had had a bit of engine trouble and that I had had to turn it in for an overhaul, and I should have to borrow somebody else's. One's own aircraft is adjusted to one's height, and every cartridge case is inspected in case it has a dent that would cause a stoppage. Now, in my borrowed aircraft, everything had been adapted for a short man, and it was not until I was taking off that I realised I was without my beautiful silk garter.

I knew this was going to be a hot assignment. We had to rendezvous with the three 1½ Strutter Sopwith photographic aircraft at 8000 feet, on our side of the lines, but the moment we approached the target the Sopwiths would dive to 2000 feet to get their photographs. Our job was to go down and look after their tails and try to stop them from being shot down – that was the moment of real danger. The Germans were expert in working out new techniques for their fighter aircraft. They seldom went up on routine patrols but would choose their time and place to attack the British formations.

On 13 July they practised a new trick. The moment the Sopwiths began to dive towards their target, a massive anti-aircraft barrage was put up between our fighters and the Sopwiths below, making it almost impossible to see the photographic aircraft we were escorting. Meantime, a German fighter squadron was alerted as to our exact position by the anti-aircraft fire. I tried to spot the photographic aircraft and to keep my eye open for enemy aircraft. It was at that moment that I saw about a dozen German fighters silhouetted against the sun on the starboard side. I seesawed my wings and turned up to meet them. Alas, my left-winger was hit first and went down in flames. The loss of young Cameron was a bad blow, and the dogfight soon became intense and vicious. I managed to get a burst into one aircraft and saw him going down, but the next moment when another enemy aircraft came into my sights I pressed the button, but nothing happened. The gun had jammed. There were now eleven enemy aircraft against the four of us who remained. The next instant I felt a burst of bullets coming through the aircraft, the bullets ripping the inside of my flying boots and going into my engine. Thank God they missed the petrol tank, but my engine sputtered and died. I was now without an engine and without a gun, but alive.

I suppose my flying was then instinct. I tried to gauge how far it would be to get back over our lines, for by now we were right behind the German lines. Without an engine there would be little chance, especially as, even with my aerobatics, flying like a falling leaf, the enemy were still firing at me when they got a chance. I was gradually losing height. I saw what looked like a small flat bit of ground, well behind the infantry lines, albeit with some shell holes in it. We all knew that if one came down among the infantry, they shot one on sight; but now controlling my glide, stalling almost to the point of losing flying speed, I put her down. It was a bumpy bit of ground, and we very soon hit a ditch and turned over, fortunately not down a shell hole. My head was jammed between the crashed top wing and the ground. I was cross; I suppose I should have been grateful. My first thought of course was fire – I had to get out. I withdrew my head sharply and broke my nose, but I did manage to roll out of the aircraft and crawl far enough away. The sun was on my face as I lay on my back looking at the little weeping angel of Amiens. I was alive.

Chapter 7

PRISONER OF WAR

I heard the tramp of boots and raised myself up on my elbows in the long grass. I was surrounded by a ring of German soldiers pointing their rifles at me, but I suppose my nose had been bleeding a good deal and my face looked a bit of a mess, for a young German officer came towards me and asked quietly if I was wounded. I shook my head and just pointed to my broken nose. He helped me up, and it was then I saw that I had had the luck to land almost on the doorstep of a German anti-aircraft battery.

The German 'Flak' looked upon themselves as being a part of the German Air Force with whom they worked closely, and were, I believe, under the same command. At any rate, this young officer could not have been nicer. He led me back to his headquarters at the battery, sat me down, gave me a drink of hot cocoa, and sent for a doctor, who came, reset my nose and plastered it up. I must have looked rather a sight. The gunners had put their rifles away and clustered around. I do not think an enemy aircraft had landed on their doorstep before. I asked the young Lieutenant the time, because my watch had stopped when I crashed. When he told me that it was not yet ten o'clock, I realised that the Germans did not adopt British Summer Time – it was going to be a long day for me.

I must have been at the battery about half an hour before a German staff car drew up and out jumped a cocky little officer with what looked like half a tin plate hanging around his neck. It was to be nearly sixty years later when my book, *The Ultra Secret*, was first published in America that I received a letter from a Mr Viegers, now living in Texas, asking whether by chance I was the young Captain who had crashed close to his battery on that July day of 1917. I was, and I was able to thank him for the way in which he had looked after me.

I was driven away to what proved to be a forward intelligence post some five miles further behind the anti-aircraft line. It was a low brick-built house, and I was greeted by a rather portly middle-aged officer in the same way that we should have greeted a German pilot back at my squadron. There was a strange detente between those who flew and fought in the air. One moment you would be doing your best to kill each other but, once down on the floor, you became another airman. So now the rather portly officer greeted me, 'Hello, I am an officer; I am a sportsman, hello.'

I must have looked a bit funny with my bloody face and bandaged nose, but I was taken into the living quarters of the house and offered a wash and a brush-up. The officer suggested that after my crash I might wish to lie down on one of the bunks reserved for prisoners as they were brought in. It was not to be very long before I was joined by a pilot from one of the Sopwith 1½ Strutters that had been shot down also; then a young naval triplane pilot was brought in from further up the line. The Germans were obviously having a busy time collecting the victims of the aerial battles.

I noticed in the intelligence centre that the German officers had Russian prisoners to look after them, but it was not until later that afternoon that I found that my precious pipe and tobacco, which I always carried when I was flying, had been stolen. I complained to the German officer, but he thought I must be mistaken, and that they had fallen out when my aeroplane was upside down. Nevertheless, all three of us were grateful for a lunch of ham and potatoes.

Then, of course, there came the interrogation. Once again the portly officer explained that he was our friend; he was a sportsman; he played polo – we could tell him everything. In fact, one told him nothing but one's number and name, and it was he who proceeded to tell me what squadron I came from, what was the name of my commanding officer, approximately where our aerodrome was located, and all about our 'funny little' Nieuport aeroplanes, as he called them. Their intelligence must have been very good and was obviously closely co-ordinated with the operations of their squadrons.

Later on that afternoon, the officer came over and quietly gave me the notecase which he told me had belonged to a member of my squadron who had just been killed.

Young Sheppard, a fine young Australian, had distinguished himself in the squadron when he used to go out Hun-hunting on his own. His great buddy was my left-winger who had been shot down in the morning. Sheppard must have gone out to avenge his friend's death; alas, he met his own. No. 29 Squadron had had a bad day.

Shortly afterwards, the officer called me over to look through the very powerful mounted field glasses they used for observing our operations. My CO had obviously thought it necessary to have a morale flight of the squadron, and as I watched my old chums flying across the evening sky led by the CO himself, I recognised that he was flying my own aeroplane that I had had to leave behind.

Then we were joined by several members of the squadron with which we had fought in the morning. I noticed that one of the pilots was carrying the cushion out of my aeroplane; he was, I learned, the leader of the squadron. We shook hands and he laughed as he showed me how the cushion I had been sitting on was riddled with bullet holes, and remarked, 'One inch nearer and you would have been a soprano.' I had not realised what a close call I had had.

We all sat down in the open air around a long wooden table and had drinks of excellent hock, our fat friend interpreting as we chatted with the pilots. They wanted to know why we still carried that out-of-date gun on the top of the wing. I explained to them that until quite recently it had been a very useful way of knocking down another aeroplane from underneath, but it was rather hard to make a case. They tried to pump one on the coming offensive. It was now quite obvious that they knew where the Passchendaele push would be, but wanted confirmation from anybody they thought could give it, especially the timing and the day. One had to pretend complete ignorance on the subject, uncertain whether that was not equally indicative since the whole front on both sides was alive with activity. The straw palliasse in the wooden bunk was not the most comfortable place to sleep on the first night; yet while I was a prisoner of war I grew so used to my board beds that when I got home I could not sleep on an ordinary mattress.

The following morning all three of us were taken off once again to a small prisoner's cage containing a little brick house on the edge of one of the German aerodromes. I did not know exactly where it was as I had rather lost my bearing by now. We were to spend about five days in this first cage until sufficient prisoners had been gathered together to move us on. It was here that I first began to learn about being really hungry.

Our sole food was a few bits of black, rather sour bread, and a few slices of very red, soft sausage, which I swear had been made from cats and dogs. There was one concession: we were taken out for walks suitably guarded. Walking through fields of ripe wheat, we picked the heads of corn, rubbed the grain out in our hands and chewed it. The cherries, too, were ripe, and we were able to gather a few of these from the trees as we went along. What really saved our pangs of hunger were the cheap German cigars which we were allowed to buy. Everybody always carried money in their pockets when they were flying and now it came in handy. German cigars were wonderful at stifling one's longing for real food, but food was obviously very short in Belgium at that time. Nevertheless, I will never forget some of the Belgian women coming up to the barbed wire and handing us little crusts of bread which they must have saved from their own meagre rations.

The little sitting room of the house was, I felt, bound to be bugged and it was not long before I found a microphone hidden behind one of the pictures. One of the other pilots wanted to pull it out, but wiser counsel prevailed, and I put the picture gently back over it. We all now understood that we must not say anything about the coming push, but we did elaborate on the vast numbers of the French armies which were coming up from the south. It was quite untrue, but we thought that it might give the Germans something to think about.

The next phase of our journey back into Germany was probably the worst that I ever experienced. We were taken to the rail-head and herded into a closed cattle truck with a batch of Russian prisoners who were obviously too weak to continue their forced labour on the Western Front. Indeed, they were too weak to stand, and lay about on the floor in heaps, their unseeing eyes peering out from their drawn faces, giving some indication of what the rest of their filthily smelly bodies must have been like inside the ragged clothes they were wearing. No longer resembling human beings, they were probably destined to die anyway. After a slow, bumpy, dirty journey, we were all turned out at Cologne station where pathetic German women spat at us as we moved off to a dungeon below the platform. Here again for the whole night we were packed together with those miserable scraps of Russian humanity. The stench was appalling, and as they were infested with every form of louse and bug, we soon began to scratch ourselves and realised that nothing, but a hot disinfectant bath would get us clean again.

Although still itching, we had a better journey in a proper railway carriage up the Rhine to Karlsruhe, the large collecting camp where prisoners were kept for several weeks until clothes and food parcels arrived for them. It was a bit of a surprise to find so many of one's fellow pilots who had trained with us in England and gone through the same experience in France. Here we were duly disinfected and every stitch of our clothing sterilised.

It was here, too, that I received letters from my mother, father and sister. I had, unknown to myself, been reported killed in action and my poor family had gone three weeks believing I was dead. They were very private letters, which I have kept until this day. I never really knew what a splendid fellow I was until I read my own obituary notice from the local paper some eighteen months later when I got home. I, too, wrote my weekly letter home and had to rewrite my first one because I was unable to persuade the censor that the word 'bastard', when applied to the pilot who had shot me down, was really one of comradely appreciation.

I asked for another uniform with my captain's rank, and for some tobacco. There were Army and merchant navy captives in the camp as well as Flying Corps, and one of the old sea captains, bless him, gave me an old pipe and some tobacco. Just after I arrived there was an auction of the food parcels of an unfortunate prisoner who had died; I remember paying ten pounds for a tin of salmon which lasted me a week. Some of us were also able to persuade the German cooks to fry our black bread in such fat as they had; otherwise, until our own food parcels arrived, we fed on vegetable soups and occasionally a stew of horse meat. It was hot in Karlsruhe that summer of 1917. I bought a hand towel from another prisoner and sewed myself a pair of shorts; they were a bit skimped, but wearable.

By August, a large batch of about one hundred of us were packed off to another camp at Trier, on the Moselle river, and were housed in an old school where Karl Marx had once been a pupil. At least it was to prove warm in the bitter winter that followed.

There was a high fence with wire around the school grounds. In another building were some fifty French prisoners who insisted on standing under the hot showers (we were allowed one a week) until the water ran cold. They were an odd lot, entirely selfish, and would fight each other at the least provocation. I even saw knives come out over the possession of a lump of sugar. We managed to play football in the large courtyard; this was unpopular with our French friends. One or two would dress up in their best uniforms and insist on walking across the courtyard to protest at our sport. Of course, they served as a sporting target for a football.

There were two splendid fellows; Georges Couprie of the Chasseurs Alpins, and a lanky Algerian Frenchman called Jacques, with whom I and Jimmy Stevenson, an ex-Bradfield lad against whom I had played football when I was at Charterhouse, used to play bridge in French. There was a small courtyard outside our room where a one-time French opera singer, now a cook for the French officers, would sing in a glorious tenor voice in time to the ancient pump at which he was drawing water.

In the deep winter of 1917/18, we gathered the snow and made a skating rink in the courtyard, and old skates were bought for us in the town. It was good exercise, if a bit dangerous, but the snow banks served another purpose. Some of us had started to dig a tunnel where the house abutted on to the boundary fence; we took the 'spoil' out each night and buried it under the snow around the rink.

It was fortunate that the Commandant of the camp had once been a military attaché in London. He spoke excellent English and genuinely liked the British, which made life easier for us; however, he did not have the same affection for the French prisoners. When one day he called all the British to a private meeting, he told us that our tunnel had been detected and advised us not to proceed with it. He insisted that we tell the French nothing about his warning. Luckily, there were no French in the escape plan, so no one got hurt.

Once there was an air raid on the railway yards by British bombers. There was panic among our guards; we were all shut indoors and anyone who tried to look out of a window invited a shot from an excited German. It was good for morale. Jim and I passed our time with a box of watercolour paints and brushes we had obtained from the town. Jim had been a scout pilot, and both he and I recreated our dogfights on the Western Front. Some of these watercolours I gave to the RAF museum at Hendon.

After the tunnel affair, it must have been decided that either Trier was not a very safe camp, or that the bedbug problem was getting too bad. These little insects lived in the crevices of the iron bedsteads and normally only came out at night to feed, but if one heated the bedstead with a candle they could be induced to take a daytime stroll up the wall. One day we heard that a Dutchman, who inspected the prison camps on behalf of the British government, was due to look us over the following morning. We spent a hectic few hours getting the little bedbugs to come out, and when the inspector arrived we were having bets as to how many bugs we could squash with our slippers on the wall. The noise could not be ignored, much to the embarrassment of the Germans.

Early in 1918, we were once again sent off east to Schweidnitz in Silesia, home of some of the Prussian barons, including the famous Richthofen. This time our camp had been a lunatic asylum, but had the merit of having quite large grounds, and both the main building and the large wooden huts were warm. They needed to be as winter set in early in this eastern province. The prisoners were about seventy per cent RFC, with some Army and merchant seamen. It was a well-run camp with a sympathetic Bavarian, Hauptmann Schmidt, as Camp Commandant. I took on the job of camp liaison officer with the Commandant and got to know him well; it gave me the opportunity to learn some German.

The new camp was poorly guarded and in the first week Tom Mapplebeck and a couple of other prisoners scaled the wall and got away. Once again, the cookhouse was close to a perimeter fence and a few of us decided to start a tunnel. There was room to spread the 'spoil' under the wooden floor, but space was limited, so it was decided that only thin people could make the attempt in order to keep the tunnel small. My shoulders were too wide. Quite a few got out in the dead of night and set off for the Austrian border in twos and threes.

Alas, some nocturnal travellers spotted some of them and raised the alarm; they were all caught and put into solitary-confinement cells in the main building where many of us slept. One large door separated us. The sergeant of our guards always kept his keys on a ring attached to his belt, and there was a well-contrived drama when a number of us staged a violent quarrel outside the guard house. Out came the sergeant and, while we argued and jostled around him, a piece of soft soap was pressed against the large key we had seen him use on the door; we managed to get hold of a bit of wire and melt down some of the tin foil from our food tins and cast some sort of a key. Luckily it worked so that food and encouragement was given to the prisoners in the nights which followed.

Our food parcels came regularly and kept us in reasonable health, though Quaker Oats for breakfast every day became a little monotonous. There were gas rings in the large eating hall so we could heat up tins of food or fry sausages; and once a week we had a vegetable and horsemeat stew 'on the house'. Food for the population of the town must have been very scarce. From our windows we could see on to the street. One day we watched a very ancient, very bony old horse pulling a load of wood; it dropped dead in the street and within an hour all the housewives in the district had left a bare skeleton in the road.

Schweidnitz was apparently similar to all POW camps where prisoners were confined for any length of time. There were those which got hold of roulette wheels and kept their gambling devotees occupied. Vast sums and even properties were signed away on IOUs, but I doubt if they were ever redeemed. The gamblers also joined the drunks. It had been easy at Trier to buy cheap moselle; rather sour wine was also readily available in Schweidnitz for those who were ready to spend the money they could get through Holland. More than one went off their heads, some dangerously, and had to be taken away.

Then there were those like myself who concentrated on trying to keep fit. We persuaded the Germans to let us play football on a flat field outside the town. There were half a dozen Carthusians, all of whom I had known at the school, and in fact most of the younger Flying Corps joined the keep-fit brigade. We even used to plod through the snow during that very cold winter of 1918/19 to the bath-house where one could turn on a shower of ice-cold water through a three-inch pipe. Most of us also tried to learn German, and in my case I also read law books which my father sent me. There was a band and a dramatic society, which saw, I suppose, the first venture on the stage of Richard Goolden. Much of the music was from *Chu-Chin-Chow*, which I shall always associate with Schweidnitz. Hauptmann Schmidt had allowed us to arrange for a cricket net with stumps, bats and balls sent out from Holland. This equipment was a great source of joy in the summer until a new Prussian general came to inspect the camp and promptly confiscated it.

Many of us made maps and accumulated some German money, which we carried about on our persons, since our quarters were subject to surprise searches. One day we were suddenly ordered into the large empty chapel which formed part of the camp and were taken off in groups to be searched. I do not know if anyone ever tried to play the organ again – the pipes were full of paper money and maps.

We had our tragedies too, some caught pneumonia. There was a devoted British Army doctor who organised us and instructed us how to nurse the patients. We were able to buy some bottles of German champagne and managed to keep them going on it with day and night shifts.

There was a bridge foursome with Jim Stevenson, two others and myself, who shared a corner of the big dormitory. The trouble was one got to know each other's play almost too well; we had to swap around partners to keep a level game. We played nearly every evening of the year we were in camp, but towards the end of 1918 excitement began to grow that at last the war was coming to an end.

The final German push in France was proclaimed a war-winner by the German newspapers, and there was general gloom; then came the turn of the tide and the Armistice in November. Our band played 'God Save the King' in front of the Commandant; the German guards threw away their rifles and joined in the cheering. They offered us their medals and Iron Crosses for a piece of soap. The starving population of the town marched on the camp intent on taking our stores of canned food. Hauptmann Schmidt was demoted, and the sergeant was made Commandant of the town and camp, but it was Schmidt who set up a machine gun opposite the camp gates and warned that he would open fire on the mob if they broke in.

Then came the news in banner headlines across the local paper of the Kaiser's abdication. Our Dutch friend came to tell us that as we were a well-stocked camp so far to the east, we would have to remain where we were until all the camps in western Germany had been repatriated, as many of them held recent captives with no proper food supplies. We were free to come and go into the town and countryside, but we would return to camp at least once a day for news of our departure. In fact, two months were to go by before we got home in mid-January 1919.

There was an old beer house close by where one could get odd snacks in exchange for a tin of corned beef or real coffee, and gradually Jim and I began to explore the countryside. We would put a tin of butter in our pockets and set off to a farm where the family would supply a splendid meal of goose in exchange for the butter. The exercise in that cold winter was welcome. The townspeople too were welcoming until early Christmas, when the local regiment returned from the war, holding what seemed more like a victory parade through the town with bands playing; so, we took ourselves back to camp for safety.

There was a kind gesture at Christmas when the old couple who ran the beer house asked Jim and me in for Christmas dinner. They had got hold of a goose and we supplied plum pudding, some butter, sausages and real coffee. It was a splendid meal, accompanied by a bottle of hock. There was no love lost on the Kaiser, who was held responsible for the war and all the misery it had caused. We drank a toast to the elimination of all would-be demagogues. Little did we know what the fate of Schweidnitz would be at the hands of the invading Russians the next time round.

By the time we came to leave, we had made a number of friends in the district who were genuinely sorry to see us and our tins of food go. But, only three days before my departure, there was a small miracle. Friedel Paterok, a very lovely, blue-eyed, fair-haired Polish girl came down from Breslau to stay with her aunt at one of the farms which we visited. She and I spent the rest of our time together in Schweidnitz. I used to visit the camp each day to collect some food to supplement the hotel meals and I finally gave her all the food I had left. Somehow, it does not seem strange to me that I remember every moment of that brief encounter.

We were packed eight in a carriage on the long journey back to north Germany, where we were due to take a ferry to Copenhagen. We very nearly did not arrive. At Frankfurt-on-Oder, in the middle of the bitter cold night, someone connected our coach to the gas mains at the station. There were no lights in the carriage, but we suddenly noticed the smell. We opened the windows to the cold night air and all hell was let loose – fortunately no one died.

Copenhagen welcomed us with open arms and many a pretty face. The oysters and champagne were excellent. Two of the Danish princes expressed a desire to dine with us, so a party was organised at the Café Vivel. A splendid meal topped by speeches of friendship would have been the highlight of our two-day stopover had we not been presented with the bill for the whole shooting match!

It was a rough crossing to Leith, enlivened by the need to keep a constant look-out for floating mines. A number of us were issued rifles and spent the daylight hours shooting at the mines in order to hole them just below the waterline, so that they would sink.

Chapter 8

OXFORD

We disembarked next day and entrained for Edinburgh. I found I was the senior officer of the train, which had also picked up another group of prisoners at Leith. At Edinburgh I was ordered by a staff officer to fall in. With a band playing, we marched into the great hall to the cheers of all the lasses who were waiting to give us food and drink. It was a marvellous homecoming.

I suppose I had not been prepared for the complete change, both in speech and customs, which I found had so altered England during the eighteen months I had been away. I found it difficult to talk to people; life was a mixture of the rejoicing of the youth and the bravery of the bereaved. No one was interested in what one had gone through; no one wanted to talk about the war anymore, only about an exuberant anticipation of a land fit for heroes to live in. Somehow I had to throw off those sombre years of war and prison camps and readjust myself to the new society.

I felt that probably the best way to rehabilitate myself would be to try to go up to university. Luckily, soon after I returned to England in 1919, I saw a notice in the newspaper offering shortened undergraduate courses at Oxford to those who had been robbed of their university careers by the war. Most of my friends who would have come up to Cambridge with me had been killed in the war, so I no longer had any reason to go there. As Oxford was near my home in Gloucestershire, I wrote and applied for a course.

Within a week I found myself in the study of the Dean of Christ Church in his lovely old house, which formed part of the north-east corner of the famous Tom Quad. Tommy Strong, as we later learned to call the Dean, was a rather slight but impressive figure in his clerical frockcoat and gaiters; but I was at once struck by the quietly spoken words of this white-haired priest with his twinkling blue eyes. I stood at attention when he entered, but his 'You're no longer in the Army now; please relax and make yourself comfortable,' spoken with a friendly smile, was to set the tone of a friendship which was all too short. We talked briefly of my war experience, of my future hopes and aspirations, and finally I was accepted to undergo a short fifteen months' degree course.

This was an idea which, the Dean explained to me, he had himself instituted for 'young men like yourself, aged beyond their youth by war, who had lost those precious years when young men's dreams range over the age-old arguments of religion, politics and love; so that they may have a chance to regain the thoughts of living instead of dying, and adjust themselves to a newer and more compassionate order of society'. Little wonder, as he was to tell me later, that he was destined to become the Bishop of Ripon because, as he said, the bench of Bishops wanted someone who understood the young people who would now have to fill the gaps of the lost generation. They could not have chosen a wiser priest, though his loss to the House (as Christ Church was called) later the following year was indeed a sad one.

The Dean told me to go along and see the Senior Censor, who made all the arrangements for undergraduate accommodation and studies. Mr Owen lived in his own comfortable quarters close to the Deanery; he was well rounded in every direction. The Dean had evidently telephoned him to say that I was coming, because my welcome was of the same kindly, informal character as the one I had received from the Dean himself. He told me how glad he was that some people like myself were going to come back and help the college regain its traditional ways of making boys into men. He was afraid I should be unable to have rooms in the college for the first term, the summer of 1919, but after that he would find me rooms in the college where I should have full opportunity of making new friends. He asked me to get in touch with him again a short while before the term started, and he would let me know where I was to go and who my tutor would be. The friendly smile on his rubicund face, together with my welcome from the Dean, were a happy prelude to my wonderful but all too short time at Oxford.

About a week after we had settled in at Oxford, the Dean asked six of us to go to his house. He must have done some homework on our backgrounds, for he now asked us if we would be prepared to start up again those field sports for which the House had been well known before the war. The Dean gave us some records to help us and also assured us that he would make arrangements with our tutors to give us extra tutorials so as not to jeopardise our examinations.

The Dean was as good as his word. My tutor, Don Carter, who was a well-known character at the House, gave me a tutorial in his rooms in Tom Quad once a week.

Our first job was to restart the small hunting club, known as Loders. It had always been kept to twelve members and met together every Sunday evening for dinner. We made Alan Apsley our chairman. He was the son of Earl Bathurst, in whose park at Cirencester both Alan and I had trained in the yeomanry. I took the job of secretary and split the work among our few members.

But now it was summer-time, and I was playing tennis for the House, partnered by Roger Weathered, who was also the amateur golf champion of Britain that year. We were coached at tennis by John Masterman who became so well known for his job of turning round the German spies we caught during the Second World War. George Hayter-Hames volunteered to look after the polo and the House beagles. We all gave him twenty-five pounds to go up to the horse sales, Tattersalls, in London and buy six ponies. They were not in the top class, but neither were their riders. Fortunately, the well-known polo player Philip Maygor offered to come to teach us the game, while he himself was able to school his own ponies. The polo ground was Port Meadow where I had had my first flight in an aeroplane, and luckily there were still good stables there for the horses. Later, George wrote round to a number of packs of beagles which had survived the war and begged for a hound. There were only two old bitches left of the pre-war House beagle pack but there were also the kennels and now a rather elderly kennelman who came back to help us. I acted as secretary, looking after the cash side and also the transport. Also, I was whipper-in, which gave me endless exercise when it came to hunting hares around Oxford. Although George had walked the new hounds out a good deal together, they were hardly a hunting pack to start with. We had a lot of followers from other colleges, all of whom contributed to our funds. By the spring of 1920, the House beagles were once again established.

Prince Paul of Serbia, another of our members, decided not to go on with his pre-war polo, so he sold me his saddle and kit cheap. Little did the poor fellow know that his brother the King would be killed, and that he, Paul, would have to take over the running of Yugoslavia, of which Serbia was to form a part. His accession meant that the holidays at his hunting lodge in Yugoslavia, to which some of us had been invited, were no longer possible. We gathered, however, that many beautiful girls would also have been invited, so that the sport would have been mostly indoors. Edward 'Ruby' Holland-Martin found good hunters at reasonable prices for me and some others. He was well in with the horse world. Alan and I used to leave Oxford at 8 a.m. on Saturdays in his pale green Ford 'tin Lizzie' to have a day's hunting with the Heythrop. I had managed to buy a splendid horse on which I was also able to win some point-to-point races at the end of the season. Alas, the following year I was not rich enough to refuse a wonderful offer for him, only to watch him come third in the National Hunt Steeplechase at Cheltenham. I also saw him run out by a loose horse at the Canal Turn, so close to home, in the Grand National. He was up with the first five horses. One only has one wonderful horse in a lifetime, so people tell me. I had a number of hunters after him, but none matched Playful Picton – out of Playmate IV by a sire called Picton, both well known in the racing world. In the spring of 1920, I organised the revival of the House Grind – the name of the Christ Church point-to-point. In all those equine activities I also had the help of Chetty Hilton-Green, who had been at my prep-school with me at Eastbourne. He had been Master of the Eton beagles before the war and was destined to become one of the most able Masters of hounds of a famous pack.

The Master of the Heythrop was a friend of the Bathurst family. His daughter, Eileen Daley, was a splendid horsewoman and used to give me a lead over the stiff fences and ditches of the Heythrop country. Often, Alan and I would pack our dinner jackets and stop for a bath and dinner with the Daley family after a good day's hunting.

I had come back from prison camp into a wonderful world. Wherever one went there were lovely girls, but sadly, there was a shortage of young men after the slaughter in the war. At Charlie Scott's house near Broadway, I met for the first time and danced with the lovely Barbara Cartland, aged only nineteen. I had come to Oxford to settle myself down to the job of being a country solicitor in my father's office, but now the thought of working in a small office from nine to five appalled me. Instead, it seemed as if the sky was the limit. There were other factors too, I think. I had travelled round the world at sixteen; then I had been a cavalry officer, and finally a fighter pilot.

It must, I know, surely be difficult in these days of universal air travel to realise what flying meant to a young man of nineteen some seventy years ago. It was as if a new dimension had suddenly been added to life. In our little wood and canvas scout planes, the forerunners of the fighters of today, the open cockpit fitted round one like a glove. The machine became part of one, and suddenly one was no longer earth-bound but could soar into the sky like a bird. One could dive and climb and make the earth turn on its side, or even upside down; one could play with the clouds and avoid their indignant 'bumps', scaling their white peaks, while down below the toy trains puffed their way along the miniature railways, and little model villages clustered round their tiny churches in the patchwork of green, brown and golden fields. Like some golden eagle, one somehow felt detached and strangely elated. Then, for me, had come the tumble down to earth like a wounded pheasant, and the claustrophobia of a prison, and the realisation that death had been so close and life so precious.

Little wonder then that I yearned for freedom and the green fields and fresh air. Meantime, it was the peace of ancient Christ Church and the friendly bells of the tower and spires of Oxford, together with my newfound friends, which more than anything 'refitted' me; it was Tommy Strong who was architect of the refit for a new and exciting young world.

The winter of 1919/20 was one of the most hectic times I can remember. As well as hunting and helping to run the beagles, there was work to do for my law degree.

I used to visit the Cripps family at Cirencester. Lettice, a cousin of theirs from a well-known family who lived near Bibury would call in on her way to the meet of the Vale of the White Horse (VWH) Bathurst hounds. There are few more glamorous sights than a pretty girl, riding side-saddle, in her faultless habit, straight and slim, on a thoroughbred hunter. I danced a lot with Lettice that winter and even borrowed an aeroplane from Leslie Holden, who was commanding the Australian Training Squadron, still in England, at a nearby aerodrome. I landed in the grounds of her family estate in order to make an impression. Her father was furious. I realised, anyway, that I was unlikely to earn enough cash to keep her in hunters.

Leslie Holden took my father up on the one and only flight he ever made. Alas, he shut his eyes and clung to the sides of the open cockpit the whole time, until he landed.

Will Muir had taken over the Cotswold hounds. He and Clara asked me to go and stay for the North Cotswold hunt ball where Charlie Scott was once again Master. The Muirs now lived in a lovely old, restored monastery not far from Cheltenham. It was built on the slope of a hill so that my bedroom had an old oak door leading out on to a gravel path, which led to a very old chapel, some hundred yards away. We had returned from the hunt ball rather late, at about 3.00 a.m., and I had tumbled, tired and happy, into bed. Outside it was cold and frosty. It must have been about 5.00 a.m. when I was suddenly awakened by a knocking and a curious brushing sound outside the old door. This was followed by the crunch of boots on the gravel path, disappearing into the distance. Sleepily, I turned over, wondering at the thoughtfulness of a gardener on a cold, dark winter's morning driving the peacocks away from the door so that I could rest. It must have been their tails which caused the brushing sound, I thought.

It was a late breakfast when I greeted Clara with the story of her efficient gardener. She went pale and then hesitatingly apologised for not warning me that I had been put in the haunted bedroom. Apparently, the monks come from the chapel along their well-worn path, still trying to find a way into the monastery through the old oak door and when they cannot get in, one hears them going back up the path. She was terribly apologetic, but being, as I thought, a very non-psychic person, I dismissed it all in good humour. But Diana Guise, who often stayed with the Muirs, told me that she was constantly followed about the house by ghostly footsteps, much to the annoyance of her small dog.

Tragedy was to come later when Will was killed while out hunting with his beloved hounds. Clara, with her two very young children, was devastated. However, she did remarry a few years later. Her second husband, coming home one night, unaccountably swerved on the drive, the car rolled down the slope, and he too was killed. Was it a ghost he had tried to avoid? Clara herself died shortly afterwards. Kim, their son, whom I had seen soon after his birth in 1916, was killed in the Second World War. One of the races at Cheltenham is named after him. Was there a curse on the old monastery?

At Easter 1920, there came to stay with us Erica Horniman, one of the two girls I had played tennis with when invited to their home near Charterhouse. She had fulfilled all the promise of the lovely girl I had last seen six years earlier. This time I really fell in love. Somehow, I felt our mothers had had something to do with it.

In the summer of 1920, I and my Christ Church friends were asked by the Dean if we could restart the House commemoration ball - the commem ball, as it was called. Every summer before the war the ball had been held in a great marquee in Tom Quad with supper in the great dining hall, and it had been one of the highlights of the season for the young undergraduates and their girlfriends.

I agreed to take it on and co-opted a fellow Carthusian to help me, Eric Sachs. He was to become one of our best-known High Court judges. Luckily we had the pre-war records to help us. Eric looked after the tickets while I found the town of Oxford was delighted at once again supplying the food and wine. We had two great marquees in Tom Quad for the suppers and danced in the wonderful great hall. I engaged Harry Roy and his famous band. The whole thing nearly got out of hand; we expected to sell some five hundred tickets but demands poured in for more than a thousand. We had to have two consecutive nights with three sittings for supper, each night. Harry Roy alone demanded two cases of champagne each night, to keep his band going.

I had asked Erica to come to the ball together with my mother and sister. I asked her to marry me.

One could almost feel the joy of all the young men in their white ties and tails and the girls in their very best dresses as we all danced the night away, until, traditionally, the first rays of the rising sun fell on Tom Tower at about four o'clock in the morning. There had been only one or two dicey moments in the supper tent when Winston Churchill, who had a large party, sat through two suppers. It was a splendid way to celebrate our engagement.

I dutifully entered my father's office where I began to learn the rules for conveyancing property. I had no money except what was left of my prisoners-of-war pay. Now I became immersed in the judgements of learned judges of the nineteenth century; I suppose it was the combination of the claustrophobia of a prison camp and the hopes and joys of a new world after the war which made me rebel.

It was only then that Erica told me that her father had left her money – quite a lot. She too longed for an open-air life, since her parents now lived in London. We decided to try our hands at farming on the Cotswolds.

My father was obviously very disappointed, but he was understanding. Without regret I left my little top-floor room in the office with all the old deed boxes and its view over the old brewery.

Chapter 9

FARMING

My father was naturally disappointed that I should not be going into the law, but once the decision was taken I lost no time in signing on as a pupil at a dairy and corn farm not far from Highworth in Wiltshire. As at most of the big dairy farms, there was a large herd of shorthorns; but the new black and white Friesian cattle were also starting to be imported from the continent. There were two other pupils, and we lived in the pub at Highworth where we kept our horses, both to ride about the farm and to hunt with the VWH. We were not allowed to do any practical farming or dairying ourselves; so, I decided to go north, where I had a good introduction to a Scottish family in Ayrshire. Here I helped in the real work and learned the hard way on the poor, often rocky, land of Glenluce.

The farmer had just installed a milking machine for his herd of one hundred Ayrshire cattle. The milking and feeding of these cows was done on a contract basis. It was from the Scot who rented the cows that I learned all the tricks of feeding mash, that mixture of oats, middlings and beans which supplemented the turnips and hay. The farmhouse food was frugal too. Never have I eaten so many oats in one form or another, but they were dear folk, and I had got mud on my boots and hands. It was a sad sight to watch calves of but a few days old being sold at Newton Stuart for a few shillings. It did not pay to rear more than enough to replenish the dairy herd, and any workable soil near the sea of Luce Bay was more valuable for growing early potatoes – 'tatties'. I came south again in the spring of 1921 as Erica and I had decided to get married in June.

I had been keeping my eyes and ears open for a small farm and was lucky to find one for sale on the Cotswold Hills only a few miles up from Cheltenham on the Cirencester road. It lay on a southern slope just to the west of the lovely little Cotswold village of Coberley, and bordered on a farm at Seven Springs, the real source of the Thames. There was a very small farmhouse adjacent to an even smaller farm cottage, and a further range of four cottages along the lane which went from Coberley to Birdlip. It was not very difficult to join up the small farmhouse and the cottage to form one very comfortable Cotswold house, the whole of the ground-floor of one of them making a long timbered room with a great open fireplace at the far end.

The eighty acres which comprised the farm were of excellent soil, bordered on the south by a sheltered little valley with a small stream which joined up further down with the stream from the Seven Springs, so it formed the first real tributary to the Thames. It had at one time been part of a larger estate, so that the farm buildings were well built to withstand the Cotswold weather. To the west of us, at Birdlip, there was the steep, thousand-foot escarpment reaching down to the Gloucester valley below, while on the hills opposite was the old 'Cuckoo pen', so called by the Romans because they could not understand the language of the ancient Britons who gathered in these small fortified areas when the Romans were about.

The water supply was from a spring which was inclined to run very slowly in the summer, so I very soon dammed up the stream in the valley. It not only made a delightful pool, which I filled with rainbow trout, but it also ran a dam which was able to pump up clear water to the house. Nor was there any electric light; however, I installed one of those little Lister engines with a range of glass batteries which lasted us for several years until we could afford a self-starting generator. Fortunately, there was a telephone to the house so that it became quite habitable. The row of four cottages along the lane was surrounded by a large kitchen garden, together with the usual pigsties, so we were able to use part of the garden as our own. I became quite proficient at ploughing with the horses. I had a pair of splendid Clydesdales until I eventually bought an International tractor with great iron wheels with spikes on them, which dragged a two-furrow plough behind it. After growing corn for a while, I decided to go in for a mixed farm, including keeping some sheep and starting a small herd of Redpoll cattle.

The limestone soil of the Cotswolds produced excellent wheat and roots, while even on that light soil one was able to make about two tons of good hay to the acre. I had been recommended to buy Welsh Clun sheep as the most profitable sort of animal for the hills. However, they were pretty wild. They just thought that the Cotswold walls were something to jump over, and I had to employ one of the small boys from the village (at half a crown a week) to find my flock from time to time. I very soon changed to a Border-Leicester.

It was about this time that Professor Boutflower, who was Principal of the Cirencester Agricultural College, persuaded the Cotswold farmers to go in for the wild white clover and rye-grass leys and the use of basic slag which produced the most wonderful sheep keep on the limestone soil. It meant that one had to grow one's hay separately, but the wild white clover leys were certainly a success.

Alas, an industrially minded government under Stanley Baldwin seemed to care little for the farmer. Few governments in this country have ever understood that highly prosperous agriculture means a highly prosperous country. Farmers plough back their profits into the land, buildings and machinery, and maintain a splendid home base for our engineering products. But prices began to fall in the face of cheap imports. Milk fell from two shillings to one shilling a gallon, which was hardly enough to make it profitable to produce. The hungry 1920s had set in.

Our first daughter arrived in 1923, and our son followed three years later. It was hard going but with my wife's income we managed to keep a horse for hunting and ponies for the children. It is hard to believe these days, that on wages of twenty-five shillings a week, the farm worker could live pretty well. He had a free cottage with a good kitchen garden and a pigsty; he got free milk and coal, and in our case was able to gather firewood from some of the woodlands round about. He invariably kept a couple of pigs, as we did, which were fed on surplus potatoes and green stuff from the garden mixed with a little wheat feed which was supplied to him from the farm.

At Michaelmas there was the great pig-killing in the village, and it was pigmeat from the great sides of bacon hung up in their cottages, together with fried potatoes, which constituted the workers' main diet for the week. Then at the weekends there would be a joint of beef at a shilling a pound. Farm workers mostly baked their own bread from the stone-ground flour from Coberley Mill. A few chickens were kept for eggs. It was a healthy diet. There were excellent apple trees in the kitchen gardens, and the swedes which we grew for the sheep augmented the winter vegetables. Our horses lived on the excellent hay that we grew together with our oats, and bran was supplied by the mill. After hunting there was always a linseed and bran mash for them, and I suppose I shall always associate the smell of boiling linseed and saddle soap with those marvellous hunting days.

Right from the days when as children we rode ponies bareback on Minchinhampton Common, through my schooldays when I hunted with the Beauforts in the holidays, and then my time in the Gloucester Yeomanry where I was in the saddle for hours every day, I have loved horses. Now that we lived right in the middle of Cotswold country, hunting became part of our life. We had a splendid vet in Cheltenham, who disliked using motorcars and would arrive on horseback. He had two remedies for all cattle and horses. First, an enormous pill about the same size as a golf ball into which, I always believed, he had packed every sort of medicine he possessed, so that it was bound to have some effect. The other was lots of cold water. There were, of course, none of the modern injections and drugs, and one had to rely on the good health of one's horses and adequate doses of cooked linseed and Epsom salts.

As for the cattle, I had learned one excellent remedy when I began farming in Scotland. One turned a sick cow out on the ploughed land where it was surprising how much earth the cow would eat and, nine times out of ten, get better. It must have been a very old-fashioned remedy, but it worked. Milk fever was another of those things which was just becoming prevalent because, hitherto, cows had not been forced to produce such vast quantities of milk. The injection of manganese into the bloodstream was a major operation.

Cuts and bruises on horses – often from touching the tops of stone walls – were hard to deal with until penicillin came into operation. Stone walls seemed to carry an unpleasant poison, and after hunting one had to be very careful to examine one's horse very closely – even for a scratch.

In the 1920s and 1930s the Cotswold hills were covered in pasture with small woods conveniently placed some miles apart, and I know nothing to equal waiting beside a covert on a cold December morning with a good horse between one's knees. There is a strange stillness, horses and riders alike sharing a suppressed excitement; then a hound speaks, and then another. All eyes are on John, the first whip, sitting motionless down at the corner of the covert, his pink coat just visible in the shadow; then silently he raises his hat – the fox is away – and suddenly hounds break covert in a cascade of music. Will, the huntsman, blows gone-away, surely the sweetest sound on a grey winter's morning. A few moments to let the hounds get away and then with the thunder of hooves you pick your spot in the big wall ahead.

Motorcars were still fairly new, and few people even had a horsebox, so it was a question of hacking anything up to eight or nine miles to the more distant meets. Fortunately, living as we did not far from the kennels, we managed to get to most of the meets five or six miles away. However, if one ran away from home, it was a very different proposition from putting your horse in a box and driving: a long, cold hack home on the old Roman roads, along the tops of the Cotswold hills with a tired horse and the knowledge that one would not arrive there before dusk.

We used to stop at a pub where the landlord would be pleased to serve us with whisky, one tot in each boot to keep our feet from freezing, and a double down the throat. One had to be fit and hardy, but it was a way of life that only those who really enjoy their horses understand. At first, I always did my own horse when I came in, as I had learned in the cavalry. I always washed him down, groomed him, fed him and bedded him down before I tended to my own needs. Soon, however, we were able to afford a groom, a splendid man called Tilling, who earned a top wage of thirty-five shillings a week and a free cottage, so that when I came back after a long, hard day I was able to have a bath before a high tea of eggs and bacon, and a comfortable lounge chair in front of the great wood fire.

It was Tilling who, when our daughter Pamela became old enough, taught her everything about hunting. At first he took her out on a leading rein, and I would keep an eye on them, but soon she wanted to go on her own.

Chetty Hilton-Green, who became Master of a famous pack in the Midlands, told me that he always kept a large-scale map of his country and plotted the runs taken by the foxes on every hunt. In this way, after about twelve months, he knew pretty well which way the fox would most likely run and, like other experienced older huntsmen, instead of spending a long time casting around at a check, he was often able to lift his hounds on to the scent almost immediately. But he complained that had the ladies hunted the fox as assiduously as they hunted him, he might have done even better.

Not far away from our farm was a lovely estate where Nigel Norman and his wife Patricia used to give me wonderful pheasant shooting. One stood down in the valley while the pheasants were driven out of the coverts way up on the hills. It was shooting at extreme height and only the very best shot would kill. Nigel was one of the pioneers of private civil flying. He built up his own aerodrome at Heston and was an invaluable help in later days when I was operating my secret photographic aircraft.

During the General Strike, everybody wanted to drive a train. I applied and was told to stay where I was and produce food. Large numbers of undergraduates from Oxford and Cambridge managed to become train or lorry drivers. There were some ugly scenes in the towns, but they did not badly affect the countryside as many of us at that time made our own electricity and had our own water supply. Trying to make a living off some eighty acres of ground was becoming a hard job. I managed to get hold of another forty acres from the neighbouring estate which bordered us on the western side, so that I was able to extend my sheep enterprise. But one had to accept that farming in the Cotswolds in the twenties was a way of life and not a way of making money.

Our son was born in 1927, and I had to start thinking hard about educating the two children. Now, tragically, the contagious abortion which my best cow had caught when I took her up to the Royal Show had spread through my herd. There was no quick remedy in those days, and, without calves, there was no milk, nor could I dispose of any of my stock except for slaughter. I could not afford to wait three or four years to get them back into production, so they had to go. I tried fattening some store cattle, but the price of beef was so low that it hardly paid. It began to look as if I should have to let the land and find a job. I had heard glowing stories of Rhodesia and thought perhaps I ought to go and have a look at the place with the idea of going out there to farm. Then a strange thing happened.

I received a plea from Oliphant Shaw, who lived at Wooten-under-Edge and on whose sheep station I had had such a wonderful time when I was in Australia. His son was now farming a fairly large place in Rhodesia. His Australian wife had left him, and he was spending too much time at the long bar in the Salisbury Club – could I spare the time to go out and get him back on his farm? He offered to pay all expenses. It was a chance I could not turn down. I decided to go out and see what the farming prospects were like.

I arranged to sell my remaining cattle and most of the sheep, also to let most of the grass to my neighbours during my absence. One farm worker could look after the few sheep and the growing corn while the faithful Tilling would take care of the horses and my children's riding. My wife said she could cope quite well and in those days even humble farmers, like ourselves, could employ a nanny, a cook and a housemaid.

Now I had to pack my bags and prepare to go off too Africa.

Chapter 10

AFRICA

I boarded the *Kemandeen* at Liverpool Docks on a cold wet evening, shortly after Christmas 1927. She was a cargo ship which did the Liverpool-to-Rangoon run and was one of the few lines which put in at Port Sudan, where I wanted to go. The British crew consisted of the Captain and four officers. The rest of the crew were Indian Laskars and there were cabins for about eight passengers. On this trip there was a young wife who was joining her soldier-husband in Cairo and a gorgeous Burmese girl who had been sent to England by her obviously very rich husband to buy clothes and jewellery. She was accompanied by a ferocious chaperone and, try as he would, the Chief Officer failed even to be allowed to talk to the girl. He used to smile at her across the dining-room table in the saloon, but even that provoked some rage on the part of the chaperone. There was also a white hunter who was going out to fulfil a job in the Sudan and two or three business people on their way to the Far East.

She was a comfortable little ship and luckily we had a very smooth passage across the Bay of Biscay. We put into Marseilles to collect some cargo, then on again to Port Said. The ship's Indian cook was an absolute marvel at making curry and we had a different one every night of the week. There was little room for recreation except a well-deck in the stern of the ship where we constantly played skittles and a couple of the Laskars were told to put them up again as we hit them down. It was a gentle, pleasant sort of voyage. There were no games masters or anybody else to push you around.

At Port Said there was the same Gully Gully producing baby chickens out of his sleeves as I had first seen in that port on my way back from Australia in 1914. The Red Sea has the reputation of being one of the hottest places in the world, and when we arrived at Port Sudan, in the country of the old fuzzy-wuzzies of Kipling's stories, and went ashore, the heat really hit one. Fortunately, it was a dry heat, and everything was sparkling; even the water in the harbour was so clear that one could see the bottom. I did not waste much time before I boarded a beautiful white train with sleepers and restaurants and every device to keep the dust out and fans inside to keep the air cool. The British in the Sudan knew how to look after themselves.

We arrived in Khartoum early the following morning. I had already obtained from the white hunter the address of a suitable hotel. But to my surprise, I was met by my sister and brother-in-law, the Governor of Mangala Province, who had been summoned back to Khartoum for a conference. When I told him where I was going to stay, he said that that was quite impossible – as a relation of his I could stay only at the General Gordon. It was a reminder of the protocol so strictly practised in the outposts of the Empire, where everybody knows everybody else's business. It was, as a matter of fact, a godsend that my sister and her husband were in Khartoum because I had to spend four or five days there before boarding the Province boat to go south up the Nile. There were parties and dinners and tennis, and one got a very good flavour of the sort of life which those close little communities led and the sharp eye which was kept on those attractive women who were, in any case, the focus of much attention.

While we were in Khartoum, Alan Cobham, the aviator, touched down on the river in his flying-boat. He was, in fact, making the first trip into Africa and was pioneering the route which we eventually took when British Overseas Airways opened up the Southampton-to-Johannesburg route in 1947. Some parts of Khartoum were still very primitive. Along the waterside were still a number of those ancient wooden water-wheels where a patient camel walks around and around forever raising an endless chain of buckets from the river below. The old wooden structure creaked much the same as it must have done since the times of the Pharaohs. We learned that one of the other provincial governors was going to accompany us down to Mangala as it looked as if my brother-in-law might be away from his station for some time. Governor Brock had just got married in Khartoum so the three-week trip up the Nile would be a honeymoon for him and his wife.

That trip from Khartoum to Mangala was one of the hottest and laziest but most interesting that I have ever made. The splash of the stern paddles became one of those noises whose sudden cessation make you wonder what on earth has happened, while the beat of the little engine down below, which was kept going by loads of wood taken on board every two or three days, at least made one feel that the boat was alive. On the top deck was a large governor's bedroom,

F.W. in 1939.

F.W.'s parents and himself, aged thirteen.

We regret to hear that Lieut. F. W. Winterbotham, only son of Mr. and Mrs. Fredk. Winterbotham, of the Culls, Stroud, is reported to have been missing since July 13th. When of military age he joined the Royal Gloucestershire Hussars, but was, subsequently, at his own earnest request, transferred to the Royal Flying Corps, in which he had recently been appointed Flight Commander. The only details received are contained in a letter from a friend, which says: "He was last seen falling in flames after a combat with twelve enemy machines. He had shown the same daring skill and gallant spirit as of old—the same spirit which had until a week before obtained for him the appointment of Acting Flight Commander." Mr. Winterbotham is clerk to the Stroud Board of Guardians and other public bodies, and the greatest sympathy is felt for him and Mrs. Winterbotham at the sad news.

Reported missing: from the *Stroud Journal*, July 1917. F.W. was shot down and made a prisoner-of war for the next eighteen months.

The young airman: F.W. joined his squadron in the Royal Flying Corps in France in 1917.

The hunting man: riding in a point-to-point, 1919.

First family: Pamela, Tony and Susan in 1932.

F.W.'s third wife, Petrea, who died in 1986 after forty years together.

Sally, daughter of F.W. and Petrea, in 1956.

The father: F.W. visits his son, Royal Naval Cadet Tony, before Tony joins his first shift, in 1943.

F.W. joins BOAC; boardroom scene, Berkeley Square, 1945.

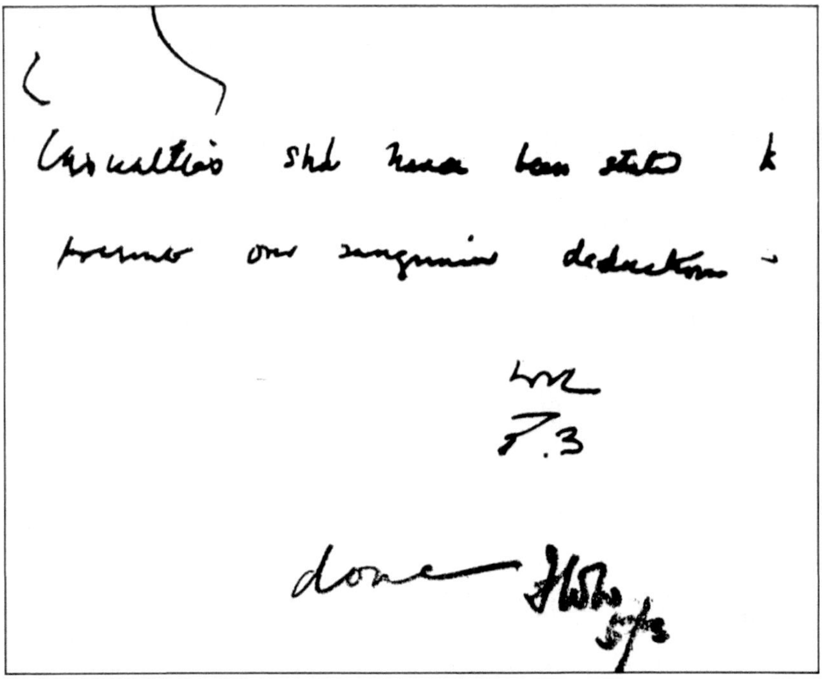

Orders from Churchill on Ultra. An example of the many notes sent between the two during the war.

Ports of call: Kisumu, Kenya. Planning the first BOAC air route from the UK to South Africa.

The chairman of BOAC, Lord Knollys, presents F.W. to Princess Elizabeth at Heathrow, 1946.

The farmer: F.W. at home in Devon in 1975.

On the farm with Petrea.

several other cabins, and a comfortable lounge where we ate. But during most of the daytime we sat outside in our deckchairs under the welcome shade of the awning.

Birdlife on the banks of the Nile was quite amazing: great spoonbills, huge flocks of crested cranes, white ibis, and storks standing like old gentlemen high on their long legs. There were, too, endless ducks scuttling around among the blue water-lilies and, some distance from the bank, water buck and gazelle would show themselves from time to time. The trip was not to be without incident.

About a day's journey out from Khartoum, we had to turn off the river up a side channel to pick up the wife of one of the district commissioners, who had been bitten by a dog. It was thought that the dog had not been rabid, but no chances could be taken. We took her back to the main river where another boat was waiting to take her quickly back to Khartoum. Then news reached us of the murder of a district commissioner by the unpredictable Newar tribe who lived on the west bank of the river. Boatloads of the Sudan Defence Force were being hurried to the scene and we were asked to stand by in case extra transport was needed. The Commissioner, Ferguson, had apparently been given no chance. He had been speared to death, as had General Gordon before him. Retribution for the tribe was swift. They had mostly fled inland, but they had been unable to take their cattle with them; to seize their cattle was probably the worst punishment that one could inflict. Cattle were their wealth and their currency.

We went on our way upstream, stopping to buy a live sheep for our food or load up with more wood to keep the little engine going. Gradually, we were leaving the country of the dark-brown Arab and getting into the centre of Black Africa. No longer were the villagers wearing their dirty 'nightshirts' which had hitherto seemed the normal form of clothing. Now clothing was being abandoned. As the villagers gathered on the banks of the river to watch the Province boat go by, the tall statuesque ebony-black men wore nothing, while the women's concession to modesty was a little bunch of green leaves attached to a string around their waists.

After about ten days we came to Malacal, a junction of the White Nile and the Sabat river, which like the Blue Nile flows down from the mountains of Ethiopia. This was a fairly large settlement of grass huts. The men's hair dyes were various colours of yellow and brown, a mixture of some sort of ochre and cow dung. They wear no clothes at all, their arms and legs are like long black sticks, everything about them is long. The women, too, have a habit of suckling both their newborn babies and their year-old offspring at the same time. The older child is strapped to her back and is able to haul up the long milk bar and feed itself over her shoulder. Over hundreds of years the tribe have protected themselves by living behind marshland where the water was deep enough for them to wade through with the water up to their mouths. Their enemies, who were shorter, could not make it and so the Dinkas thrived.

Malacal was to become the staging post for the first British Overseas Airways flying-boat route to South Africa; and the passengers used to be taken upriver for a short trip before their overnight rest in the tented camps. One American had told me that, having passed a number of these naked Dinkas on the riverbank, he begged the coxswain of the boat to take the passengers back. He was afraid that his wife would never respect him again.

We, too, stopped over for a day at Malacal and stocked up with the inevitable sheep and wood for the boilers. Going south, we should now be passing through the great area of the Sud, hundreds of square miles of swamp on which float endless islands of papyrus, the tall green stalks with their spray-like heads standing ten or twelve feet high, as far as the eye can see. The whole area acts as a vast sponge-like reservoir for the Nile as it flows on down to Egypt. Only one channel is kept free for the boats. It was this papyrus which was used by the ancient Egyptians to make their paper.

On the southern edge of the Sud roamed the great Bor herd of about a hundred elephants and Brock told me that before leaving Khartoum he had obtained permission from the Game warden for me to shoot one of the old bulls, if we were fortunate enough to see them. Our luck was in. We spotted the herd, half-hidden by papyrus, rumbling gently through the now shallow parts of the Sud. We studied them through our binoculars – there were certainly a number of bulls with tusks long enough to warrant one of them being shot. It was an exciting moment as we got down into the little rowing boat and made our way to the edge of the great, floating reeds.

Luckily, the cook on board was also an experienced hunter. He had filled a little piece of cloth with wood ash and tied some string around it to make a tight ball which he then held up and gently flicked with his finger. The fine ash came out and floated away in the soft wind. It was the simplest form of wind gauge I have ever seen. Fortunately, a slight breeze was blowing from the herd towards us. But they were only about a hundred yards from where we stood. To move, we had to jump, as quietly as possible, from one floating tuft of papyrus to another until we could hear the elephants but no longer see them.

Nevertheless, as we got nearer, something startled them. They started to raise their trunks and their ears, and you could just see some of the taller ones over the tops of the papyrus as they all started to move, splashing through the swamp. Fortunately, they were going across our front, but it looked as if it would be difficult to get a shot. Then suddenly, a bare twenty yards away, the papyrus parted, and I saw the enormous head of a bull elephant, trunk in the air and flat ears spread out, trying to catch a scent or a sound that would give him a clue to his danger. I stood absolutely still, hoping the elephant would not see fit to charge. But then he turned a little sideways, his eyes on me. I fired, and at once there was pandemonium as the whole herd crashed through the marsh in front of us. But my bullet had found its mark, and the bull went down immediately. It is difficult to describe one's emotion. The whole business had been terribly exciting – and yet now I wished I had not done it.

It was not until I was on board again that Brock reminded me what a dangerous position I had been in. There were no trees to climb and nothing to get behind if the animal had charged, and it is doubtful whether my small bullet would have pierced his skull, which is probably the only way to fell an elephant coming directly towards you at close quarters.

For several days now, we had paddled our way through the Sud. Day after day our view had been the great papyrus swamps. There were no sandbanks with crocodiles lying on them, but we were soon to see both again as we left the swamps. There were often ten or twelve crocodiles with their great mouths wide open, which is their way of keeping cool, lying on little sandy beaches. They would quickly slide into the water as the boat approached.

Now, again, we were in big-game country. There were more elephant with white birds perched on their backs and picking off the ticks; there were endless hippos in the water, either their great jaws opening into the sun or only their nostrils and eyes appearing above the surface. There were little villages where all the inhabitants, now all ebony black and unclothed, would line up on the riverbank to watch the boat go by. Great flocks of pelicans would fold their wings and dive like a bullet for fish. It was very hot.

Finally, we drew up alongside the little wooden quay of Mongulla Province, where my sister and her husband were normally stationed. There was not much to see: a few sheds, a block of administration offices, the Governor's house, and a number of round thatched huts. I suppose in deference to the Governor, some of the Africans wore loincloths or shorts. Others, who had evidently come down from neighbouring villages, slung their blankets over their shoulders, a useful way of carrying your bed around, and all carried their long-handled spears, the working part of which was made from locally smelted and beaten-out metal. The overall smell was of cow dung. The hair of some of these warriors varied from bright red to dark yellow ochre. It was here that the law was administered by my brother-in-law, and it was from here also that he had to look after all the people of his province. If there was a drought and likelihood of a famine, grain would be sent down from Khartoum – the people did not starve. They grew millet as their ordinary staple food.

In exchange for this mother-care of the whole population, the heads of the village had to pay a small tax in either cattle or grain. There was a doctor too, who was available to go out to the districts, and district commissioners and their assistants who would look after the welfare of the villages and settle local squabbles. It was an admirable system. It put an end to the little tribal wars and the pillaging of women and food. It settled the grievances and generally allowed the African to get on with growing his crops in peace.

Soon the time came to move on. I was to travel from Torrit down to Nimali on the Uganda border where I would catch another boat to Lake Victoria. The Sudanese boats could not go much further than Juba due to rapids on the Nile. I made the trip in a truck with a cover fitting closely everywhere in order to keep out the tsetse fly.

At Nimali, now in Uganda, I boarded the little paddle steamer, and we made our way further up the Nile to Lake Albert. On the way we saw some of the famous white rhino. Surely Uganda must be the most fertile and prolific country in the world, well-watered by the rivers and the lakes – everything and anything seemed to grow almost before your eyes. I went down to the engine room of the little boat where a small boy was keeping the boiler going by throwing on logs from time to time. Between whiles he sat on a great pile of wood reading the Bible, which was open on his lap, upside down. He told me he was a mission boy and proudly recited the words 'Allah, Allah, there is only one God, Allah.'

After crossing Lake Albert, we wound our way up to Jinja where Lake Victoria spills out over the falls at the start of its two thousand miles down to the Mediterranean. On the great inland sea of Lake Victoria, another little boat took me along the shore to Entebbe, and then across the corner of this great lake to Kenya. Here I boarded a train drawn by an enormous wood-burning engine which huffed and puffed as it drew us up hill and down dale through jungle and across plains with the inevitable thorn trees looking like great umbrellas stuck in the ground.

There were zebra, giraffe and buck, farms, cattle and little settlements at the many stops we made to replenish the wood fuel until, at last, we arrived at Nairobi. We had been climbing all the way from Lake Victoria as we left behind the heat of the Nile Valley for the uplands of Kenya and the cool evening breeze. Little wonder the British found this climate ideal. It seemed a happy land too. Everyone was relaxed and the Africans themselves seemed contented. And why not? The white farmers grew plenty of cheap food for them.

I had been invited up to stay with one of the early settlers in Kenya, Mrs Rutherford. She had a farm up the Solai valley which was north of Nairobi and close to lovely Lake Naivasha where, for the first time, I saw that wonderful sight of the great flocks of flamingoes rising from the water like a pink cloud. There was a little railway which ran up the valley from Nairobi and Mrs Rutherford had come to Nakuru station to meet me and drive me up a few miles along the dusty road to her farm.

She was a spare, tough woman of about sixty. A rather wrinkled face was burned a golden brown by the Kenyan sun, but her bright blue eyes beneath her white hair were full of fun as she described the first time she had arrived in a buggy with an old horse. As they drove up this dusty track between the high grass, she was accompanied on one side by a black mamba snake travelling shoulder-high through the grasses. The place abounded with lion and the small, thatched mud house was surrounded by a high thorn fence to keep them out. Now, we drove up to a low brick bungalow and three or four round African mud huts, one of which was to be my bedroom. There was also a large thorn-encircled boma into which the cattle still had to be brought every night. The farm spread out in the valley below, the mounting hills behind forming the escarpment of the Rift valley, in the distance the Kenya highlands.

She told me she had chosen the farm because it had an ever-running little stream, a rare thing for a farm in Kenya. Soon the railway had come to Nakuru and on up the Rift valley. She laughingly warned me to be careful how I stepped over the equator which ran between my hut and her bungalow. Here the African night came down swiftly at six o'clock. For some years Mrs Rutherford had run the farm on her own with an African houseboy and two other boys looking after the cattle, but now she was getting on and had engaged a white manager who was desperately anxious to improve the grassland. I promised

I would go into this question of appropriate grasses when I got back to England. Most of the land was rather undulating and unsuitable for ploughing corn, although just across the valley an Italian farmer had arrived and ploughed up some hundred acres of rich soil on which he was planting his maize.

Close by there was a large estate belonging to Lord Delamere who claimed the right to stop the train for Nairobi to Nakuru station any time he wished. Just before we arrived, there had been an incident. The Indian stationmaster at Nakuru had failed to keep the train waiting for his lordship and the story had come out from Nairobi of a message despatched immediately to headquarters by the stationmaster. It read, 'The Lord hath kicked me, please advise.' The railways were run almost entirely by Indians, and they were very efficient.

There was little game in this area because cultivation had driven them out, but there were still zebra as there are everywhere in Africa, and a few gazelle. I decided I would wander round and have a look at what game there was. Mrs Rutherford gave me the warnings which I had already received in the Sudan: always shake out your boots before putting them on in the morning in case of scorpions; never sit and rest on a rock without seeing that it is clear of scorpions or snakes; and never stand under a tree without making quite certain that the branches above you are free of both snakes and leopards.

About a quarter of a mile above the house up the escarpment was a rocky ravine, the home of a large troop of dog-faced baboons. I had been warned not to go too close to them as the large males could be dangerous. I did however get close enough to see the family life which was going on in this sheltered spot. It was obviously too steep for lion to raid it and the mothers, and their babies were playing just like any large family. It was from here that the little stream rose that came down the hill past the house. Even this was subject to control by the laws in Kenya: nobody may draw off more than a given amount of water from any stream or river running through their property, as it has to feed others as well.

I spent three days in this delightful corner of Kenya. The night before I left for Nairobi, there was a small earth tremor. Nobody seemed to be bothered about it. They were fairly frequent up the Rift valley, that strange crack in the earth's surface that runs from the River Jordan halfway through Africa. We took the little train back to Nairobi where I dutifully went to write my name in the visitors' book at Government House. Here, to my astonishment, I met Joe Cripps. I had not realised that after he had joined the army he had landed the job of ADC to Greig, the Governor of Kenya.

Nairobi was certainly a flourishing town. I stayed overnight at the excellent hotel. The streets were thronged with Africans and whites alike. Everybody seemed contented and happy, and Kenya itself was certainly prosperous, but there was a little nagging doubt whether it was really a white man's country, despite the heights of the hills where the cool evenings made life bearable, but the children grew tall and lanky and lacking in energy.

It was Rhodesia that I particularly wanted to see since it was there that the climate was favourable for permanent settlement by Europeans. On the long railway journey from Nairobi down to Mombasa, the principal port of Kenya, we crossed the flat plains and famous game reserves. Lion were visible from the train as were every other sort of African game. The land here was much more fertile than in the Sudan. Mombasa was hot and as yet undeveloped, but it was a busy little port, and we were glad to get aboard the ship which was to take us down to Beira. In the days when Kenya had first been looked upon as an overflow area for the Indian continent, these ships used to ply to and from Bombay to Mombasa bringing large numbers of Indian immigrants into Africa. The Indians became the shopkeepers and the railway workers and prospered in the jobs which Africans had not yet learned to do.

She was a small ship, and we were told that there were only eight or nine passengers in the First Class going south. That evening I sat down to dinner in the small saloon with a middle-aged man, his wife and a very beautiful girl of about twenty. Both the man and his wife were dark, while the girl had blue eyes and very blonde hair, so I was not surprised to learn that she was in fact their niece. I was more surprised, however, when her aunt turned to me and asked if I were Captain Winterbotham.

She told me that Joe Cripps had spoken to them about meeting me in Kenya and said I would be going on down to Rhodesia. She had obviously found out a little bit about me because her first remark, pointedly in front of her niece, was, 'I understand that you are married.' She also went on to remind me that I had been an officer in the Gloucester Yeomanry with her brother, a Captain Wills. I had been warned. But it was not until much later, when I got to know Diana Sheffield better, that she told me she had been sent off on this trip because she had caused some disturbance with the married men of her family. I could quite imagine it. She had found a large part of her trip deadly boring but told me that she had had fun with Joe Cripps in Nairobi. Now there was no doubt she was glad to find someone to talk to.

I do not know how it was, later on in the lounge, that we got to talking about ghosts, but she was obviously quite serious when she described how she had seen the headless lady in grey throw herself from the roof of Lowther Castle where she was staying as a relation of the Lonsdale family. I had told her about my experience with the Muirs at Postlip Hall. There was a small round table in the lounge, perhaps three feet across and standing about three feet high. Diana suggested that the assembled company get up and go over to it. On her instruction we placed our hands, palms down, on the table so that our thumbs touched in a semi-circle. Then, gently, at her command, we raised the table purely by the palms of our hands and moved it about the lounge. It was a most extraordinary sensation. One of the other passengers, an elderly lady, just picked up her knitting and vanished while the two or three other passengers looked on in amazement. I could never really make out whether Diana's apparent powers were the cause of her magnetism, or vice versa; she was certainly magnetic. Now that I had been put on my honour by her aunt, I was allowed to see more of her during the short voyage, which passed only too quickly.

We put into Dar es Salaam, the capital of Tanganyika, coming into the lovely, almost enclosed, harbour through a narrow channel from the ocean. The white bungalows with their tin roofs spread about the hills around the little town reminded me very much of Brisbane. The vegetation was lush and green; there was not much cargo to be dealt with, so we did not stay long there and once again put to sea for the last part of our journey down to Beira, the port of Portuguese East Africa through which one had to pass to get into Rhodesia. There was a long wooden two-storeyed hotel near the waterfront, and it was here that Diana's aunt approached me on the subject of bedrooms.

Apparently, she and her husband and I had been allotted rooms on the ground floor, while Diana had been given a single room on the second. I was politely asked by the aunt whether I would mind changing rooms with Diana so that she would be close to them. I was by this time beginning to realise some of her concern for her beautiful niece and of course readily agreed.

It was after an early dinner that evening, just as the sun was going down over the hills to the west, that we all took a stroll along the sea wall which was planted on the landward side with an avenue of frangipani trees. They were in full bloom and their exotic scent was almost overpowering; Diana wore a cool evening dress, the same colour as her eyes. It was a heady mixture.

Oliphant Shaw, whose sheep station I had stayed on in Australia, had bought his younger son a lovely property called Nyabeira, some twenty miles west of Salisbury in Rhodesia. I gather that he had purchased it from another Australian for a pretty good price, because the Australian then went down to Portuguese East Africa and set himself up without any financial worries on a larger farm about halfway between Beira and Umtali, which is on the Rhodesian frontier.

I said goodbye to the family in Beira and the next morning went off by train. Diana, her aunt and uncle were due to follow on later so we thought there might be a chance of meeting up there somewhere. Crossing the border into Rhodesia, I thought I might well have been in the Highlands of Scotland. Most of the settlers in that district were in fact Scottish. The journey down to Salisbury was typical of that fertile country: its fields of maize and tobacco, the great tobacco barns and the teams of oxen ploughing the rich land.

Courtly Shaw met me at the station. I had not seen him since the end of the war. He was too young to have seen active service, but he had joined the Army, only to retire again at the end of the war and go out to Australia, presumably to take charge of his father's sheep station. Being some hundreds of miles away from civilisation did not fit in with his idea of life. So, his father had decided to buy him a property in Rhodesia where he would at least be within reasonable distance of civilisation. He married one of the daughters of his father's old friends and brought his Australian bride to Rhodesia. Alas, she in turn had been used to living close to Melbourne and found even the African farm too isolated from her neighbours and the town of Salisbury; she returned to Australia.

The very long bar at the Salisbury Club is reputed to have equalled the one at Shangai and it was at the Salisbury Club that Courtly had begun to drown his sorrows, which was the real reason why his father had asked me if I could go and help him. Salisbury was a town of jacarandas and flamboyant trees, one-storey houses with their lovely gardens, a single main street of mostly wooden buildings, and one large hotel. A few buildings like the post office and police station were already built of brick and the main street was tarmac, but as soon as one got out of town, the roads were just dirt.

Courtly had a magnificent Austin Seven in which we set off along the twenty miles to Nyabeira, his farm. Fortunately, it was the dry season, but the road was full of large potholes which one had to avoid lest one's wheels go down and possibly break a spring. The country to the west of Salisbury was fairly flat and farmsteads were springing up all around. On Nyabeira itself, which I believe was somewhere around a thousand acres, only part of the farm was being cultivated. There was a delightfully large and comfortable stone-built bungalow with a thatched roof which managed to keep it fairly cool. There was the inevitable windmill close by, pumping up water from an underground well, and a little electric-light generator. Close by was a splendid tennis court made from the crushed mounds of the termite ant, which possessed all the sticky qualities to make a hard surface, weather-proof as well.

The garden abounded with tropical flowers and fruit and outside my bedroom windows, which opened on to the garden, was an avenue of passion fruit. I was told that when Courtly's father stayed here, he always took his breakfast by walking up and down the avenue, picking and eating the ripe fruit. One of the things one misses after leaving Africa is the pawpaw, which I invariably had for breakfast. It is a slightly acquired flavour but is very full of pepsin; in fact, the seeds are collected and crushed for the extraction of this substance, which has a marvellous digestive effect. There were, of course, any amount of oranges as well.

We were well looked after in the house by three boys; one of them was the cook, another a butler, and the third a boy of all work. Even in the dry season away from Salisbury it gets quite cool in the evening, and it was good to have a wood fire burning. All the house boys and the half-dozen farm boys lived in their own village about half a mile away from the house. The pathway to their village was lined on either side by copious tomato bushes; the boys used to collect tomatoes in the garden before going home and spit the pips out on either side on their way.

The garden also grew a certain amount of vegetables, especially melons and pumpkin, the latter providing a large part of the food for cattle and particularly the oxen which were used for ploughing. There were three tobacco barns for drying the crop, one of the principal money-makers in Rhodesia at that time, but it entailed quite a lot of work growing the small plants from seed, planting them out and then harvesting the crop. Drying in the barns was a tricky business because the fires had to be kept going day and night. The most reliable boys were used on the night shift to see that the fire temperatures never went down. It had happened that one boy went to sleep and the crop in that barn was spoilt.

All the fuel was wood and Courtly had wisely brought eucalyptus-tree seed over to Rhodesia from Australia. He established a system of planting so many acres every year. They were very quick-growing and after about three or four years were fit to cut so that he had a permanent supply of wood both for the house and for the tobacco-drying. There was an enormous acreage of maize but here, as in the Sudan, the monkeys were the chief trouble. They would make their way up a row of maize and with their limited intelligence would put one cob under their arm to take home and then pick another. Then they put the new one under their arm, and pushed the first one out, so that eventually they took only two home but left a string of picked cobs along the ground. As they came mostly at night, they were difficult to get rid of.

I did my best to keep us away from the town of Salisbury. However, we did go in once or twice and also paid a visit to some other friends of mine to the south of Salisbury who ran a large cattle ranch. I also made contact with the Minister of Agriculture in Salisbury, who was very anxious to import some Redpoll cattle into Rhodesia. In fact, he gave me a commission to do so, and I was able to collect a number of young heifers and a few young bulls which I sent out when I got home to England, but the agricultural position in Rhodesia, on which the country virtually depended in conjunction with its mining interests, was looking rather gloomy. The world recession, sparked off by the American slump, had not yet arrived but after talking to a number of farmers I judged the outlook was not too happy and I was certainly advised not to try and come out there at this particular time.

The manager of the great Wankie colliery, which supplied all the coal to both North and South Rhodesia at the time, was a friend of Courtly's father; he arranged that I should go up and look at the colliery on my way to the Victoria Falls. I went up by train; the manager kindly showed me round the whole enterprise and then asked me to dinner. I was a little nervous because I was catching a train at about eight o'clock to go on to Victoria Falls. However, he took me to his house and assured me that he would get me to the train on time. At about 6 p.m. he looked out of the window and to my astonishment said, 'There it is, on its way.' The headlights of that engine could be seen over a hundred miles away down the dead-straight track, so we had our evening meal in comfort, and I got over to the station in time to catch it.

The next morning at breakfast at the Falls Hotel, I was delighted to find Diana, her aunt and uncle, who had arrived the day before. They had been staying with Sir John Chancellor, the Governor in Salisbury. We had lots to talk about and spent the next two days together. We were washed with spray and almost deafened with the thunder of the great Victoria Falls. We also went across the Zambesi to a country club where there was a swimming area in the river enclosed with an enormous net to keep out both crocodile and hippos; it was good to have a cool swim.

Alas, I had to say a final goodbye as I was due back in Salisbury, then on to Durban in South Africa, where I would join the ship which was to bring me back via Cape Town to England. I met Diana again a few years later. She had married, and Ruby Holland-Martin, who knew them both, took me round to call. I think she was much happier in London than Africa and was just as beautiful.

The *Llandaff Castle* was a fairly slow ship. It took fourteen days to get home from Cape Town. It was a warm leisurely trip with the usual deck games and competitions, and fancy-dress dances mostly organised by a busy South African who was christened the 'indoor game warden'. After a doleful journey from Gravesend up to Liverpool Street station in London, my wife and daughter were there to meet me at that rather grubby terminal. It was certainly a contrast from the sunshine and the sea that I became used to, but it was good to be home again, and I had learned a great deal about Rhodesia, including the fact that it would certainly be imprudent to go there at that time.

Chapter 11

SECRET SERVICE

In 1929 I decided I should have to get a job. My ageing father had taken a junior partner, so it would have been useless to start again in the law business, and I could see no prospect of making a living again out of farming in the 'hungry twenties'. It was going to be a wrench if I had to work in London, but there was another child on the way, and I was determined to hold the family together even if it meant seeing them only at weekends.

I wrote to a number of friends asking if they knew of any possible job. It was Cicely Ritchie, one of the five little girls I had met when I first went to Charterhouse and with whom I had always kept in touch, who came to my rescue. She introduced me to a stockbroker friend of their family who invited me to lunch in London. I was a little surprised to find that a Canadian client of his was also present, and I was encouraged to talk about Canada and my experiences there. The client, who lived in Vancouver, was so delighted that he bought a large packet of shares, and I was asked to join the firm as soon as I wanted to.

That evening, I dined with Ruby Holland-Martin, now a partner in his father's bank. I told him the good news, but to my surprise he was less than enthusiastic, and repeated the same warning I had heard in Rhodesia: trouble was on the way in America, and he suggested that I might well find myself unemployed again all too quickly. It was a bit of a knock, and I had to tell Cicely why I could not accept. Within a week she had told another friend in the Air Ministry of my plight. My luck was in. Archie Boyle, head of the Air Intelligence section of the Air Staff, needed assistance. Who better than an ex-pilot who knew the world and could speak French and some German as well?

Once again, I went to London, this time to lunch with Archie and after talking of all my travels and service in the RFC, I was told that I would be put on the short-list and that I should be prepared to come to

London for an interview at a moment's notice. This was really exciting. At least I knew a bit about aeroplanes and, if I was lucky, I should no longer have to rely on my judgement of a milking cow.

I was duly summoned for an interview with the Deputy Chief of Air Staff, Sir Cyril Newall. It was now or never, and I was thankful that all my previous experiences had enabled me to 'talk of many things' and places. I also found that Sir Cyril was a relation of some family friends. My ten minutes stretched to twenty – until looking at me and Archie, who was standing patiently nearby, he uttered two magical words. 'You'll do.' Only then did he tell me what I would 'do'.

I was to start up and operate an organisation in the Secret Intelligence Service (SIS) for the Royal Air Force alongside those already in existence for the Navy and Army. I suppose I must have betrayed my excitement – there were broad grins on the faces of Archie and the Air Marshal, who now bade me good luck and expressed the hope that I would provide the RAF with better secret intelligence than the other armed forces.

Cicely and Archie were not only responsible for getting me the most exciting and rewarding job that anyone could wish for, but Archie and his wife Maria were to become two of my dearest friends during the strenuous years of an uneasy peace and an even more uneasy war. It was hard saying goodbye to Erica and our two small children, if only for a week, on a cold January morning in 1930. The snow lay thick on the Cotswolds. It was some comfort to know that we no longer had any cattle or sheep to look after, only my hunter and Pam's pony. Fortunately, Tilling, our groom, was one of those people who could turn his hand to anything and was invaluable in running me to and from Kemble station in my newly acquired Baby Austin car – a drive of about ten miles – where I caught the early train, the 'Cheltenham Flyer', which did the ninety miles to London in ninety minutes. One got an excellent egg and bacon breakfast on the train and my return fare was just one pound. I soon got to know the small band of weekly commuters from around our area of Gloucestershire, but it was always difficult not to let them know what my job really was.

On my first day at the Air Ministry, Archie and his immediate boss, Charles Blount, took me round to the offices of the Secret Service where I was to work and to meet my new boss. We entered the portals of Broadway Buildings, near Queen Anne's Gate, and were taken up in a rather ancient lift to the fourth floor where two blue-uniformed government messengers escorted us along a richly carpeted passage to a thickly padded door, behind which was the office of the Chief of SIS, Admiral Sir Hugh Sinclair ('C' to give him his usual title), whose job had been a perquisite of the Admiralty since the First World War. The Service effectively went back many years to the time when Lord Walsingham made it part of the security of the state in the sixteenth century.

The Admiral, a stocky figure, rose from behind his large mahogany desk to greet me with a benign smile. His handshake was as gentle as his voice, and only the alert dark eyes hinted at the strength that lay beneath the mildness. We talked for a few minutes, and I realised that I was being quietly looked over, much as I had been assessed by Archie Boyle at our first luncheon; again, I evidently passed scrutiny. The Admiral told me that I could be quite sure that I would enjoy the full co-operation of all my colleagues. Whereupon he put a bowler hat firmly on his head and went off to see the Prime Minister.

So, this was my new Chief. I had become an officer of SIS (often known as MI6). The Admiral was to become my friend and adviser for ten crowded years. His absolute personal loyalty and fairness to his staff were valuable qualities in the face of the needling of Cabinet ministers and the jealousies of Service life at the top.

I found my colleagues eager to help me, but it was clearly not going to be easy to get inside information on aviation matters. People who had the required technical knowledge and were prepared to sell it to a foreign country were difficult to find. Moreover, we had only limited funds at our disposal. The kind of people I needed were a cut above the common-or-garden agent whose job was usually to report on what he saw and rarely on what he knew. Having found the right people, I should have to train them in the sort of intelligence I required. Then, knowing the motives of the agent selling me the information, I should have to assess its worth. This was one side of the job, but I would also have to understand all the varied requirements of the Air Staff; the technical and operational performances of new aeroplanes manufactured abroad; the organisation of foreign air forces; the efficiency of their pilots and their staff. Finally, I needed to be able to give the people to whom I sent the information some guidance on the reasons for my assessment. I saw very rapidly that it was no easy job to begin from scratch, but it was an enormous challenge, and it was not long before another side of my work became evident: that of examining the aeronautical ambitions of those countries which might prove potential enemies.

In London, despite the financial crisis caused by the American slump, I found general complacency. Russia was the major concern in conversation on foreign affairs, but the Communist government there was gradually settling down after the years of genocide and was telling the world what miracles Russia would achieve with five-year plans and huge armed forces. However, it became clear in the early 1930s from the information which we were receiving that the Soviet military threat was no more than bluff, and it was calculated that it would be at least ten years before the Russians could raise the armies, navies and air forces that they now boasted. Nevertheless, this propaganda was taken seriously in some areas of Whitehall.

The noisy Italians in their black Fascist shirts were becoming easier to analyse, and at least Italy, unlike Russia, was not cut off from the rest of Europe. It was from studying the antics of Mussolini that I first learned to recognise the ground-rules of the dictator. Thus, if your regime begins to lose its grip at home, you must find a foreign enemy or, better still, take part in a small foreign war. You must also uncover an internal enemy so that you can eliminate the people you do not like. But in those early days, apart from the repercussions of the Wall Street crash, the Russian propaganda and the posturing of Mussolini, world politics seemed tranquil.

But I did begin to notice reports sent in from Germany which described considerable unrest in Bavaria. A party known as the National Socialist German Workers' Party, backed by former Army officers, was reportedly beginning to revolt against the Weimar Republic, which was failing to suppress widespread Communist agitation. A certain Adolf Hitler, who had been imprisoned in 1923 for leading an attempted *putsch* in Munich, was making rabble-rousing speeches.

Under the terms of the 1919 Treaty of Versailles the German Army was closely monitored and, as the Republic was forbidden to have an air force, the matter did not really fall within my area of responsibility. Nevertheless, Hitler's speeches were extremely bellicose, and they made me wonder whether they were the first manifestations of a resurgence of militarism in Germany, the seeds of which I thought I had detected in 1918-19 in the arrogance of the defeated. Soon afterwards, I began to receive reports from other agents in Germany – which were also picked up by some newspapers – that the Germans were secretly training military pilots in the Soviet Union. It was also suggested that they had some Army officers at the training camp. Having received an immediate request from the Air Ministry for more details, I asked whether our principal agent who had been reporting Hitler's speeches could travel to London so that I might meet him.

I took out this man's file from our records and found that he was a Baltic baron, aged about forty, whose lands had been taken from him by the Bolsheviks. Now resident in Berlin he was *The Times* political correspondent as well as acting for us. More interesting still, he had a British passport, he had a British wife, he had served in the Wiltshire Regiment in the First World War, and he had transferred to the Royal Flying Corps. He had been found unfit to fly but he had served in the balloon section and was described as being entirely pro-British. Apart from speaking perfect English, he also spoke fluent German, Russian and French. I was delighted, and at once felt sure that he was the man I had been looking for. His name was Baron William de Ropp.

I arranged to meet Bill de Ropp at the end of 1931 in an hotel near our office where we usually entertained agents from overseas – it was of course unwise to bring them to head office. I was somewhat surprised to see what appeared to be a perfectly normal Englishman, with fair hair, a reddish moustache and blue eyes, dressed in a smart English suit. He greeted me in immaculate English without a trace of an accent. I introduced myself as a member of the Air Staff, because at this point I did not want him to know my true job. We moved over to a quiet corner table in the restaurant and at once started to reminisce about the old days in the Royal Flying Corps. He then talked about his life as a journalist in Berlin. He and his English wife lived in a flat in the Kurfürstendamm, which was a cross between London's Piccadilly and New York's Fifth Avenue. In the 1930s there was no livelier place in Berlin.

As our meal drew on I was able to see that de Ropp was highly intelligent and had a quick sense of humour. He would clearly be able to take rapid decisions, and I guessed that he was a good judge of character. But not until the end of the meal did I raise the subject of my difficulty in getting hold of information about what the Germans planned to do about rearmament in the air.

Bill told me that he knew one of the original Nazis, Alfred Rosenberg, who had been the leader of this new National Socialist Party when Hitler was gaoled in 1923. Like Bill, Rosenberg came from one of the Baltic provinces, so they had an immediate rapport. Bill had been introduced to Rosenberg by a fellow journalist in Berlin, and from then on Rosenberg had sought out Bill not only out of straightforward friendship but also with a view to making use of him to further the Nazi cause. As well as being the creator of the Nazi ideology which brought together the myth of the Aryan superman and the notion of racial purity to provide the new Nazi type of pagan religion, Rosenberg was also the editor of the only Nazi newspaper, the *Völkischer Beobachter*, the principal instrument of Nazi propaganda in the days before Josef Goebbels arrived on the scene. Rosenberg was an intimate of Hitler and of Rudolf Hess, and, although he never mentioned rearmament to Bill, he had talked a great deal about what the Nazis would do when they obtained power. He had no doubt, at the end of 1931, that the Nazis would win power within a few years. It was, said Bill, an exciting programme, even a dangerous one. Nevertheless, he was playing Rosenberg along, helping him to understand the articles in *The Times* attacking the National Socialists and generally functioning as an English contact. Rosenberg had told Bill that the Party was held rigorously at arm's length by the British Embassy, which appeared to have been warned off this new movement. It was therefore necessary to get English contacts who might be persuaded to understand the Nazi aims.

Bill was confident that the information I wanted could be obtained, but he asked for time to think it over and undertook to get in touch with me shortly. Although he had been very matter of fact when he was talking about the Nazis, I detected an undercurrent of excitement, which I felt myself, at the prospect of the upsurge of this new party.

I had to wait several weeks before I heard from Bill again. He had clearly thought the whole matter over very thoroughly. First, he confirmed my information about the training of German pilots and other officers in Russia and revealed that the details had been leaked by the Russians as a snub to the anti-Communist Nazis, who seemed to be gaining ground in Germany.

Second, Bill told me that he had spoken to Rosenberg since our luncheon and that it seemed likely that he, Bill, would be put on the Nazi payroll as their English contact, whose job would be to interpret the articles in *The Times* to Rosenberg; to try to influence Geoffrey Dawson, the newspaper's editor, to be sympathetic towards the Nazis; and to do all that he could to make important British contacts for the Nazis. Then came a startling suggestion and one which entirely changed the course of my life during the thirties. Bill proposed that he should bring Rosenberg to London and introduce him to Dawson, together with one or two MPs or others in public life and give me the opportunity of meeting him myself. If it was possible, Bill maintained, I might find myself being invited back to Berlin, where I could then make the contacts I needed. He again emphasised that the Nazis were desperately keen to get British connections in high places; if he could arrange this visit it would confirm his job as Rosenberg's agent.

Rosenberg's proposal to visit Britain excited me a great deal and I discussed it at once with the Admiral. Permission to go ahead was given after a few days, but my Chief warned me that the invitation must come from me, as a private person and friend of de Ropp, and that I must be extremely careful to whom I introduced Rosenberg, with the understanding that if I got into trouble my job would be at risk. I duly sent an invitation to Rosenberg, through de Ropp, written under the letterhead of the Royal Air Force Club. A visit was arranged.

I had learned a smattering of German in the prison camp, but since Bill was an expert interpreter I decided that it might dispel suspicions if my German was poor. I had no doubt that some contact of the Nazis in London would check up on me, to find out who and how important I was. They would see my name in the Air Force list, with an office in the Air Ministry in Kingsway – though that office was really used for storing filing cabinets – where I was seen occasionally. I made a point of making my number with the doorman as I came and went between the Air Ministry and my offices in Broadway Buildings.

Meanwhile, I was learning more about my job in other fields. In 1930, the RAF's main role had been keeping the peace in the Middle East, and one of my first tasks had been to assess intelligence sent in from new agents in that area. We had a good man in Jerusalem who was able to watch the sheikhs. His best sources were the sheikhs' young boyfriends who were handed on from one sheikh to another.

April 1932 came and went but no Rosenberg. It seemed he was too busy to come until autumn. Well, at least I could make use of the time to learn more about him. Bill told me that Rosenberg was well read and had based the Nazi philosophy on the writings of Houston Stewart Chamberlain and Nietzsche. By 1930 he had become the political philosopher of the NSDAP, as the National Socialists called themselves before they became known as the Nazi Party. He had remained close to Hitler and as the editor of the Party newspaper was a man of considerable influence. However, Bill felt that Rosenberg was much too introverted to deal with the swashbucklers who had since joined the Party and were now thrusting themselves towards the top.

Rosenberg had married a childhood sweetheart, but this marriage had petered out. He had remarried in 1925. But neither Bill nor I ever met his second wife or his daughter: Party members did not bring their wives and families into public politics.

This then was Rosenberg, through whom I was to establish my Nazi connection.

Chapter 12

ROSENBERG

It was a magnificent autumn day in 1932 when I met Bill and Rosenberg at Liverpool Street station. Rosenberg turned out to be a well-built man, aged about thirty-six years, with dark hair, and a rather hard face. He bore no resemblance to the photographs I had seen of him – clearly he had put on weight. His smile was agreeable, and his handshake firm and he wore a suit which was unmistakably not English. At first he was a little too jolly, but he eventually relaxed enough to indulge in the earnest conversation I wanted to hear.

That evening we all dined together at the same restaurant where I had first taken Bill to lunch. Rosenberg launched into his theme, complaining about the hostility shown towards the National Socialists by the British press and the aloofness of the British Embassy in Berlin. He felt sure that the National Socialists' ideas would be welcomed by the British if only we knew about them. He said that they were determined not only to establish Aryan rule in Russia and Eastern Europe but also to bring law and order to Germany, crushing the Communist disruption. The only way in which they could interest the British in their aims was to make influential contacts in Britain who would, perhaps, themselves visit Germany, see what was going on and tell the British public through the press.

I asked Rosenberg to expound to me the policies which the Nazis would follow if they became the power in Germany. He said he would prefer that his Führer should do this if and when I visited him. This was an intriguing idea, and I invited him to explain what his own job would be in the new Germany. This prompted a disquisition on the new ideology he was struggling to develop. He had just written a book called *The Myth of the Twentieth Century* in which he criticised the 'turn the other cheek' attitude of Christianity. He called instead for a return to the ancient gods of the Nordic peoples, to the worship of the sun, of power and authority, and above all of themselves, the supermen, the Aryans.

As I listened to this revolutionary and began to grasp the range of the new ideology that he was proclaiming, I grew alarmed. After all, it had been only fifteen years since the Russian Revolution. Were we now going to see another revolution, and would a future Germany seek to impose her ideology on the world just as Russia was declaring that she was going to impose Communism?

The Germans were excellent organisers, and Rosenberg gave me a good idea of how the Nazis were going to organise the German people. They were not, he explained, going to make the same mistake as the Communists and try to eliminate all private enterprise, but they were going to impose government authority. They would do away with trade unions, and people would be directed to their jobs. Only this way, he said, could they overcome the dreadful unemployment and the inflation of their currency, which were leaving their people wide open to Communist doctrines. The youth of the country especially was going to be organised and one of Rosenberg's tasks would be to train them in the new Aryan ideology.

I made up my mind to try to delve a bit deeper into the subject of Rosenberg's new religion because now, near the end of 1933, it looked as if the Nazis would soon be sweeping into power. I was beginning to see why Bill had been so keen for me to meet Rosenberg. I could understand, too, how hard it was for Bill himself to convey in his reports to MI6 what was really happening in Germany.

The following day Bill had arranged a lunch for Rosenberg with Geoffrey Dawson, the editor of *The Times*. This was important for both of them: it gave Bill the prestige necessary to make him useful to Rosenberg, and it gave Rosenberg an insight into the freedom of the press in Britain. Dawson also found the meeting of interest and proved an attentive listener. Rosenberg believed that he had made a good impression and was exultant when I met him later in the afternoon. De Ropp, too, was delighted, for it was to be the beginning of a much closer association between them.

That evening, I was holding a small cocktail party at the Royal Air Force Club. I asked Archie Boyle to come along as my Air Ministry boss and to make it quite clear to Rosenberg that I was a member of the Air Staff. I invited Alan, Lord Apsley, and Bobby Perkins, both members of Parliament, to bring along two or three of their MP friends. Nigel Norman also came and brought several members of the Guards Flying Club.

The following day I had made arrangements for a lunch with Oliver Locker-Lampson, leader of a right-wing group calling themselves the Blue Shirts. When Rosenberg heard that their objective was to counter Communist propaganda he was enthusiastic. It confirmed his belief that I was sympathetic to the National Socialists.

Handling Rosenberg's visit was a tricky assignment. I wished to ingratiate myself but not too much; I wanted him to see something of England but not to get a misleading impression. I drove him round the Surrey countryside, took him to see my old school, Charterhouse, showed him a typical English pub, and generally treated him as an important visiting dignitary. It seemed to succeed. Rosenberg appeared certain that I was the sort of contact he needed; he also accepted Bill as a valuable German agent. We now both hoped to get right to the heart of the Nazi Party.

In February 1934 Rosenberg, true to his word, invited me to visit Berlin and to meet Hitler to see for myself what National Socialism was all about. By this time the Nazis were in power, Hitler was Chancellor, and my visit had taken on a new significance. I asked my Chief if I should be allowed to go. Eventually the Foreign Office gave permission. My Chief warned me once again that I would be on my own if I got into any trouble.

As the overnight train from Holland drew into Berlin I was quite unprepared for my reception. While the train moved slowly along an almost empty platform my coach came to a halt right opposite a red carpet. Two black-uniformed SS men came to my compartment, took my hand luggage and helped me down on to the platform. I saw Rosenberg in a smart new Nazi uniform standing some ten yards away. Behind him in a semi-circle were a number of tall, black-uniformed, white-gloved SS guards with their hands on the two pistols in their belts. There was a 'Heil Hitler' salute from Rosenberg and then a welcoming handshake, a few words of greeting, a click of many heels and then the Nazi Movement Drill Number One went into immediate action.

This was the first time that I had encountered it, but I was to do so many times in those early days of the 'revolution'. You turned sharply in the direction of your car or your hotel, or wherever you were making for, and you did a half-walk, half-run for it. You jumped into your car, the engine of which was already running, and clutched whatever you could to prevent yourself making an undignified backwards somersault as the car jumped away. I rapidly found myself in a black Mercedes and I just caught sight of the bodyguard jumping into a second black Mercedes, when we were off, speeding along the broad street in two minutes flat from the time I stepped from the train.

The reason, of course, for the rapid-movement drill was that ever since the Munich marchers had been shot up by the police, the top boys of the movement had taken care not to be easily picked off. So, the drill was established. I even saw Göring doing it surprisingly lightly for a man of his size. These tactics, like the interminable 'Heil Hitler' salutes, eased off gradually as the regime became stabilised, but the habit died hard even up to 1936.

I stayed with Bill and his wife in their flat on the Kurfürstendamm. They put me up on a divan in the sitting room. The flat was both central and comfortable, and after the experience of my VIP arrival I was glad to be able to rest a while and I wanted Bill to brief me thoroughly on my visit. Bill told me of the profound effect the knowledge that I had direct access to the head of the Foreign Office had had on Rosenberg and I decided to emphasise this point on my return to London. Rosenberg had told Bill I should meet the Führer the following morning.

Chapter 13

HITLER

Although I had learned a certain amount of German in my PoW days, I knew I could not keep up with rapid and highly important conversation and I had agreed with Bill de Ropp that I should pretend not to understand German, and that all conversations should be interpreted. This would take up more time, but it was vital to get the precise meanings behind anything said by Hitler. I proposed to try and assess the truth behind all the important statements by watching the speaker closely. Bill had an excellent memory, so that together after an important meeting we could put our heads together and draw up an accurate account of what had been told us. I do not think we missed a trick in all the important meetings. I had also been warned by Bill not to get into any discussion about politics.

It was a cold February morning even for Berlin when Rosenberg came round to pick up Bill and myself in his large black Mercedes. We were driven swiftly round to the Old Chancellery to meet the man himself, Adolf Hitler.

I was used to the drill now as we quickly got out and ran up the wide steps into the great hall, its floor covered in large black and white squares of marble. There was a loud click of heels as some twenty or more black-uniformed SS guards sprang to attention. The officer of the guard came forward to inspect and greet us with the now familiar Nazi salute.

The motionless, black-uniformed men, each one standing on one of the white squares, looked exactly like the pawns on a chess board. The whole scene had such an *Alice in Wonderland* look that I half expected to see a white Queen come tripping down the red-carpeted staircase.

The black SS guards were also stationed on either side of the stairway every three steps, and I had my first experience of being visually but thoroughly frisked as we went up and were ushered into a red plush waiting room. In due course I got used to this visual frisking. I suppose the guards were well trained to spot any unusual bulge about one's person. Rosenberg paced about, rather nervous at being kept waiting by Hitler.

I was to learn that the smiling gentleman who eventually came out from seeing his Führer was Fritz Todt, who had just been given the go-ahead by Hitler to build the great autobahns across Germany. He had every reason to be pleased. These motorways were primarily to meet the needs of the military. Rosenberg asked me to go ahead by myself and, as I passed through the great doors, a black sentry on either side, I was once again visually frisked.

It was a lovely room, some sixty feet long. The honey-coloured wood floor gleamed as the sun shone through the tall windows on my left with their attractive fan-shaped tops. Right at the far end sat Hitler behind what looked like an antique painted desk – little moustache, slick of hair and all. I felt him watching me closely as I made the long walk all by myself. I had little doubt he was waiting to see if I would give the Nazi salute. I did not. I stopped in front of his desk. He was smiling now and as he stood up and shook hands I was to realise that without any high heels to his shoes he seemed quite short. Rosenberg and de Ropp had now come up, Rosenberg certainly delighted that there had been no mix-up over my welcome. Hitler moved out from behind the desk. He was wearing his indoor uniform of black trousers and brown shirt and tunic. He now gave me a formal welcome and then opened the conversation by asking about my flying experiences in the First World War and whether I had been well treated as a PoW. I was able to give him an account of the strange accord between the British and German pilots in the First World War and of how, if a German pilot was shot down on our side, we had them brought to our aerodrome mess and gave them a welcome meal and a rest before they were taken away to the PoW 'cage'.

Hitler was smiling broadly now and his large rather bulging blue eyes shone as he told me that this seemed to be the only chivalry left in war, and that his new Air Force would be taught this, and that I must meet some of these men and find out for myself. It was a good start. He went on to tell me that the Versailles Treaty and the Weimar Republic were now dead and that his new Air Force already had some 500 aircraft. I was a bit taken aback at this figure which had been so casually tossed at me, but I was aware that they had been training pilots in Russia and must have a certain number of aircraft available. I think too, at that early stage, Hitler included the Ju-52 transport aircraft which could, I knew, be turned into bombers without much difficulty.

Anyway, the admission of the beginnings of an air force was as simple as that, and here, in this great room, where the Great Hindenburg had reigned as head of state for the past nine years, the 'Little Corporal' put an end to the era of armed-forces limitation and stirred the hope of a nation for a return to prosperity and work. He went on to tell how back in the 1920s the Communists had planned a take-over of this poor and hungry nation. He was more excited now, but his voice was hard as he said, 'Unless we destroy the Communists, they will destroy us.' Turning directly to me he said how he wished he could talk to some of our British Embassy or politicians the way he could now talk to me.

I do not know how long my interview had been scheduled for, but to Rosenberg's joy Hitler now suggested that we should all sit down on the four chairs around a small table. This was the only other furniture in this large room.

Hitler then went on to talk about a visit he had had from Anthony Eden, junior minister at the Foreign Office, whose message had seemed to be that the British government did not like what he was doing. Hitler said the only thing that impressed him was the knife-edge crease in Eden's trousers. Anyway, the meeting was a wash-out. Nor had I heard of it before. It was when I paid a courtesy visit to the British Embassy a few days later that I found out that no one in the Embassy was allowed to speak to the Nazis and that the only information they could get about Hitler's intentions was from conversations at other Embassy cocktail parties.

Hitler, spotting my evident interest in his boasts about a great new air force, promised to let me hear more before I left. I had made it a rule that I would never ask any direct questions in Germany which might lead people to think I was trying to get information by the back door, but now I was getting the green light to meet the people who were to create the new Army and Air Force.

Now he turned to me and said, 'You must remember that I have had to sell half my birthright to the Army.' This was such a sudden remark that I failed to realise its significance at the time. What he had meant was that the Army, always a powerful political force in Germany, had their own ideas about priorities of revenge for the First World War and the great invasion of Russia.

When I said to Hitler that he obviously felt very strongly about Communism, he rose to his feet. I could not help noticing that his already rather protuberant eyes seemed to bulge further out of their sockets. Looking up at him, it seemed as if he had become a different person. I saw his little moustache bristle, and the back of his neck go red. Then he began. In short, staccato sentences, he shouted as if we were some vast audience, and for a full three minutes poured out vituperation against the Communists. To me it was the most extraordinary sideshow I had ever seen. Bill looked across the table to see how I was taking it. It seemed so ludicrous that I found myself smiling. Hitler looked down at me. In an instant he became quite normal, his eyes ceased to bulge, he smiled back at me and in a normal voice said, 'That is what I think of the Russians and what needs to be done to them.' He added, putting a finger to the side of his nose, 'Please tell your politicians in England to – for once – keep their noses out of it.'

During this curious 'oration' Rosenberg had sat back in his chair as if mesmerised by his Führer's performance. Hitler's evident ability to sway the crowds seemed strange to me, but I was to see it in action at the 1936 Nuremberg Rally.

But now, with a handshake and a smile, we left him standing by the round table. As we were leaving a self-important man came barging up behind us, asking Bill de Ropp what we had been up to with the Führer. Putzi Hanfstaengl was evidently a sort of press relations officer; he had not seen Rosenberg, who was ahead of us. Rosenberg stopped and gave Putzi the dressing-down of his life. The Black SS guards in the hall below sprang to attention. But more was to come.

Rudolf Hess, Hitler's deputy, and what we now call Party Chairman, had a large office in the basement of the Chancellery. Rosenberg led the way down the steps into a well-lighted underground room. At the far end sat Hess behind his desk, one shining jackboot showing through the centre space – apparently he was famous in the Party for his immaculate dress. He was evidently inspecting us, but the pose was spoiled by the way in which he kept his eyes slightly downcast. It was only when we got talking that I noticed a slight glint in his eyes, which one could detect only at close quarters. There was no handshaking, but he asked if he could help me on any point. I asked why he thought it necessary to dress all the Party members in the brown-shirt uniform. Hess was very frank about it, saying that the British with their great Empire responsibilities were much more self-reliant and sure of themselves than the German people. For them, togetherness was a method of gaining self-reliance and it showed too in the rapidity of the growth of the Party over the last few years. I did not mention the fact that it also gave the Party faithful a better opportunity to shake collecting tins under one's nose in the streets. Nevertheless, there was truth in his explanation. I did not intend to get his views on racial questions. He seemed busy and I thought it best just to thank him and move out. The fresh February air was good. Rosenberg dropped us off at Bill's flat and we got down to recording every important word and moment of that strange meeting.

Chapter 14

THE PEOPLE AND THE GENERALS

Rosenberg had told me that he had to go down to Weimar to meet local party supporters. He thought Bill and I might like to accompany him. We set off next morning in Rosenberg's black Mercedes. The road to Weimar passed through some very attractive country but I was surprised to find how much of it was poor sandy soil, not rich agricultural land. However, it did grow good timber. Lunch of jugged hare and a bottle of hock in an old timbered inn at Wittenberg was served by a rather flustered landlord in traditional red waistcoat and white apron.

Rosenberg seemed more relaxed than he had been in Berlin – the strain of life in the capital must have been very wearying in the early 1930s. Already he had lost some of the exuberance I had seen in London. He had become dull and preoccupied much of the time; his complexion was sallow, and it was difficult to get him to smile. He was taking himself far too seriously and only became lively when carried away by his own enthusiasm for some project such as the sterilisation of the unfit.

After lunch we went for a walk around the ancient town and, as we gazed up at the old church, Rosenberg indicated one of the reasons for his atheism. 'You know,' he said, 'if we in Germany hadn't spent thirty years fighting among ourselves over how we were supposed to say our prayers, you British wouldn't have had the chance to annex half the world.'

We drove on through the green valley of the Elbe into the hills and forests. How beautifully kept the forests were, every tree straight, in what seemed to be unending rows of weedless precision. Forestry is a great art in Germany. The State Foresters are men of great importance;

they even have a uniform. Complimenting Rosenberg on the neat rows and the apparent absence of ill-formed trees I inadvertently set him off again on one of his pet subjects. Not only were all the trees to be perfect in Germany; the people, too, were to be subject to a strict genetic code.

Even then, not long after they had come to power, the Nazis had begun a programme of sterilising anyone who had produced a mongoloid or abnormal child. After all, the Third Reich was going to last for a thousand years, and we all knew that long before that there would not be enough food to go round. 'If the great Nordic races, and that includes the English,' explained Rosenberg, 'are to survive, there will be no place for weaklings or fools. Is it not better to have a healthy, happy people by using such sciences as we have? Already, too, we are selecting true Nordic women for our breeding experiments.'

I asked Rosenberg what the Nazis proposed to do about the elderly. Would they copy the Bushmen of South Africa and abandon old people so that lions and hyenas could finish them off? Rosenberg laughed uproariously but avoided answering my question. I wondered uneasily if all this would apply to Britain if we failed to survive another war against Germany.

Rosenberg had a splendid driver called Herr Schmidt, a tall, Scottish-looking man of about thirty-five, with reddish hair and a ginger moustache. A racing driver before joining Rosenberg's staff, he was a cheerful fellow who ate with us and chain-smoked. But despite his good driving we did not arrive in Weimar until after dark.

It was raining, but nothing could dampen the ardour of the local Nazis. As the Mercedes drew up outside the hotel the 'Heil Hitlers' became a roar. Here was a hero of the revolution come to Weimar, the home of the dead republic, and Weimar was going to demonstrate its enthusiasm. Floodlights caught the bright crimson of the beswastika-ed banners which, though drooping in the rain, formed a solid canopy of colour above the streets. It hardly seemed real and yet it was somehow thrilling. I remember thinking that a band would have completed the picture but looking back on my time in Germany, it seems to me that bands were reserved for the military. I do not recall hearing one playing at the head of the SA or the SS, for instance. Perhaps it was believed that such music might detract from the personalities of the leaders. Certainly, in terms of noise, Hitler's voice was quite sufficient.

There was no racing into the hotel here. As I stood on the hotel steps with Rosenberg my hand was gripped a hundred times by Party members of all ages, some of them weeping with emotion. It is just not good enough to suggest that National Socialism was forced upon the German people; the great majority took to it wholeheartedly.

We were already rather late, but we were given a cold snack before leaving the hotel for an enormous hall where the rally was to take place. I had no idea what to expect but the tension was building up and I found it contagious. The wild enthusiasm of these masses of ordinary citizens celebrating the toppling of democratic government was so at odds with my own way of life that I felt as though I was present at the revival of some great mediaeval pageant. As we entered the great building – Rosenberg, Bill, myself and two of the local bigwigs – some 5000 heads turned and watched in silence as we walked up the long aisle to the front row. Before us was a large amphitheatre, with tier upon tier of choristers, several hundred of them. They were men of all ages, from the young and eager to the old, moustached, bespectacled Teuton so familiar in our fairy stories. On a dais between the choir and the body of the hall stood a lectern from which Rosenberg would give his speech.

The whole audience and choir had risen to their feet as we entered. Now, as we reached our seats, they gave the 'Heil Hitler' salute; arms shot out beside and behind me, one just missing the top of my head from the row behind. Three times they shouted 'Heil!' as one man, down went the arms in silence and everyone took their seats. Despite the hardness of the chairs, there was still an odd feeling of unreality about it all. I did not want to embarrass Rosenberg so I too gave the Nazi salute this time; I was afraid I might have been lynched otherwise. I could not recognise what the choir was singing as the noise was overwhelming, but I caught odd bits of Wagner at his loudest.

The rumour that Hitler had a collapsible spring support up his sleeve must surely have been true. Rarely have I seen a more pathetic sight than when, at the end of a rousing Nordic speech by Rosenberg, the whole choir sang 'Deutschland über Alles' with their right arms outstretched, starting a little higher than the shoulder but slowly falling as the song wore on. A sharp tap of the conductor's baton and up they all went again, only to sink gradually once more.

When the rally ended, Rosenberg, who had a great many people to talk to, handed me over to a group of young Nazis – cheerful boys, proud that they could speak English – and we moved off to a beer-cellar. We talked no politics, the beer was good and flowing freely when suddenly a waiter came up to tell me that an Englishman, on the telephone from Berlin, was asking for me.

Experience has shown me that members of British embassies abroad, no doubt because of the diplomatic immunity they enjoy, come to feel an extraordinary sense of personal security. An ordinary

United Kingdom citizen visiting countries with somewhat nervous governments has no immunity and no such sense of security. The Air Attaché on the other end of the phone, which I was certain would be tapped, had no notion of the chill which ran up my spine.

My colleague in Berlin was as jolly as ever but I was icy. He told me that he had mentioned the first of my talks to the Ambassador, Sir Eric Phipps, who had demanded to see me at once. I pointed out that I was not subject to the whims of the Ambassador but promised to get back as soon as I reasonably could.

Thoughtfully I returned to my table. I had to do some quick thinking. I was wondering how the Air Attaché had got through to me in that beer-cellar. He must have telephoned Rosenberg's office, probably for the first time, and then through all the various connections down to Weimar until at last he reached me. This process would have given the Germans ample time to put on their recording machinery, and I did not doubt that everything that the Air Attaché and I had said had been recorded. But I felt that I had been sufficiently abrupt on the telephone to indicate my displeasure and had cut short any explanation of the real reason for my recall to Berlin.

Soon Rosenberg came over to my table. I made a quick decision and explained to him that, as he knew, my government was a little nervous about individuals, especially ones with important official connections like myself, visiting Germany at that time and I feared I was in trouble with my superiors. How soon could he get me back to Berlin? I could not tell whether he swallowed my excuse, though my companions certainly did. More beer all round and not to worry! Anyway, I bluffed it out until midnight, then went across to the hotel.

The next morning, I was awoken by a knock on my door. It was Rosenberg. He came over and sat by my bed. I have no idea how long he had been preparing his little speech, but as he sat there and quietly sympathised with me in my troubles with authority, he told me of the glories of defiance of the old order, of the splendid thing I was doing in standing up for the new. He personally would ask Hitler to see that no harm came to me for coming over to see him and his colleagues. He had rearranged his whole programme so that we could return to Berlin a day sooner.

On our way back we called at the House of Nietzsche – one of the main reasons, I suspected, for Rosenberg's visit to Weimar. It was a large house, steeply gabled, standing well back behind dark pine woods. Inside were huge carved pinewood staircases, doors and cornices; the whole place had an overbearing air. Beyond the hall in a gloomy book-lined library were about twenty young men and women working away at the author's works. I presumed they were compiling some sort of anthology.

I was in no mood to be gentle when I went to the Embassy on our return to Berlin. The Air Attaché explained that the Embassy never seemed able to get any information direct from the Nazis so my visit to Hitler had excited the Ambassador. I next visited Sir Eric himself, having made a mental note not to disclose all I knew to him but to confine myself to the question of the number of aircraft that Hitler had told me about, since I knew he had divulged something of this to Eden. I was most careful not to mention that I was going straight on to a special luncheon party given by Rosenberg for fear that the Ambassador should seek to quiz me again later. I quietly said goodbye and walked back to the flat.

Horsher's was a splendid restaurant with dark oak panelling and resplendently Victorian red plush decor. In the dining room stood a great table groaning beneath a heavy collection of silver and shining glass. The waiters were wearing black knee-breeches, white stockings, red waistcoats and white aprons.

I was just wondering how Göring (whom I expected at the luncheon) would react to our meeting when two men in their late thirties were shown in. After a quiet exchange of greetings and messages with Rosenberg, the latter turned to me and said that it was a great disappointment to him that Göring was not able to come today but that he had sent two senior members of his staff to represent him. They were then introduced to me as Commodore Ralph Wenninger and Commodore Albert Kesselring. Both names rang a bell in my memory.

Every year the German Army published a list of the officers filling the various appointments at their War Office, and I had for some time studied the German book carefully because I had the idea that if a secret Air Staff was to be formed it would probably be based on a military pattern. By the end of 1933 I had noticed that each department of the German War Office had an attached officer added to its staff. One of the names seemed familiar from my First World War flying days and after careful examination it became clear that these attached officers were mostly ex-First World War Air Force pilots. I had little doubt that this was an Air Staff in training, camouflaged in the German War Office until the day when Göring's new Air Ministry would be inaugurated and the new German Air Force launched on the world. At that time, of course, it was still officially non-existent.

Wenninger was tall and fair, with agreeable manners, a ready smile and, from what I could see, not too many brains. He was elegantly dressed, and he looked comfortable. Kesselring was altogether different: square, swarthy, with an almost rude manner, he was wearing an ill-fitting coat and trousers, which had evidently been borrowed for the occasion.

Next to arrive was Herr Lörzer. He was introduced to me as the man who ran all gliding and civil flying club operations for young pilots. Finally, the main guest appeared, General Walther von Reichenau. So, Hitler had given the green light for me to meet some of his top Air Force and Army people. Kesselring was shortly to become Chief of the German Air Staff. General Lörzer was to command all flying training. After what Hitler had told me about the tension between the Army and the Nazis, I was a little surprised to see the enthusiasm with which Rosenberg introduced the General. He was obviously a Hitler fan. Later I was to discover that General Reichenau had had the ingenious idea of making every Army officer and conscript take a personal oath of allegiance to Hitler. Some of the older generals were not in favour of this because it weakened the authority of the General Staff in relation to the Nazi Party, but it had reinforced Reichenau's position as the principal Nazi favourite. He was a good-looking man, tall and slightly balding, a typical monocled, duel-scarred, square-headed general of the High Command.

Rosenberg sat at the head of the table; on his right was Reichenau; I sat next to him with Lörzer on my right; opposite were the two air commodores on Rosenberg's left, and then Bill de Ropp. For me this was an ideal seating arrangement because the General would be turning towards me when he spoke, and Bill would be able to hear everything across the table. As we sat down I noticed that Bill's eyebrows were twitching a little, as they always did when he was excited; it was clear that he thought this was going to be a very important meeting.

Rosenberg began by saying that I had asked Hitler if I could learn more about the proposed invasion of Russia, so the Führer had invited General Reichenau, the invasion's principal planner, to talk to me. Rosenberg's speech was a little formal, as if he were trying to stress the importance of the occasion, but it certainly made me sit up and take notice. Here was the top man sitting down to tell me all about it; I could hardly believe it. I thanked both Rosenberg and the General for sparing me their valuable time, which appeared to ease the somewhat strained atmosphere, and the General started talking in almost perfect English. He reminded me that Anthony Eden had suggested a ban on the building of all bomber aircraft; would I give my views? I thought that this, without prior warning, was rather a fast one to bowl at me. But it was not difficult to answer. I replied that this suggestion by the politicians was founded on a wish to stop the bombing of innocent civilians as a method of warfare, but unfortunately politicians are not technicians and the officers opposite me would no doubt have understood that if such a ban was imposed it would put a stop to the building of civilian transport aircraft as well. To give only one example, the Germans' own Ju-52 transport aircraft were so designed that the baggage compartments, which were at the centre of gravity, could be transformed into bomb bays at a stroke. At this, Kesselring looked down at the table and I saw that he was blushing slightly, but they had asked for it after all. I concluded by saying that, although Eden's aims were laudable, I did not see how his suggestion could possibly be put into practice. The General had listened intently; now, nodding across to his two junior officers, he said, 'There, you have your answer. Now I want to tell the Major about my plans for the Communists.'

By this time the red-waistcoated waiters were serving the soup, but I scarcely noticed what I was eating, nor I think did Reichenau. I could hardly believe what he was telling me. Here I was, in 1934, in Berlin, being told the whole plan for the invasion of the Soviet Union. Moreover, as detail followed detail I began to see that the German Army had developed a completely new strategy of warfare.

The General began by explaining that in the coming invasion of Russia speed and surprise were to be the predominant components. He pointed out that the invasion would have to be carried out between the melting of the snows in the spring and the onset of the frosts in the autumn, and to achieve this in a country as large as Russia they would invade by moving enormous tank spearheads at a speed of about two hundred kilometres a day. As the conversation was carried out in English, Rosenberg could not understand a word and he sat stolidly at the head of the table. Wenninger, who did understand English, was looking increasingly concerned, while Bill was gaping with astonishment. There was no question of this being rehearsed propaganda. Not wanting Reichenau to stop here, I objected that such warfare might be tricky in Russia with its great areas of marsh and woodland. By way of reply, the General placed his left hand on the tablecloth, the three middle fingers wide apart, and pushed them across towards the silver candlesticks in the middle; he added that as Russia was very large the German tank spearheads would be able to go round the marshes and woodlands and not through them. The speed of their advance would be so great that either the Russians would be cut off and surrounded or they would have to take flight so suddenly that they would not be able to take any equipment with them.

I then said, 'Well, how about your own equipment at that speed?'

'Ah,' replied Reichenau, 'this is just what we are planning; you see the vast tank spearheads will be rather like an arrow, broad at the base and fanning out. As they proceed, motorised infantry will come up and take over the flanks that they have opened up. Artillery, too, will help them defend these flanks while we push further and further ahead.'

'But do you not expect any sort of opposition?' I asked. 'Surely the Russians have plenty of guns if nothing else?'

Reichenau now glanced at the two commodores and said, 'These gentlemen are going to take care of that; we are going to destroy all opposition from the air.'

For a moment I thought that this might have prompted their question about bombers, but if they were planning to destroy enemy artillery and tanks from the air the attacks would have to come from low-flying aircraft and large bombers are not the best or most manoeuvrable aeroplanes for this purpose. 'Perhaps,' I thought, 'they are going to build some sort of fighter bomber that is fast and easy to handle at low altitudes and can carry just one large bomb.'

Scores of questions rushed through my mind, but I was anxious not to halt Reichenau's flow of information. I was careful to pick on points to query which I hoped would stimulate rather than stop him.

Surely, I enquired, at a speed of two hundred kilometres a day it would be extraordinarily hard to feed and supply the troops? The Russians, I knew, had a policy of always living off the land; could the Germans do the same? Reichenau hesitated, and to my dismay nearly stopped, uncertain whether to answer. But after a moment he resumed. The motorised infantry, as they raced forward, would not have to carry food or ammunition themselves; it would all be brought up separately, much of it by air, and of course the infantry defending these broad flanks would also have tanks and massed artillery. There would be special aerodrome units.

This was yet another crucial point. I wondered how the Germans were going to keep their fighter bombers, or whatever was to be their aerial artillery, close enough up behind the tank spearheads? Were they going to build aerodromes as they went along? 'Yes,' Reichenau replied, 'if necessary, but one must remember that there are only going to be a certain number of these spearheads.' He did not say three, but I had assumed that number from the way he had enacted it with his hand.

General Reichenau seemed absolutely certain that his forces would be able to pull all this off and he now turned to de Ropp and myself and said, 'You see, the whole war in Russia will be over in the early summer. No doubt it will take a good while to mop up the vast Russian forces which have been split up and surrounded.'

Again, I did not want him to stop, so I said sceptically, 'Well, we've always been taught in our history books that the Russian winter has proved the greatest Russian general.'

Reichenau put his fist quietly on the table and with great emphasis said, 'There will be no Russian winter. It will be a German winter. All our troops will be comfortably and warmly housed in the great cities and towns of the Communists.'

It was a dramatic climax to a most extraordinary preview of what the great German Reich proposed to do in the not far distant future. The General's face was glowing with enthusiasm, eager for the excitements of an aggressive war. It was the first time I had heard the word 'Blitzkrieg' but some inkling of its potential had already formed in my mind. Would they send similar tank spearheads into Europe? What sort of defence could anyone put up against such power?

I hoped such thoughts did not show on my face. A delicious charlotte russe had been put before us but Reichenau was not eating. I on the other hand was not going to miss it; indeed, I thought a break in the conversation might encourage him to think of more to tell me, so I turned to Lörzer and questioned him about his young pilots and their flying clubs, or whatever he preferred to call his initial training centres.

Meanwhile the General was speaking to Rosenberg, clearly asking him whether this was the sort of information I wanted to know. It was clear that Rosenberg had not understood a word, for he was nodding in a rather foolish manner. Kesselring looked anxious and rapidly gave Rosenberg the gist of what had been said, whereupon Rosenberg turned to me and, speaking in German, said, 'I'm sure it's not necessary to ask you not to pass any information on to the Communists.' After Bill had translated this for me, I looked suitably horrified and assured him that it was certainly quite unnecessary to ask me. This seemed to satisfy everybody.

I kept wondering what sort of question I should be asking at that very moment, when I had such a talkative exponent of this new method of warfare in full flood. If the tanks were to have this close air support, I eventually decided to ask General Reichenau, would they be able to build forward aerodromes as quickly as they needed them?

Oh, yes, he replied. There would be special aerodrome units flown in behind the tank spearheads. These men would provide complete aerodromes, together with a full aerodrome service. But Reichenau added that, since the war would be over so quickly, it would hardly be worthwhile repairing any of the badly damaged aircraft; anyway, there would be plenty of new aircraft to fall back on. This suggested the manufacture of vast numbers of aeroplanes if they were to have at least a hundred per cent reserves.

Reichenau explained that the tanks and infantry would also be supplied by air, enabling them to maintain their speed of advance. There would be no heavy supply lorries holding things up.

As we rose at the end of the meal Reichenau remarked confidently that he hoped that what he had been able to tell me would convince my friends in London of the Nazis' intentions. He bowed from the waist and departed.

How would the Germans produce the vast quantity of armaments and aircraft necessary for these plans? The efforts made to achieve such prodigious feats must soon become obvious for us to see. At least I now knew what to look for, and it should not be too difficult to obtain enough information to judge whether Reichenau's vision was capable of being put into effect. My principal job now would be to find out exactly how the new German Air Force would prepare for war. In particular, was it feasible to use aircraft as advance artillery?

The lunch party was now over. Wenninger and Kesselring departed, but Rosenberg suggested we sit down with him and Lörzer and have a talk. To my astonishment he then asked me which of the two German officers would in my opinion make the best Air Attaché in London. He hastened to add that, of course, 'He would be accredited at first as a civilian attaché,' but he did not think 'that would fool anybody'. In any case it would not be for very long. Wenninger, with his elegant clothes, his ready smile and his reasonable English seemed the obvious choice; in any case I did not think he would be likely to learn very much that we did not want him to know. Had Kesselring's surly silence during lunch been a pose to ensure that I should not choose him for the Air Attaché's post? Or had he been brought along to give me the impression that I had a choice although they had no intention of sending Kesselring? I could not tell, but certainly he was never surly when I later came to know him better.

I had not been able to talk much to Lörzer during lunch, but I now found him eager to tell me how he would at last be able to train his young pilots on powered aircraft after years of frustration when they were only allowed to use gliders. I assumed that Lörzer, although dressed in civilian clothes, was really in command of the new flying training schools for the Luftwaffe. Ever since I had discovered from Hitler that he was going to form a new air force; I had known that I must talk to some of the pilots: it was they who would really tell me what were the flaws and virtues of their various aircraft. It occurred to me to invite Lörzer to bring five or six of his young pilots over to England in their light aeroplanes later that summer. I assured him that we would entertain them at a civil aerodrome. Lörzer was enthusiastic and said that he would get permission from the Führer as soon as possible. He took his leave and Rosenberg dropped us back at the flat.

Chapter 15

HIGH-LEVEL ESPIONAGE

My interview with Hitler, together with Rosenberg's lunch, had provided me with a clear picture of what the Nazis planned to do and how they intended to do it. Hitler and his colleagues seemed determined not to fight Britain again; was this impression to be trusted? I was certain that Hitler had not been bluffing. As for Reichenau, he had been too spontaneous and enthusiastic to be anything but genuine.

As I thought about all that Reichenau had said about his Blitzkrieg, I realised that the Germans had the intelligence to see the potential of the aeroplane. It was clear that Hitler likewise had seen the potential of the Air Force as a strategic weapon. The Germans were going to use aeroplanes as artillery, in defence of their destructive bombers, and as transporters as well as bombers. With fighter aircraft to protect them presumably, it was going to need an awful lot of aeroplanes.

The next day I took my leave of Rosenberg and thanked him for his hospitality. He reminded me of what Hitler had said – that Britain should mind her own business – in rather more polite language. He evidently felt that my visit had been a success, for he asked me back later in the year for the Nuremberg Rally.

Back in London, that March of 1934, I was glad to see newspaper reports of a speech by Hitler predicting the end of the Versailles Treaty. At long last the press was taking notice of him.

My Chief asked for a full report on my visit as soon as possible, with a copy for the Foreign Office and three more for the service ministries. After I had done that, I composed a paper extolling the virtues of the National Socialist movement, explaining what it was doing for Germany and what it hoped to accomplish. I included the main points that Hitler had made, in particular that Britain should keep out of future wars and added that I had met Reichenau. I had this report copied on Air Ministry paper with 'Copy to the Foreign Office' typed along the bottom. I then made sure that it reached the Nazis by leaking it to one of the embassies in London which we knew had contact with them.

The following extract (dated 14 May 1934) from Rosenberg's diaries demonstrates that the Nazis did indeed get hold of this report.

Major Winterbotham was here on vacation from 27 February up to 6 March. Then I arranged for him to meet Reichenau, Lörzer, Hess, two commodores, and finally Hitler. Major Winterbotham conveyed the greetings of the British airmen. The Führer said that the Air Force had been the truly knightly weapon of the World War. As for the rest, the English have been a dangerous enemy because Germany was forced to keep two-thirds of her aeroplanes on the English frontline. Moving to present times, the Fuhrer gave expression to his conviction that no doubt the French were superior in numbers of aircraft, but he considered the English stronger in value. As for the rest, he might be in favour of considerable reinforcement of the English Air Force, primarily for the following reason: that he was to demand for the defence of Germany a certain percentage in relation to the fleets of our neighbouring states. Now this necessary percentage was approaching the British numerical strength, a fact he did not mind very much because various inferences would be drawn from it; England could have twice as many aircraft and even more, this would be only welcome.

The conversation took a satisfactory course and Winterbotham made a brilliant report in London. I went to Weimar with Winterbotham and de Ropp, to show him the style of our meetings. I showed him the Goethe-Haus, the Nietzsche-Archives. All these things, especially the frame of mind in Germany, deeply impressed Winterbotham; everything was so far from any propaganda.

My true and more alarming report produced immediate reactions. Lord Londonderry, the Secretary of State for Air, and his Under-Secretary, Philip Sassoon, asked me to visit them. Lord Londonderry was delighted, because he had been having enormous difficulty in persuading the Cabinet to take notice of the Nazi upsurge but at least I had produced some facts.

Archie Boyle was also thrilled by my detailed information, though he was less flattering about the Air Attaché's behaviour; a change was made in that appointment shortly afterwards. Sir Robert Vansittart, Permanent Under-Secretary at the Foreign Office, was also pleased with my report. As for my Chief, he invited me to his flat a few evenings later. Here, over a bottle of port, I described some of the Germans I had met. He was much amused, and these private visits to him became a ritual each time I returned from my German trips. However, at the Foreign Office I had caused havoc. My report had upset certain people in Cabinet circles. The Secretary of State for India, Sir Samuel Hoare, a former Minister for Air, was most displeased. Both my Chief and I were puzzled by this. If Sir Robert Vansittart appreciated my information, why didn't Sir Samuel Hoare? Was there some hidden political motive?

It was soon time for me to deal with Lörzer's visit with the young pilots. I was lucky enough to obtain the co-operation of Nigel Norman, who owned and ran Heston aerodrome; this meant that the visit could properly be described as 'private' because the aerodrome was used by a number of private flying clubs. Nigel was fascinated by the idea of the visit from young German pilots who, although they were new Luftwaffe recruits, would come as civilians. He put the Secretary of the Guards Flying Club in the picture. Archie Boyle at the Air Ministry had already given the visit his blessing. A cousin of mine, Lindsay Everard, who was an MP and Chairman of the Flying Clubs Association in Britain, also offered his help. Herr Lörzer had agreed to accompany me and look after the young pilots.

I later learned that as a result of this visit the young Luftwaffe fighter pilots were ordered by Hitler to revive the tradition of chivalry in the air as practised in the First World War. Another outcome of this visit and one most useful to me was the founding of the Luftwaffe Club in Berlin in 1935, of which I was made an honorary member the following year. This gave me the opportunity to talk to the young German pilots.

It was in this way that I first heard one day in 1936 of the new dive-bombers, called Stukas. So, this was the secret aerial artillery General Reichenau had told me about. According to the young pilots these single-seater aircraft had to dive vertically at their target and aim their bomb before pulling out. They told me of how dangerous and difficult it was training with them; of how the terrific speed built up in an almost vertical dive with a heavy bomb on board was inclined to snap the wings off the aeroplane; of how, when the pilot pulled the aircraft out of its dive after dropping the bomb, he was almost pushed through his seat with the 'G' force. I was told that there had already been a number of casualties and that much needed to be done before the technique became operational. This was vital information, for it was now clear that this form of aerial artillery was to be the second principal component of Blitzkrieg. Unless the

Germans could perfect it, they would be unable to undertake the aerial destruction of opposition to their tank spearheads.

I consulted RAF officers in England about dive-bombing and found them uniformly sceptical. In their view the technique was so dangerous and was so wasteful in trained men and materials that it would never be used. I was disturbed by this inability of the English to understand the potential of the dive-bomber, for I was convinced that the Nazis would persevere with the development of this new concept in aerial artillery. It would be extremely difficult to counter-attack either by air or by anti-aircraft methods. But the Air Ministry technical branch were untroubled, because they thought the Germans would never use dive-bombers.

When Ralph Wenninger and his wife arrived in London, they were welcomed by Archie Boyle and there was a suitable sprinkling of RAF officers at the first cocktail party that the Wenningers gave in their flat in Kensington. Wenninger brought me two bottles of wild-raspberry liqueur. This must have been Rosenberg's idea, for I had told him that this was the only sort of liqueur I found drinkable in Germany. I just could not stand the sickly-sweet green potions which Rosenberg himself seemed to enjoy. Wenninger was given the usual careful conducted tours arranged by the Air Ministry. He was shown our Staff College and our training facilities, but there were three things which he was never allowed to learn anything about: our progress in radar; our brilliant system of control of the whole of our fighter air force from Fighter Command, which included our system of enabling our fighters to home in on approaching enemy formations; and our production of the Spitfire. This aircraft was later to catch the Germans completely by surprise.

Wenninger, like all the foreign attachés, used to visit Archie Boyle from time to time. On these occasions Archie would let me know in advance so that I would be in the Ministry when Wenninger was there and would be summoned by Archie to meet him in his office. In this way I managed to maintain the fiction that I was a member of the Air Staff and nothing more. Rosenberg himself seemed satisfied according to the following extract from his diaries for 11 July 1934:

> The Air Ministry emphasises that it will help us honestly but one should not try making them believe things, because they are receiving exact information anyway. The next Air Attaché for Berlin, who is closely connected with Winterbotham, will be a good man as opposed to the present one, who is a rather simple-minded man. Corresponding to that the German Attaché will be shown round in England.

By the end of 1934 I had a new ally. Desmond Morton had been the member of our office team charged with uncovering intrigues in foreign politics, but now he was given the special task of acquiring and collating all possible information on German armaments and war factories. His first priority was to be aircraft and aero-engine production. This took a great load off my shoulders, and it meant that I could concentrate more on the role of the Luftwaffe, its training and strategy. Together, Desmond and I would be able to arrive at a much more accurate forecast of growth and performance. He obtained a complete list of existing German factories from Control Commission Records, together with their capacities. This made it easier to observe any extensions to existing factories or the construction of new ones.

By the beginning of 1935 estimates of German intentions and many other bits of the jigsaw were arriving in London. Estimates of Hitler's target varied from 3000 to 5000 first-line aircraft. At that time, it was difficult to forecast which was correct, but we took a conservative view of 4000, which proved to be right in 1939 but had been whittled down to 3000 by July of 1940.

It so happened that Desmond lived next door to Chartwell, the home of Winston Churchill, where he was often a guest at Sunday lunch. I was at first unaware of this and wondered why it was always on Friday nights that he would come to my office to help me work out estimates of progress of the build-up of the Luftwaffe, but I soon found out that on Sundays Desmond would give these figures to Winston Churchill. The following week there would inevitably be a parliamentary question by Churchill in the House of Commons to ask the Prime Minister whether it was a fact that such and such figures for the strength of the Luftwaffe were now correct. I never knew whether the Prime Minister had any idea how Winston Churchill had obtained his figures, but Baldwin always gave the bland reply that he did not have any information on this subject.

Morton was a vital partner in our joint efforts to ferret out the truth of the Luftwaffe expansion, but early in 1935 a piece of rare intelligence good fortune came my way which made our mutual search much easier. The new British Air Attaché in Berlin had been a prisoner of war with me in 1918 and was an old friend, so I had given him some idea of my connections with Rosenberg and the Nazis, enough to know that when an envelope addressed to me one day dropped through the Embassy letter box it was important to send it on to me in London as quickly as possible through the diplomatic bag.

The envelope contained a sheet of paper about ten inches by eight which was clearly a photostat of a single page from a book. At the top, above a black line, were letters and figures indicating that it was part of Volume D, Chapter 3, and in the centre the word geheim, meaning secret; and on the right-hand side was the page number thirty-two; at least that is my recollection. Beneath the black line came the heading 'The Establishment of Flying Schools', under which was a column which ran right down the page listing the names and locations of the flying schools of the Luftwaffe. There were some twenty-five in all. That was all there was in the envelope. To begin with I suspected it might be a hoax, but when I looked at the list carefully I realised that quite a few of the names coincided with those that I already knew about from other sources. Obviously, if the symbols at the top were authentic, this was just one page out of a book. However, I was not going to risk sending it straight over to the Air Ministry without checking more of the details myself, nor of course was I willing to compromise the source, if he were genuine, by sending the list to agents overseas; so, I picked out a number of the flying schools listed and sent their names to separate capitals in Europe for verification.

A few weeks later when I was beginning to get confirmation of the existence, or preparation for the existence, of these flying schools, a second envelope arrived from Berlin. This time the page was from the same volume, but the chapter and page were different and below the line was set out the complete establishment of a new German fighter squadron. I could hardly believe my eyes. Here I was fishing in every European pond for any scrap of information which would help me fill in the framework of the new Luftwaffe and here on my desk was what purported to be a leaf out of a secret volume on the organisation of that new German Air Force. The second envelope had been accompanied by a typewritten note giving only a name and an obvious accommodation address in a Berlin suburb, with a request that under no circumstances was the information to be passed to the French.

My liaison over intelligence with my opposite number of the French Deuxième Bureau, Colonel Georges Ronin, was extremely close. We exchanged every bit of information we could about Germany. But now I was asked to withhold from him information from my new source. That source must be well informed. It seemed likely that he was on Göring's staff, a man who was either passionately anti-Nazi or extremely greedy. Further extracts from Göring's 'bible', as I called it, continued to arrive throughout 1936, 1937 and 1939. I suppose I must have had some thirty of these photostats giving all aspects of the Luftwaffe build-up. They were of course always invaluable, but they were of the greatest use now, at the beginning of 1935, when I had not yet been able to convince either the government or the Air

Ministry that my conclusions about the Nazis were correct. There was no demand for money enclosed with these photostat reports until five or six of them had been received towards the end of 1935. That demand was a substantial one. My Chief asked me for a careful assessment of the value of these reports.

Money had never been readily available from the time I had joined the Secret Service at the beginning of 1930, so I told the Admiral that I would prefer to give up many small sources to concentrate on this one, so vital was the information. I showed him some of the reports and the conclusions which they had confirmed, and he seemed quite satisfied.

In due course a moustached and bespectacled passenger arrived at a Berlin station off the Hamburg train and deposited two small suitcases at the left-luggage office. The ticket for the deposit was sent to the address in Berlin, and a day or two later another moustached and bespectacled gentleman collected the suitcases. It was the copybook method of transferring payment. The envelopes continued to arrive.

I would have liked to have arranged a meeting between this source and myself outside Germany so that I could identify exactly which pages from the 'bible' I wanted, but I hesitated to do so in case I compromised him. From 1935 to 1938 I remained patient and took what was given me. Then with war imminent in 1939, I thought we should meet in case he could be persuaded to defect and bring with him the whole order of battle of the Luftwaffe. An invitation was sent to him to meet me in Switzerland. A rendezvous was actually fixed for Zurich, where I waited for three days, but nobody turned up. I was not altogether surprised; if the source held a senior position in Göring's Air Force, he might well have been moved out of Berlin when things began to hot up. This guess of mine was probably correct for after returning from Zurich I received no more photostats.

Chapter 16

THE SHOWDOWN

In February 1935 I was ordered by Charles Medhurst, the Director of Intelligence at the Air Ministry, to accompany him on a tour of the Middle East, where it was the RAF's job to maintain law and order. It occurred to me that some Cabinet ministers considered me to be too eager in pursuing the German rearmament question when it was manifestly against government policy to admit what was happening. The Air Staff were presumably persuaded that a month or two out of Europe would cool me down.

On my return to London I found that no more pages from Göring's 'bible' had come in, but much fill-in material from other sources around Europe had appeared. The picture was becoming clearer; but it was now time for me to go to Paris to visit my opposite number there.

Georges Ronin was about the same age as myself and he had also been a pilot in the First World War. He spoke no English and had a very keen sense of humour. We got on well together and we became good friends. We would compare all the information on the German Air Force that both of us had collected during the previous three months.

I planned to find out as delicately as I could why I had been asked not to pass the Göring 'bible' information to the French. I had brought with me some extracts from the flying-school report, and I let Georges know that they had been supplied by an exceptionally important source, and I asked him not to pass the information on verbatim even to his French Air Ministry. Georges wanted to know if there was any particular reason why he should not do so. I smiled at him and said, 'Well, that's what I'm trying to find out.' And then for the first time since I had known him he confessed that he himself was not sure of his own General Staff, though he did not know how far the treachery went. As long as I gave him the outline of the information so that he could fill in his own picture, he promised that it would be so mixed up with all his other data as to be untraceable. I knew Georges well enough to tell him at this point that our source was within the German Air Ministry itself. He grinned and said, 'Now we're getting somewhere, aren't we?' So, whenever I received the photocopies during the next few years I would pass them to Georges minus the page or chapter references at the top, and he in turn never allowed them to leave his own office except in a disguised form.

With hindsight I suppose it is not surprising that I found it difficult to follow the devious path of British politics during the middle thirties. The apparently deliberate failure of either of the main parties to believe any information concerning Germany's rearmament or her aggressive intentions frustrated all those whose job it was to collect it and puzzled those in the services charged with ensuring the safety of their country. One could only conclude that if the government were to accept the information I and others were providing, they would be forced to take some action, and that for reasons of political expediency they preferred to procrastinate for as long as possible. Winston Churchill, well briefed by Desmond Morton, was continually asking questions in the House of Commons on German air rearmament. Yet on at least one occasion Baldwin rose to answer the question, in his pocket the latest estimates which I had sent to him at his urgent request that morning, only to declare that he had no information on the subject. Then, in May 1935, referring to German air strength, he told the House of Commons, 'I was completely wrong, we were completely misled on that subject.'

My Chief, the Admiral, usually a calm man, was infuriated by Baldwin's words. It was a deliberate statement, so the hunt for a scapegoat would doubtless soon be on, and the Admiral was determined that neither he nor I should be the quarry. In late June 1935, he called me to his room to ask that I summarise all the evidence I had ever obtained right from my first meeting with Hitler and bring him samples of the latest data that I had received, for, as he put it, 'We've got a tough situation on our hands now.' I soon completed the summary, and promptly took it along to his office together with actual photographs of the Göring 'bible' pages. He looked it over, rang for his secretary and told her to inform the Prime Minister's secretary that he would be round at 10 Downing Street shortly.

Now that he had a complaint from the Chief of the Secret Service, Baldwin took the opportunity he had been waiting for to let somebody else take the blame. He ordered an enquiry into the whole subject of German air rearmament at Cabinet Committee level, to be held in July. My Chief warned me to prepare my case with great care. This I did, and a few weeks later, as we drove in his car to the meeting, he again warned me that if I failed to convince the Cabinet of my views I might very well lose my job. 'There are plenty of people', he said, 'who would be only too delighted to get it.'

We entered the conference room. At a long table facing us were the three Committee members: Philip Cunliffe-Lister, later to become Lord Swinton, as chairman; on his right Lord Runciman, wearing a stiff high collar, and Sir Kingsley Wood on his left. They all greeted us, but looking to my right I was surprised to see not only Lord Londonderry, the Minister for Air, but the Chief of Air Staff, Sir Edward Ellington, flanked by Air Vice-Marshal Christopher Courtney, as well as Archie Boyle and the young RAF officer in charge of the German Section at Air Ministry Intelligence. I had met Lord Londonderry and his assistant Philip Sassoon on my return from Germany in 1934. They had both been delighted with my evidence, so I knew he would be on my side. I also felt that Chris Courtney and Archie Boyle would back me up. On our side were my Chief, Desmond Morton and myself. The Air Staff looked very glum, and I wondered whether they were going to be helpful or oppose my evidence.

Lord Swinton began by asking the Chief of Air Staff to state the Air Ministry case. I was grateful for this as it would tell me exactly what I had to confirm, but the CAS appeared quite unbriefed and told the young Flight Lieutenant to open the proceedings.

He did not seem very sure of himself but, to put it briefly, he challenged all my information and figures of personnel training, aerodromes, flying schools and aircraft production as absurd. I think the Committee were as much taken aback as I was, but now they were going to get it straight in the neck. It was a rule in our office that precise details of where and from whom information was obtained was never disclosed, but my own category of reliability was given on every report I sent to the Air Ministry. It was of course fortunate that by now I was receiving the priceless photostats of some of the most important pages of Göring's secret volumes on the establishment of the complete Luftwaffe, and to these I could award the category of absolute reliability. I had agreed with my Chief that I could now reveal the source of my information, but not the way in which I obtained it.

I opened my case by asking Air Staff if they were aware that a complete air staff was being secretly trained in the German War Office. Blank disbelief, until I told of my meeting with the Chief of Luftwaffe Staff at lunch, and with an air commodore whom I had been asked to approve as Air Attaché in London. It was a large leopard among the Air Staff pigeons. I could see the CAS in quiet conversation with Chris

Courtney. Lord Runciman's only remark was 'Did you really talk to that man Hitler?'

As I now read out the list of training establishments, the whole Air Staff seemed taken aback. The CAS listened to every word with an expression of sheer disbelief. He had not been well briefed. The young officer went red in the face and still clung to his statement that the Nazis could not build so large a number of aircraft over the next three years. I asked Chris Courtney if he could remember the numbers of aircraft the British had built in those fateful years of 1917-18. He agreed that the figure of three or four thousand over the next three years was possible, and here Desmond Morton came in with full details of the tremendous expansion now being made to the known aircraft and engine factories and the new factories being built. The opposition was silenced. We were home and dry.

Lord Swinton turned to me and said, 'Thank you, I think you have made your point.' He then thanked the Air Staff, who now filed out. Archie Boyle gave me a quiet wink, and Lord Londonderry a grateful smile. On our way back to the office, the Admiral congratulated Morton and myself on our performance. It was, in a way, a turning point in my career in MI6. We all had a drink in the Admiral's flat.

Shortly afterwards, Lord Swinton took over the job of Minister for Air (Lord Londonderry had been made Baldwin's scapegoat), and as a result of this meeting gave the Air Staff the go-ahead for the Spitfire programme, and also the construction of great shadow factories for its mass production in the Midlands. If he had not done so, we should not have won the Battle of Britain in the air, and in turn would not have won the Second World War.

Lord Swinton soon sent for me to ask how co-operation between the Air Ministry Intelligence and my department was progressing. I explained that the Air Ministry personnel preferred to keep their collating to themselves. Then and there he sent for Archie Boyle and told both of us that in future there must be much closer co-ordination. He then suggested that I find a suitable person to help me as it looked as though I would be having plenty to do.

At long last some momentum was building up, and people were taking notice. It did not take me long to recruit John Perkins, a great friend and an aviation enthusiast, who was also Parliamentary Under-Secretary to the Minister of Air. He had also been one of the people I had asked to help me entertain the young German pilots the previous year.

I learned later that as a result of the Cabinet Committee meeting that I had attended, Baldwin had agreed to set rearmament preparations in motion. This could now be done, he felt, without provoking too much comment and it undoubtedly helped when, after Munich, Chamberlain gave the go-ahead for full-scale modernisation of Fighter Command. But it was all too little, too late. It was not until November 1936 that Baldwin finally admitted his mistake in not taking German rearmament seriously:

> 'I put before the whole House my views with an appalling frankness. Supposing I had gone to the country and said that Germany was rearming and that we must be armed, does anyone think that our pacific democracy would have rallied to that cry at that moment? I cannot think of anything that would have made the loss of the election, from my point of view, more certain.'

So here at last was the admission why certain ministers did not want to know what I had to tell them. But I believe that Baldwin was profoundly wrong; the stakes were too high.

Chapter 17

DETENTE

By March 1936 Hitler evidently believed that he was strong enough to challenge France and Britain to see if they reacted. In contravention of the Versailles Treaty he marched into the Rhineland. Both London and Paris were taken unawares. Hitler had also sent several Luftwaffe fighter squadrons into this demilitarised zone. After both London and Paris had concluded that they could do nothing about them, it was revealed that these few fighter squadrons had been flying from one aerodrome to another, changing their insignia from time to time, to give the impression that Hitler had a vast concentration of fighter aircraft to meet anything that the British or the French could put up. So, Hitler got away with it, which must have encouraged him to think that the British and the French governments' lack of action meant they were funking the issue. I have little doubt that he now felt convinced that the more he thrust his gigantic rearmament programme down our throats, the more embarrassed our government would be and the less likely to start interfering in any future plans for expansion. His bluff had come off.

When I finally revisited Germany in the summer of 1936, I found a very different Rosenberg from the one I had got to know in 1934 – more withdrawn, much fatter, and rather crumpled. He was absorbed in his ideology, preparing plans for the dissemination and control of his new religion, not only throughout Germany but right across the rest of Europe, including Finland, the Finns being 'true Aryans'. He explained that he had delegated some of the conduct of foreign affairs in order to give himself more time to organise his priesthood, but he had retained the job of keeping Hitler personally informed about foreign press comment and had trained a public-relations staff to deal with foreign press correspondents in Berlin.

One warm evening in our favourite little café-bar on the Kurfürstendamm, Rosenberg opened out about his plans. He told Bill and me that he had actually started to build a great cultural centre, rather on the lines of an enlarged Vatican City, in southern Germany. It was to be the centre of the Nordic cult throughout a 'unified' Aryan Europe and great colleges would be built there. Bill had told me that he had made friends with an important Nazi called Erich Koch, who was the Gauleiter, or Governor, of the province of East Prussia and also a friend of Rosenberg's. It was suggested that I go up to East Prussia to see something of Koch's successful work in that province.

Karl Böme, the young member of his press-relations staff whom Rosenberg had delegated to look after me, with instructions that I was to see whatever I liked, had just become Professor of Journalism, a chair no doubt invented for members of Rosenberg's staff. There is a German expression *gute Kerl* – meaning 'a good fellow' – which I mistranslated as 'a good Charles' so I used to call Karl 'a proper Charlie': he was flattered. He was a cheerful, handsome man of about twenty-seven or -eight, fair, always dressed in well-cut shirt and breeches. He liked to be smart, and he was the joy of most of the barmaids on the Kurfürstendamm. He had a quiet, rather plump little wife who lived in Hamburg, and who sometimes came to Berlin in terrible tweeds with her wire-haired fox terrier. As I have said, wives were not encouraged to appear in official Nazi circles – this was a man's world.

It was a Nazi requirement that those of their members whose work involved contact with foreigners should learn the appropriate language. Charlie was struggling with English, and gratefully used me to practise on.

Rosenberg was due to visit Lübeck, that wonderful Hansa city on the Baltic, for a few days. He suggested that Bill and I should go too, and that Charlie was to come along to ensure my complete freedom. It was hot midsummer in Berlin, so we were only too glad of a chance to visit the sea. As usual when a high Party official was due, forests of crimson banners festooned the city, ruining the lovely old buildings. There was not the same enthusiasm as further south. The Baltic peoples have always had a strong streak of independence, and they were somewhat cautious in their acceptance of the Nazis. Nevertheless, there was a small crowd waiting outside the main hotel to watch the arrival of Rosenberg; he therefore advised the canter technique into the hotel. This was the last time that I was asked to perform this drill because the leading Nazis now felt much more secure.

The following day was Midsummer's Day and Rosenberg proudly announced that he would take us to see the new Nazi version of the Festival of the Solstice in Lübeck's ancient fortress. There, on the circular roof of the ancient keep, stood a circle of identical Hitler youths, shoulder to shoulder, all of them exactly the same height and shape, fair hair, blue eyes, dressed in their pale khaki shirts and shorts, 'totally Aryan'. The battlements now echoed, with centuries-old pagan litanies chanted by the circle of Aryan boys. At midday there was a shadowless silence as the sun hung for a moment directly overhead, and then a paean of praise rang out for the Aryan sun-god. The whole performance had been in deadly earnest.

In the Luftwaffe Club back in Berlin most of the talk was about the pilots' training programme, their 'crash courses', as they called them. So, I thought I would look at one of the aerodromes where these took place. While I was trying to organise this, I received a note from the Air Attaché asking me to go to see him. Events had taken a bizarre turn.

Hitler, I was told, had decided to order real detente between the Luftwaffe and the Royal Air Force. He claimed to have been worried by the exaggerated reports of the Luftwaffe build-up in the British press, and now he asked for two senior officers from the Air Ministry, together with their aides, to come to Germany where they would be shown exactly what the Luftwaffe was doing. The Attaché told me that the invitation had been issued by Erhard Milch as the Secretary of State for Air, and that the Air Ministry were going to reply shortly with the names of the people they would send. There was a note for me from Archie Boyle saying that he thought it would be better if I kept out of the way of the delegation since this was an official visit, which would be carried out in full uniform.

I came to the conclusion that Hitler must be getting desperate about British neutrality. He must have thought that if he could make official contact with the Royal Air Force and show them some of the might of the modern Luftwaffe, it would pressurise the British government into keeping out of the coming conflict. I was keen to hear Rosenberg's reaction to this latest move. I had not long to wait for he soon sent a message round asking Bill and me to go to see him in his office. He was cross, he said, because he had not been consulted on this move and Hitler had gone over his head straight to Göring. It was, incidentally, interesting to note that Göring had not sent the invitation himself. He probably did not approve of it but had to do what Hitler ordered and so passed the job on to Milch, no doubt so that he himself could escape any criticism that might arise later. At any rate, the Air Staff would at last be able to see for themselves that I had not been talking nonsense.

Two air marshals accompanied by two more junior members of the Air Ministry staff duly arrived in Germany and I was to learn later on in London exactly what they had been shown. They visited the Air Staff itself and the Air Staff College. They were shown the new Richthofen Fighter Wing, now in the summer of 1936 equipped with the Me-109. They were shown the production line at Heinkel's factory on the Baltic coast and the newest aircraft, the Heinkel 111, the Junkers 86 and 87, and the Dornier 17. Bombers and dive-bombers were demonstrated to them, and they were given the performance figures, which must have frightened them somewhat. However, this did not satisfy Air Marshal Courtney, who asked Milch for his production programme, upon which Milch produced his 1934 programme, which he said was due for completion in 1938. It comprised thirty bomber squadrons, six dive-bomber squadrons and twelve fighter squadrons, some 2340 aircraft in all; and he then said that to date some fifty per cent of the programme was completed, meaning 1116 first-line aircraft. However, because these figures did not agree with those I had given the Air Ministry, Courtney said that he was under the impression that more had already been built. Milch admitted the error and told him that the figures he had given had been completed nine months earlier. Thus, at the end of 1935, they already had fifty per cent of the programme completed.

I was to learn from Rosenberg later that Göring had been wise to keep out of this detente because Kesselring, who had become Chief of Air Staff, openly denounced Milch for giving away the Luftwaffe secrets. In fact, Rosenberg gave the impression that there was a good deal of in-fighting going on between Göring and his principal officers. Two weeks after the mission returned to London, the newly promoted Major-General Wenninger was given similar details of the Royal Air Force, according to current planning. These revealed that the RAF would have 1736 first-line aircraft plus an immediate reserve by the end of 1938.

There was, however, one especially interesting point about this detente. Milch not only asked our delegation in Germany not to take any notes, but he also asked them not to pass the information to the Foreign Office because he did not wish it to be passed to the French. He clearly felt that once it was outside the hands of the Air Ministry it would somehow be given to the French. When Courtney told me of this provision, it struck an immediate chord. I knew that Milch, when he had been chief of the civil airline Lufthansa, had been very friendly towards Britain, and the outcome of this detente also made it clear that he did not wish to go to war against us. None of the planes we had learned about so far were long-range bombers, so it did not look as though Milch had built an air force with Great Britain in mind. Had he, I wondered, been the source of my photographs from Göring's 'bible' with the similar request that it should not be passed on to the French? It seemed quite possible now, and the fact that Kesselring was denouncing Milch for giving us information fitted the picture; there seemed to be a Göring-Kesselring faction who were bloodthirsty for revenge against England, while Hitler, Milch, Rosenberg and, I suspected, Hess, and maybe other members of the Nazi hierarchy, were playing for British neutrality. Goebbels was evidently preparing for both.

Chapter 18

ERICH KOCH

I benefited greatly from Hitler's policy of detente, because now we knew the performance of the German aircraft which would make up the Luftwaffe and we knew the Germans' own estimate of their production programme. At long last our civil servants and politicians were beginning to grasp what was going on in Germany and seemed likely to look more favourably in future on the information which I might be sending them. It was just as well that Hitler's act of open showmanship had occurred when it did, for obtaining information was proving increasingly difficult. In addition, Rosenberg had been squeezed out of the Foreign Relations Department by Joachim von Ribbentrop. However, it would still be possible to obtain data on factory and aeroplane production, although this would now be hived off into Desmond Morton's industrial-output section. My job would be to find out more about the general efficiency of the Luftwaffe, its training and tactics. I would also keep a watching brief on dive-bombing training, aircraft armament and performance and the possible production of any new type of gun or bomb. As always I would be listening for any hint that a new secret weapon had been invented, for news of German radar research, and for any suggestion of advances in their development of aerial photography and code techniques. But first I would have to concentrate on discovering more about the Germans' intentions against Russia and try to gain a clearer idea of the dates when they were likely to begin war operations and of the probable order of procedure.

With Charlie Böme once again detailed by Rosenberg to look after us, Bill and I set off for Königsberg to meet Erich Koch, the Gauleiter of East Prussia. From him we hoped to obtain information about the Russian front.

Since we had a special Ju-52 at our disposal, I asked Charlie if we could see as much of the country as possible. It was an amazing land to the east of Berlin, densely covered with forest interspersed by small lakes. From the air the little areas of water glistened in the sunlight like so many mirrors nestling in the deep green velvet forests which stretched away to the horizon. There seemed few areas of good land, and it was here in the east that I knew that a number of military aerodromes had recently been carved out of the forest, so I asked the pilot to see how many of these we could count. He happily found and flew over five or more of them within reasonable range of our direct route. I saw that these aerodromes were all of exactly the same pattern, designed to hold about two squadrons. But now the skies around us were filled with operational aircraft, a considerable advance on those I had seen before – proper military types which made our old Junkers machine look as if it were standing still. This was certainly an opportunity I would not have missed; it was the visual proof of the information from Göring's 'bible' which had been backed up by our other sources. If what I had seen was being repeated all over the country, the present effort in Germany would certainly be able to meet Milch's programme and supply a large pool of fully trained pilots in reserve.

At Danzig we had to land for customs. One could easily imagine the irritation of the Germans at this restriction, one of the less sensible provisions of the Versailles Treaty. After leaving Danzig we flew on along the Baltic coast and up the long canal leading from the sea at Pilau to Königsberg some miles inland. I noted the range of new concrete shelters for U-boats under construction at Pilau.

At the aerodrome to welcome us was Erich Koch with his broad smile and noticeable lack of 'Heil Hitlers'. We approached the waiting cars at an ordinary walk. The tension so evident in Berlin seemed much less.

Erich I discovered to be a veritable cock-sparrow of a man: he had been born and brought up in the Ruhr, a railway worker by trade, and he was a passionate socialist. He had, however, seen no future in trades unionism under the Nazis, so had wisely decided to achieve his ambitions by joining the Party in 1925. A natural organiser, whose stocky frame exuded energy, he had survived the in-fighting in the Party and managed, when Hitler came to power, to be given the job of Gauleiter of East Prussia, an area cut off from the rest of Germany by the Polish Corridor. Here he hoped to carry out his socialist plans with little interference from Berlin. I liked this enthusiastic man as soon as I met him, for he had none of the arrogance of the jumped-up Nazi yet was close enough to the Party hierarchy to know a great deal.

He had soon discovered that almost all the agricultural land in the province was in the hands of the old Prussian families. As a result of poor estate management, they were all heavily mortgaged to the state. It was therefore easy for Koch to foreclose these mortgages and take over the properties. But he left the barons enough land around their houses to run a home farm and he allowed them to continue to use their titles.

When Koch had chosen a site for one of his settlements, instead of building the houses in the middle, he put the factories at the centre on the railway or river. Most of the light industries, some of which were evidently connected with the rearmament effort, he brought out from his native Ruhr, together with the people who already knew how to operate them. The houses, shopping centres, sports grounds and swimming pools were then located outside the factory area with plenty of roads leading in. The houses, in this way, could be planned on a garden-suburb principle with all their amusements close at hand. Koch was immensely proud of what he was doing and took us to see some of the houses near Elbing. The new tenants were genuinely delighted to see him.

On our return to Königsberg, we found the town a forest of red banners in honour of Hess, who was staying at our hotel. This time he was more relaxed than when I had first met him in his office near Hitler's in Berlin.

Koch had had the idea that I might like to visit an amber mine, one of the very few in the world. I was told that the reason for the amber's presence was that long ago, when this whole area had been covered in great pine forests, some giant storm or meteorite had cut down a wide swathe of trees from East Prussia to Sweden. The pines, felled in full vigour, had oozed great quantities of resin which in the course of time had been buried and turned into amber.

Amber in lumps as large as potatoes must always have had scarcity value, but I had not expected the mine to have such strong police protection. The manager appeared uneasy as he showed us round, and when we returned to the cleaning and processing plant, after visiting the great open-cast mine, he grew increasingly anxious. At length he took Charlie aside and asked if it was all right for foreigners to see what was now a war factory. Charlie gave him the okay and laughed with us over the idea that we might be seeing anything we should not. The manager explained to us that the amber was melted down and purified to make especially fine resin which was used for insulating electrical wiring. Instead of probing further and so making the man more agitated, I said that it seemed such a waste of a lovely material which was so valuable for necklaces and beads and was particularly admired in Moslem countries; he assured me that the market for necklaces had been cornered by the British and that the resin was unique for certain classes of insulation at extreme altitudes. The final answer to that one came in 1944 with the V weapons.

It had not escaped my notice that since Hess's visit Koch had grown rather subdued. Before long he explained that Hess had told him his province would be visited by a number of generals from the Army in the near future. A look of alarm came into his face when I said that I supposed this was in connection with the Russian invasion. However, I went on to tell him what Hitler had told me and about my conversation with Reichenau in Berlin. Then he let himself go. He said that just as he was getting his province into some sort of order, the whole place was going to be overrun by the military, who were going to build concrete this and concrete that and railways and spoil this little province. He told us that he had decided to come back to Berlin with us if we would give him a lift.

I was sorry to leave East Prussia. As we flew back over the sand dunes which divide a large inland lake from the Baltic Sea, both Erich Koch and I felt sad about what was in store for this province. We both knew. He asked me to come back again. I liked him and felt he would talk more freely another time. I certainly intended to return.

Chapter 19

STRENGTH THROUGH JOY

The detente between the Luftwaffe and the RAF continued in 1937. The Luftwaffe itself was starting to flex its wings in public. In July Ernst Udet, who was evidently responsible now for aircraft production, came over to the Hendon Air Show; and both Milch and Udet turned up at Zurich in Switzerland showing off their Me-109 fighters and the Do-17 bomber, which proved to be faster than the fighters from the various countries which took part in that air display. Also, on show there was the Daimler-Benz 600 aero-engine. Air Marshal Goddard had pulled off a remarkable bluff when he met Udet in Berlin with the RAF mission. He persuaded Udet that the only really good high-performance bomber was one with two engines. It was not until during the Battle of Britain that the Luftwaffe – unable to carry sufficient fuel for the two engines over long distances – found themselves unable to reach or interfere with our Atlantic sea routes.

In July the principal designer of the Bristol aero-engine, Roy Fedden, was invited to Germany for a tour of the Messerschmitt aircraft factory. On his return he told me that he had never been so frightened in his life both by the rate of production and by the performance of these latest German fighters, the Me-109 and the twin-engined Me-110. No doubt that was the object of the exercise.

In the course of that summer, Desmond Morton began to receive very interesting information about German shortages of materials required for rearmament. It seemed that both steel and aluminium were now scarce, and a contact in one of the aircraft factories advised us that the target for 1938 would not now be completed until the spring of 1939. This was indeed good news. It no doubt explained the contradictory reports we started to get about the total first-line aircraft which would eventually comprise the Luftwaffe; they had obviously run into difficulties.

In September 1937 the Germans held some quite large-scale manoeuvres to which certain foreign military and air attachés were invited. According to the information given to them, the Germans fielded over 1300 aircraft, all new and modern machines. The Stuka dive-bomber was seen in action for the first time. As it dived out of the sky it cannot have seemed all that intimidating, for none of the military was altered to its potential; at that time, it was not fitted with its screaming siren device. Certainly, none of the senior British or French officers at the demonstrations saw it as dangerous. They did not seem able to envisage the effect it would eventually have as it screamed down like a demon to drop a large bomb directly on to the troops and guns below. Perhaps it was the absence of a spearhead of advancing tanks trundling along the ground at the manoeuvres which lulled them into indifference.

In September 1937 the Nazis sent a special aeroplane over to Britain to collect a number of visitors who had been invited to the Nuremberg Rally. I was one of them. Bill and Charlie came to meet me at Nuremberg, and we went off to the hotel rooms which Rosenberg had reserved for us. Apparently Rosenberg was unlikely to be at the rally himself and I later found that he had been down to Austria, doubtless preparing his Aryan propaganda for the Anschluss in 1938. I watched the parades in the stadium with growing unease and was as baffled as ever by the ranting exhortations of the Führer. But the most interesting part of my visit was lunch at an *Arbeitsdienst* camp.

Young men between the ages of fifteen and eighteen, after they had finished their spell in the Hitler Youth organisation, were drafted into these camps, where they were put to work building roads and reservoirs and undertaking drainage and forestry operations. It was a kind of pre-military training designed to keep them fighting fit and out of mischief under firm discipline. The young men I saw were a splendid sight, with their sun-burned and muscular bodies stripped to the waist as they laid drainage pipes along a trench.

I lunched in the camp mess room with the young Commandant, who must have been all of twenty-three years old, and I asked him what was the secret of their enthusiasm for their work. He explained it quite simply: these young people had a cause which had been offered to them by the Führer. They understood perfectly well that they would soon be drafted into the armed forces and that they were going to be part of the great new German Reich. 'It's exciting for them, you know,' he said. I suggested that it must be tricky keeping such high-spirited youngsters under control. He evidently mistook my meaning because he replied, 'One teaspoonful of bicarbonate of soda per head per day, and sex doesn't even start to rear its perverted head.' I was to see them in their thousands giving a display at Nuremberg the following year.

When I returned to London I found that the Air Ministry had issued an invitation to Milch to visit England with a delegation on much the same lines as the one which we had sent to Berlin the year before. Milch and his delegation arrived in October in one of their new Heinkel 111s and were shown our own Air Staff College and some of our units which had not yet been equipped with modern aircraft. We were especially careful not to let any of them see a prototype Spitfire. However, by now we wanted to make it clear to the Germans that, although we were not prepared or preparing for war, we were alert to the possibilities, so we took them to see one of our new shadow factories to show that we could expand our production of aircraft at great speed should it be necessary.

The game of bluff and counter-bluff which we were playing with the Germans was often a very close-run thing. At one party given by Fighter Command for the visiting Germans, Milch asked what progress we were making with our development of radar, a question which caught his hosts completely off balance, for this particular invention was still high on our secret list. How much did the Germans know about radar themselves? How much did they know about our experiments? We were fairly certain that we were ahead, but this supposition was not yet proven. Early in 1939 a small radar saucer with a central aerial was seen near the Baltic Sea by one of our contacts, a discovery which alerted the Air Ministry to call a special meeting, with scientists Robert Watson-Watt and Henry Tizard present, to discuss what I could do to penetrate any German experiments in this area. At this meeting it was decided to provide me with a young scientist to assist me in this sort of scientific work and so R.V. Jones became attached to my section – a partnership that was to have such excellent results later on. When war broke out we discovered to our great relief that the Germans had only a very short-range experimental radar outfit, which did not become efficient until we started our retaliation bombing later.

Not long after Milch had returned to Germany, Charlie Böme came over to stay with me. I had invited him while I was at Nuremberg. I wanted him to see what life was like in Britain. I felt it would do no harm and might knock a little bit of the Aryan nonsense out of him. I showed him some of our country pursuits, taking him out shooting and to a meet of the Cotswold hounds. I myself was riding and Charlie seemed very amused at our pink coats and top hats, which he considered very Olde Worlde stuff. Nevertheless, he got thoroughly excited when we found a fox. He was amazed at the good roads that we had in Britain, and he said he did not know that we had built autostrades everywhere. I explained to him that this was the ordinary London-to-Gloucester road and that we had not yet gone in for the German type of motorway.

Just before the end of the year Hitler began to make speeches about how oppressed the German minority was in Austria, declaring that it was high time that Austria returned to the Fatherland. We had seen these tactics before it was clearly just a matter of time before he moved to take over Austria. I knew that in that event it would be the end of detente between the RAF and the Luftwaffe.

As it happened, the occupation was a little further off than I expected, as the Anschluss was not effected until March 1938. It had been preceded by a great deal of ineffectual diplomatic activity which, as I had imagined, brought detente to an end. Had it perhaps now occurred to Hitler that we were not sympathetic to him and that there was a real chance that we might in the end fight?

By May 1938 Bill advised me that the signs were that more definite decisions were being taken on the timing of the 'expansion'; he added that security was being tightened up. All this made it vital that I go to Berlin, even though we were obtaining a good deal of intelligence about the Luftwaffe. The crucial knowledge of 'when' and 'where' we could expect to be attacked was not the sort of information that was easily obtainable by ordinary sources. But I wondered whether I should be welcome in Berlin, or whether I should now be *persona non grata.* I appreciated that I had had a good innings from 1934 to 1937, and also that Rosenberg's position in the hierarchy was growing more tenuous the nearer we came to war. I put the question to Bill: should I be running too great a risk if I came over? Rosenberg had issued no invitation, but I had one from Erich Koch to revisit East Prussia. At the same time, I did not want to involve Bill in any trouble. His presence in Berlin would be crucial for us and we had already made arrangements to evacuate him to Switzerland if necessary. I would have liked to let things cool down a bit after the Anschluss, but again the longer I left it the less welcome I might be in Germany.

But Bill was reassuring. He himself was still regarded as an essential English contact by Rosenberg, and he did not believe Rosenberg or Hitler, who still wanted to maintain contact with the RAF, would consider me unwelcome. I should have to tread carefully, but if we went to East Prussia we might learn what we wanted to know without appearing too inquisitive.

I decided to go to Germany. I needed to know how the Anschluss had affected the Nazis' plans. Were they intending to silence the West before invading Russia? Which personalities in the German High Command now carried most weight, who was applying pressure to whom, and who was Hitler listening to? Were those intent on revenge for the defeat of 1918 winning over the 'leave Britain out of it' faction?

Accordingly in the summer of 1938 I went back to Berlin. I felt that by this time, if there was going to be a war in the near future, the signs would now be obvious. And so they were. In what one might call official circles, in which previously I had moved without much restriction, I was now being treated much more warily. By contrast the pro-Nazi American press and visitors were being given the full VIP treatment. Young William Randolph Hearst of the Hearst Press, already very Anglophobe, was receiving a great deal of attention from Rosenberg's Foreign Press Department. The military seemed more sure of themselves, and the new German Air Force were too busy, no doubt getting their units organised, to entertain visitors. Nonetheless, having successfully negotiated the open-fronted, non-stop lifts of Göring's new Air Ministry, I was courteously received by the officer in charge of foreign liaison. He was polite but unforthcoming, fobbing me off with bland generalisations. In 1936 I would have been encouraged to go along for a drink at the Luftwaffe Club to meet the pilots. But this time no invitation was issued, so I decided to go along anyway. Here too there was a difference; they seemed aware of my Englishness and were politely noncommittal.

Only Charlie Böme was inquisitive. Indeed, he seemed naively curious about what was going on in Britain. One morning I was in his office when with rather too studied a casualness he asked me what slogans the English would use in the next war. He was not a very good actor, and it was obvious that this was a leading question which he had been told to ask by Goebbels' Propaganda Ministry; he had passed the question on to me exactly as he had received it, unadorned. It was no good telling him that we did not decide these things in advance and that, anyway, His Majesty's Government did not recognise the possibility of war. I was sure that Charlie did not believe me when I denied any knowledge of such plans, and no doubt Goebbels' worst fears were later realised when their own Beethoven gave us the incomparable 'V for Victory'.

Rosenberg himself was not in Berlin and Charlie apologised for his absence. It transpired that he was down south somewhere either in Austria or looking after his new 'Vatican'. So, I decided to go up to East Prussia as arranged and revisit Erich Koch in the hope that he might be able to give me some concrete information. Charlie offered to accompany us, but I told him that provided he could lay on an aeroplane for Bill and myself to travel up to Königsberg, there was no need for him to come, especially as I could see he was very busy in Berlin looking after the Americans. I felt sure he had been told by Rosenberg to attend to the Americans and he seemed relieved that we did not want him to come along with us to East Prussia, but he looked a bit askance at my remark.

I had asked Charlie to alert Erich Koch to our visit, and he came down to the aerodrome to meet us. There was not quite as much bounce about him as there had been the last time I had seen him. He seemed preoccupied and I soon discovered that the Army were in his province in large numbers; indeed, most of the senior officers were staying in the one good hotel. Koch thought it advisable that he should take us to one of his little hotels by the Mesurian Lakes, where at least we should get peace and quiet. Moreover, as he explained, it would save the embarrassment of having to introduce me to a number of generals, who might think it strange that I should be up there at this moment.

Koch appreciated the strange beauty of these long, narrow, dark-green waters which lay between steep pine-clad hills where the trees ran right down to the water's edge. I have seen similar scenery on the Wanganui river in New Zealand, but instead of the pale greenery of the New Zealand tree fern, here was nothing but the deep blue-green of pines reflected in the still lakes, whose quiet calmness seemed remote from the mad turbulence of Europe. Erich Koch had built several small hotels by the lakeside, for he had plans to open up the area as a holiday resort. The only people around were locals from the sparse villages, and it was possible to wander peacefully from one lake to another, sometimes on a sandy road through the narrow gorges, at other times in a boat through a modern lock which had replaced some old rapids.

Koch asked me if I thought English tourists would come to East Prussia. 'Yes, of course they will,' I replied. 'Well, sometime perhaps in the future.' What a waste of good holiday material that was!

We spent several days in these idyllic surroundings, and it was here that, as I hoped, Koch unburdened himself. It was evident that plans were now well advanced for the invasion of Russia, and East Prussia was, of course, going to be the launching-pad. What would become of all his plans for his people? Generals now swarmed over his beloved province, organising digging here, cutting down forests there, pouring masses of concrete everywhere, tunnelling, laying railways to nowhere: all was destruction and noise. It was heartbreaking.

Koch could not say which he disliked the most, the Russians or the generals, and to prove his point he took me round to some of the massive earthworks on our way back to the capital. One such bunker was to be Hitler's headquarters for the Russian campaign, and it was here that he nearly died when the Army tried to assassinate him in 1944. The military were certainly spoiling the countryside, and the timing of all this construction, combined with the other indications I had seen in Berlin, suggested that by now Hitler's plans had been finalised. From time to time, I noticed Koch looking a little sideways at me as if he knew that we were both going to be in for trouble, and I judged that this was probably the moment to put to him the question which I was so keen to have answered. I asked him how long he was to be burdened with these Army people. He smiled and said, 'That is in the nature of a leading question.' As he turned he looked me straight in the eye and said, 'But I have no doubt your Secret Service knows all about it.' His words shook me rather, but by that time I was sufficiently shock-proof to make an immediate disarming reply, 'Maybe. I believe they're pretty good, but as I have some admiration both for you and your province, I'd rather like to know for myself.' Even so, I wondered whether the Nazis had received some warning about me, or could it be that the clamming-up in Berlin was just a general tightening up by the security services? Koch thought for a moment, then he said, 'In my opinion it will take at least three years to complete all their construction, and by that time my poor country will probably sink under the sea from sheer weight of concrete.'

So, it was to be 1941 at the earliest in the East. This was the first and only time I ever asked a direct personal question of any of the Nazis. I felt that the matter was of vital importance and that, as it now seemed unlikely I would be welcome in Germany very much longer, I should take the risk. In any case I convinced myself that the subject of the invasion of Russia was one which Hitler himself had taken trouble to see that I was informed about. It was to me the key to the timing of any Blitzkrieg in the West.

As we travelled back to Königsberg, along one of the rather narrow roads, we came upon a repair job being carried out, no doubt in order to carry some of the heavy lorries. The whole scene reminded me of my boyhood: piles of broken hard stone being spread by hand and rolled in by an old-fashioned steamroller. There was no room to pass so we waited for a while, and when the driver of the steamroller just went on with his job Erich Koch jumped out of the car and went over to speak to him. But Gauleiter or not, the driver was going to finish the job before he moved out of the way. Koch returned to the car laughing. 'Now that's what I like to see,' he said, 'it's almost English. There's far too little independence among us Germans.' There was no aggressive impatience about this man.

I had spent quite a while with Erich Koch. His character was not complex; he was not a racist and, in the true sense of the word, I doubt if he was a real Nazi. He did, however, loathe the Communists, for he hated their genocide, their propaganda, their secret-police state and their proximity just over the border. One thing I felt quite certain of was that Koch had not been guessing about the date, nor had he tried to bluff me. He was not subtle enough for that. It had taken a long time, but patience had been rewarded.

That night in my hotel room I worked out the times backwards: if the Russian invasion was to take place in 1941 it must start as soon as the snows melted in the spring. So, if the Germans planned to launch a Blitzkrieg attack on France and the West they would have to complete it by October 1940 if they were to have time to refit their divisions and redeploy them from the West to the east Russian front. The Germans always preferred to attack in the spring so that they could deprive their enemy of any harvest and more than likely reap it themselves. All that meant we could expect a Blitzkrieg in the West in the spring of 1940 at the latest. It was now high summer of 1938. That would give the Germans another eighteen months to get their Air Force into shape – which meant for me another eighteen months to try to complete our knowledge of the Luftwaffe.

Looking back on it all, I often wonder if my conclusions, which I put down in writing for my office on my return to London, were ever seen by Churchill or any other politician or senior military commander. Certainly, I was not the only one to have concluded as I did, so I only hope my information helped to reinforce the views of those who realised that we should have to fight a war. My bosses and my senior colleagues in the Air Ministry agreed with my suggested timings, and it was partly the knowledge that the Germans had to invade Britain before the end of September 1940 or not at all, because of their Russian commitment, which helped us to recognise the Battle of Britain, when it came, for what it was: a crucial turning point with a definite time limit for the Nazis.

When we returned to Berlin Erich Koch came with us to attend the annual rally at Nuremberg. Rosenberg was also back in Berlin, so we all had lunch together the following day. It was the last time I was to see Erich Koch. During the 1944 German retreat before the onslaught of the Russian armies he refused to abandon his province or his people, and in 1945 he was captured by the Russians. After the war I heard that the Germans had stripped some celebrated tortoiseshell panelling from one of the well-known Russian palaces during their advance into Russia in 1941, and that it had been buried somewhere in East Prussia. Perhaps the Russians thought that Koch knew where it was and when he refused to co-operate they threatened to kill him. Knowing him as I did, I am quite sure he would have told them nothing even if he knew.

Chapter 20

EXPOSURE

I had holidayed in Italy in August 1936 with a beautiful Yugoslav called Josephine, whom I had met on my trip to Germany that summer (my marriage had collapsed several years before). While I was in Italy I found myself shadowed unceasingly by the Italians. They watched me right up to the last moment when the Paris express from Rome crossed the border into France. This had made me suspicious, so back in London I investigated the various tie-ups operating between European countries. There seemed to be a fairly close intelligence link between the French and the Czechoslovakian intelligence service in Paris. The Czechs had taken advantage of close Anglo-French links to try to penetrate the British Secret Intelligence Service; they had even been said to have watched the house where 'our man' in Paris lived and where I used to stay when in France. In addition, the Czechs had some kind of intelligence tie-in with the Italians. Could the Czechs have learned about me from their French connections, and had they in turn passed on their information to the Italians? Might the Italians in their turn offer it to the Germans? I began to feel that too many people were learning too much for safety. Knowledge of this kind is always worth cash to someone; sooner or later the Germans would surely discover my role in intelligence. By 1938 I felt sure that my days as Rosenberg's guest in Germany were numbered.

Now, over our lunch together with Erich Koch in August 1938, Rosenberg was determinedly taciturn. Nonetheless he had asked Bill and me to dine at his house the evening before our visit to Nuremberg, so I felt comparatively secure for a few days yet. I passed those days looking around Berlin in an attempt to gauge the mood of the people. Security seemed to be tightening up all round to judge by the number of SS personnel on the streets, and there was an air of mounting excitement everywhere, an air of expectancy. This was particularly true of young people, who seemed tense and alert. The pavements, cafés and restaurants on the Kurfürstendamm were crowded and the Kakadoo, with its large semi-circular bar and its alternate blonde and brunette barmaids, was doing brisk business. We bumped into Ralph Wenninger and his wife outside the Kranzler restaurant, and they invited us to join them for dinner, but not a word was spoken about detente, about the Luftwaffe or about the future. The meal of blue trout from the Black Forest, fresh from the large tank outside, was excellent; but I felt uneasy throughout.

Rosenberg had asked us to his house the following evening at about six o'clock to have a good long chat with us. He had installed a television set, even though it was only 1938, but it may well have been some sort of closed-circuit affair wired to the nearby radio station. In any case, it worked well, and excellent pictures of a ballet were transmitted.

No one else, besides Bill and me, came to the dinner. Indeed, I never met his wife and daughter, nor the red-haired mistress he was said to keep in Berlin; as far as I could tell he was living alone in this big house, apart from an elderly couple to look after him. To begin with we had champagne, then for dinner fish and meat embellished with estimable hock, followed by fruit. He had gone to great trouble to give us a first-rate meal, which lasted for nearly two hours. Each course was accompanied by a lengthy monologue from Rosenberg, who was plainly not his usual self. At length, he brought out a tall bottle of sticky, sweet green liqueur from a locked cupboard. By this time, it had become evident from his conversation that he was trying to give me some kind of warning. I guessed too, from the whole setup, that this was probably the last time Bill, and I would see him alone on the old basis of friendship. A sense of personal danger infused me. How much did he know?

I tried to remember if there had been any way in which I had slipped up. Had someone given me away? The Italians, for instance? But apart from my recent direct question to Koch in East Prussia, I could recall nothing that I had done which could constitute espionage in their eyes. My actions had always been beyond suspicion, my conversation simple. They had done all the talking. Rosenberg had learned a great deal about diplomacy since the days when we had first met him, but this evening, perhaps because of the liqueur he became less discreet and began talking of our special relationship. I was disconcerted, for surely I had proved a tremendous disappointment to him in my supposed role of persuading influential people in Britain to look at things the Nazi way. I had not been seen to have influenced anyone of importance, so why was he being so effusive?

In the course of his monologues Rosenberg repeated Hitler's declaration to me that three superpowers should govern the world, and he stressed the Nazis' hopes of bringing this about despite England's present refusal to co-operate and her apparent lack of any definite policy towards Germany. He reminded me that it was Hitler's belief, shared by all those in close contact with the Russians, that unless Communism was crushed now the world would fall into chaos, inflamed, as he put it, by the envy and hatred of the Communist doctrine. He declared forcefully that the Third Reich would annihilate this menace and was prepared to go it alone if Britain was for once able to keep her nose out of other people's business. He said this with one of his rare smiles, but I could not help feeling that he had accurately summed up the occupational disease at that time of so many of those who talked so much but did so little to save Europe in the late 1930s. He assured me that the German Army and the German Air Force were becoming the most powerful weapons ever known in Europe. Finally, he added a little homily about the Aryan races being the only ones who could rid the world of corruption. What more did England want?

Despite the friendly manner in which he spoke and the liberal quantities of wine and liqueur which he had drunk, Rosenberg must have prepared himself carefully for this lecture and had skilfully summed up the policies that the Nazis had been trying to put across to the British government with a mixture of bluff, persuasion and threats for the past four years. It was not surprising that the Nazis had been puzzled by the British reaction; there had been none.

The meal was over, but Rosenberg still had a final message to deliver. Perhaps I had seen a number of Italian officers around in Berlin? Well, he would like to inform me that, now that the Rome-Berlin axis was in full operation, the Germans and Italians had become very close indeed, so close, in fact, that they were exchanging intelligence information. Under the circumstances, he felt that it might be better if, after the Nuremberg Rally, I were not to come back to Germany.

I looked completely blank at this suggestion, as if I did not know what he was talking about, but of course I realised that he now knew I was connected in some way with intelligence. So, my impressions at the beginning of the meal had not been so ill-founded after all. Still, his manner of telling me that I was exposed had been delicate and gentlemanly, so I did not feel that an order for my immediate arrest was likely. I felt that Rosenberg genuinely regretted that his connection with me would have to end, but his manner persuaded me that the precautions I had always taken not to appear too inquisitive and my seemingly great efforts towards detente would mean that the Nazis would not take action against me provided that I left quietly.

I could foresee no useful role for Rosenberg in a war and suspected that even now he was probably over the peak of his power; he might well be inclined to back both ways in case the great Nazi dream did not come off. All this reassured me and offered hope that I would not be publicly exposed. That would have been too damaging both for Rosenberg's reputation and for all those who had given me their confidences and protection. Many of them had been seen to entertain me openly; they would look foolish if it were widely known that I was a spy. Rosenberg himself had made no accusations against me. It looked as if my bogus reports which had been leaked back to Berlin had convinced him from the start that I was genuine. I did, however, wonder whether it would be sensible to go to the Nuremberg Rally even if I stuck close to Rosenberg; might it not be better to make a dash for home while the going was good?

Rosenberg had been drinking pretty heavily towards the end of the evening and by the time we came to leave he was quite drunk. He had difficulty in standing upright on the pavement when he came out to see us off, and he had become morose. I was sorry to say goodbye to him like this but at the last moment, just as he turned to stumble indoors, he asked us to come with him in his car to see a little of Bavaria. Then I knew that, whatever he had heard of my real activities, he was not prepared to take any action, and I could go out as I had come in, a guest of Rosenberg, sponsored by the Führer himself, and no questions asked.

There was no doubt that Rosenberg had always been very fair with me; he had always given me the full VIP treatment when I was in Germany, and he had enabled me to see a great deal of the countryside, to meet the people and so to weigh up the mood of the Germans themselves. Over and above this he had unwittingly given me every opportunity to check for myself much of the information that I was receiving from various sources in Germany and to sift the wheat from the chaff. This latter point was especially important, for there was a great deal of chaff pouring in from refugees hoping to make a little cash, and this was to increase steadily until 1939. In addition, I had been able, through close contact with the top men and with the help of Bill de Ropp, to obtain a fairly accurate impression of what was shortly going to hit us.

The next day we drove through Bavaria in Rosenberg's limousine with Herr Schmidt at the wheel. He had driven me a great deal on various excursions around Germany and so at Bill's suggestion I had bought him a small gold cigarette case as a present. Schmidt was a little embarrassed and almost sentimental. He may have guessed that I should not be seeing him again. We drove straight to Munich and did the 370-odd miles in time for a four o'clock pint of that wonderful dark-brown Munich beer, swallowed ice cold at a little café in the shade of the great cathedral. First impressions are often best. It was hot, the beer went down smoothly, and nothing could dispel the charm of the place.

Parts of the new motorways, the plans for which had been okayed by Hitler immediately before my first meeting with him, were now operational. We drove on down into the Bavarian Hills to a favourite lakeside holiday haunt of the Nazi hierarchy, the Tegel-see. Much to the disgust of the locals the large and prosperous Gauleiters used to wear the traditional Lederhosen and Tyrolean hats, which is much like a Londoner donning the kilt and bonnet to go to Scotland for his holiday. Nevertheless, the country was beautiful. We met several of Rosenberg's friends taking a refresher before the Nuremberg show.

We drove back to Nuremberg via the mediaeval walled city of Regensburg, now deservedly a tourist attraction. All was bustle in the town of Nuremberg when we reached it. A new hotel had been built to accommodate the principal guests and Nazis of importance for the rally. Companies of Brown Shirts from various parts of the Reich were arriving and marching through the streets to those short, staccato German marching songs. They would be lining the routes for their Führer during the next week. The whole city was as usual a mass of crimson banners. Every now and again a well-known leader would go by in a large black car and the crowds would give him a 'Heil'. Especially popular was the town's own leader, Streicher. He was a really nasty-looking type who took his popularity with evident joy. Despite the grimness behind all the bustle, what with the multitude of odd-shaped brown-shirted Teutons, the crimson-bannered streets and the spotlights, I felt we were getting right back to the comic-opera atmosphere once again. The Nazi showmanship was by now terrific.

This year, for the first time, the whole place was full of Italian officers in white uniforms and gold tassels. Their free and easy manners in the hotel, where they used the lounge for lounging, offended the strict 'correctness' of the Nazis and I doubt they would have been so happy if they had understood the Nazis' ill-concealed displeasure. However, Charlie, Bill and I found a small bar with only Himmler and a few of his pals propping it up. The pretty blonde barmaid was just what Charlie was looking for. There was an entrance to this small bar from the street; it was carefully guarded and one of its double doors was shut with a bolt into the floor. All at once there was a clatter of side-arms and a curse, and there, stuck in the single doorway, was Göring. The quickness of Charlie saved the day. He slid up the bolt of the second door and the bulk flowed into the bar, beaming.

One trick I always enjoyed was the way the leaders were both divested of, and re-equipped with, their Sam Browne belts complete with daggers and revolvers, their hats, and lastly their gloves and canes. One of the leaders had only to enter a hotel or other room from out of doors when two arms would come round his waist from behind, undo his belt buckle and shoulder strap, and deftly slide the whole thing off from the back. Another pair of hands would remove his hat and then take his gloves and stick. I once timed Himmler being re-dressed in this way: five seconds flat!

Himmler looked at you with his beady eyes through his thick-lensed, rimless glasses, yet never seemed to see you. Perhaps he was only locating the jugular vein for future use. His handclasp was cold; his black uniform befitting the poisonous beetle that he was. He had no social graces whatever.

Rosenberg had arranged a luncheon for some of his more honoured guests at Nuremberg. The table was long and narrow, and I was seated just opposite Himmler. After the usual heel-clicking introduction and cold handshake he spoke not one word to me across the two feet of tablecloth during lunch. I wondered whether he had now got a dossier about me in his pocket. It was like eating opposite a cobra.

Each day of the Nuremberg Rally there was a show put on in the sports stadium, both for the benefit of foreign visitors and for internal propaganda. The Nazis, as usual, performed *en masse*. I think one of the most significant demonstrations I saw was the parade of the young men of the *Arbeitsdienst*. They drilled with polished spades instead of rifles and it was quite a spectacle to see thousands of them flashing the symbols of their work in the bright sunshine with faultless precision. Hitler was present at this particular parade, and Bill, Charlie and I had been given seats in the 'royal box' set high above the stadium. Hitler greeted us cordially, which was a great relief and probably meant that whatever Rosenberg and Himmler knew about me, they had not passed it on to him – or was it the 'chivalry of the air'? We found ourselves sitting only a couple of rows behind him and slightly to one side. Charlie, who was sitting beside me, seemed, that afternoon, to be completely hypnotised by his Führer. His eyes never left the little man, and from time to time he would interrupt my attention from the weaving and flashing of the spades with such words as: 'Look, the

Führer smiles! Look, the Führer laughs! Look, the Führer waves his hand!' I could see it all myself and I simply had not the heart to say to Charlie, 'So what?' I had never encountered this sort of absolute hero-worship before. I thought then that if Charlie could so lose himself in the worship of this little man, no wonder the youth of the nation were ready to go through fire for him.

At last, the Führer rose to his feet to make his speech and there was a roar from half a million throats. As he stood there in front of the microphone, I saw the same thing happen that I had seen the very first time I met him: the back of his neck went scarlet, his eyes started from their sockets, his face flushed, and he started one of those diatribes that are now so well known. This time it was considerably more aggressive, which made me think that time was really running out. The Third Reich was going to take its place in the world; the Aryan race was going to predominate; there must be room for every German to live and live happily; and all the rest of it. He never repeated himself, but gradually one could see the vast army of young men below us in the stadium starting to sway with crowd emotion. I wondered if Hitler would stop before it became hysteria. He judged it just right. He whipped the whole of the assembly up to a frenzy and then he stopped. His neck returned to a normal colour; his eyes went back into their sockets and his face became calm. I had been fascinated not by the speech, which obviously left me cold, but by the extraordinary hold he had over his audience and the way in which he could switch on and switch off this strange performance. I looked along the row of chairs to my right to see how other people were taking it. I noticed Franz von Papen in civilian clothes sitting towards the end of the row, his Homburg hat well over his face. He was fast asleep.

We descended the steep steps which led up to the dais on which we had been sitting and made our way back to the hotel. Here Rosenberg informed us that he had obtained special passes to take Bill and me to the Party meeting the following afternoon; we were getting the full treatment. The Nuremberg Nazi Party meeting had become an annual festival of remembrance for those who had been killed in the early days of the movement. It was held in the new Party Hall in Nuremberg. Under one of the two pillars of the doorway had been buried a copy of *Mein Kampf*, and under the other a copy of Rosenberg's *The Myth of the Twentieth Century* – probably the best place for both these books. The hall was not very large and only selected Party members, and their womenfolk had been given tickets. I think Bill and I were the sole outsiders and, as Rosenberg's guests once again, had been given seats in the front row. On a raised platform, facing the audience, sat the leaders.

The ceremony began not long after we had taken our seats. At the roll of the drum everybody rose and along the aisle from the back of the hall came the slow procession of banners. The square storm-troopers in black uniforms, their square heads engulfed in square black steel helmets, each man carrying a square black and silver banner of his district surmounted by the inevitable vulture, slowly filed past the leaders to take up their stand behind them. At last, the final banner was in place, making a great black and silver curtain behind the line of chairs on which the leaders sat.

This was the first time I had seen all the top Nazis together, and now here they were facing me, all sitting in a row on hard wooden chairs not a dozen feet away. It all seemed unreal. It was almost like being in Madame Tussaud's waxworks! What was so odd about them? Of course, none of them was wearing a hat. I had met a number of them without their hats from time to time but never all of them sitting in a row. What an enormous difference the German military-type hat with its high front made to the wearer. But here, surrounded by their closest followers, they were just fellow Nazis. No pale-blue uniform and rows of medals for Göring; now they all wore plain brown shirts, buttoned at the wrist and neck, with a plain black tie.

I suppose any line of middle-aged men all dressed alike, but so different in size, shape and face, would look funny. I managed to keep my face straight by reminding myself that these men would soon be responsible for waging yet another war, in which it now looked as if we should be unavoidably involved, along with goodness knows what suffering, and I remember wondering what would happen if some fanatic or would-be martyr could liquidate them as they sat there together – Hitler, Hess, Rosenberg, Goebbels, Himmler, Göring, Heydrich, Ribbentrop, Schirach, the lot.

Only Hitler and Hess struck me as being really at ease. The former had achieved a great measure of poise, but now, as he came to the lectern to read the names of his dead comrades, he looked not four but fourteen years older than when I had first met him. The pockets beneath his protruding blue eyes were deeper, the face sallower; but his voice was strong, and as with other men whom I have seen fulfil their destinies in a short space of time, one sensed an authority which had grown with power over the past few years. There seemed little doubt that he had been the undisputed leader of this new Party right from the start; now all who saw him knew it.

Sitting on Hitler's right was Hess, the ever faithful shadow, self-effacing, quiet-mannered, a dreamer, and yet, as he proved later, a man of decisive action if the need arose. I cannot think that Hess, a little fanatical perhaps where the welfare of his leader and his country was concerned, was basically evil, like some of his comrades. His solo flight to England during the war, at enormous risk, was his last desperate act to save his country from having to wage a war on two fronts. As he sat, quietly smiling, next to his leader, his arms folded and the well-shod leg thrust out in a typical pose, he too was relaxed. But there was always a slightly wild look in his eyes below those bushy black eyebrows.

Alfred Rosenberg, who was seated next to him, evidently found his chair a bit hard. I had noticed he often adopted the forward leaning position, which he now held, one elbow on the knee and chin in hand. This somewhat unpredictable man, whom I had watched since 1932, seemed to have lost his enormous enthusiasm and to have turned into a rather unhappy individual, as if he found the foundations of his Aryan religion less solid than he had hoped. Nevertheless, he had amply repaid me for his first visit to London, and when in Germany I had always been given a place of honour at official functions. His hair was beginning to thin on top, his face was lined, pale and loose-skinned. He seemed to be looking inwards these days, perhaps not quite liking what he saw. After all, he was much more concerned with the long-term picture and now that the moment of truth was coming nearer the stakes were not quite so neatly arranged as he and his Party had hoped; maybe he was calling on his pagan gods. I wondered how long he could hold down his job and thought that perhaps he had wanted me to see him in the seat near his Führer, albeit for the last time.

Joseph Goebbels I never knew. He looked like an evil gnome, yet they say he was passionately fond of his family; a master of his art, his task grew too big even for him. He sat down, his bright dark eyes darting from face to face. Perhaps he was trying to get some inspiration for a new slogan; maybe, after Charlie's failure, he was trying to read my mind. At least he stood by his leader to the end. Unless you are insane, it takes guts to sacrifice your whole family and die with them.

Göring: now when you are as vast as Hermann and have short legs into the bargain, it is not easy to sit for long on a normal-sized, hard wooden chair and keep smiling. Despite the carefully arranged gaps on either side of him, he bulged against his comrades and seemed to look to them to keep him upright. He fidgeted, scowled and smiled mechanically from time to time. He also got overheated and had to mop his great slab of a face. Signs of too-good living were obvious; I would say that Göring, unlike Rosenberg, lived for today and possibly tomorrow and, as we know, he did it in style. He was one of the great swashbucklers of all time. Nero must have been one of his heroes; and yet here in his vast brown shirt below the sweating face, he looked more pathetic than ridiculous. Power had sapped his better judgement; he seemed nearer to the point of demoralisation than his comrades.

Himmler never moved. He sat solidly, rock-like, his arms folded; only his eyes were never still. I suppose this was from force of habit, in much the same way as we fighter pilots in the First World War kept looking around to see who was getting on our tail. I never saw Himmler smile; always the cold, sinister, rather flat, round pasty face with a bluish chin – a man who, in his youth, had been considered mentally subnormal and had been unable to hold down a job. It must have needed the unholy inspiration of his leader to enable him to build up the black-uniformed stormtroops as Hitler's personal army and Himmler's own instrument of evil.

Next to Himmler was Reinhard Heydrich, tall, fair and good-looking. One would not guess that it was this man above all others who would uncover and nurture the beast that was never far beneath the surface of that band of subhuman monsters.

Joachim von Ribbentrop always looked out of place among these men; the sort of man you would never look at twice in ordinary circumstances, except for the uncontrollable twitch of his face; a man who showed himself during his time as Ambassador in London as quite inadequate to fulfil any job requiring intellect, tact or diplomacy, which after all was what he was supposed to have.

This was the last time I saw any of these men except Rosenberg. Somehow the comic opera had turned to sinister melodrama. The presence of such a concentrated dose of Nazis left me thoroughly depressed and I was thankful to get out into the sunshine and fresh air. Bill and I thought a drink was indicated.

That evening Rosenberg was waiting in the hall of the hotel as Bill and I came down before dinner, and one of Rosenberg's aides informed me that he wished to say an official goodbye. So, this was it. Rosenberg was now a Reichsleiter, ranking second only to the Führer himself. At the far end of the hall, he stood erect, flanked by his staff and his bodyguard, wearing a new, well-cut uniform with his badges of rank at the collar. He appeared to be at the peak of his career, one of the most powerful men in the new Reich. He had obviously made this a somewhat public occasion, maybe in order to show that I was now finished with. Shaking hands, he bade me a solemn farewell. I detected a little sadness in his voice, and I felt a twinge of sorrow at having used him in the way I had. Utterly misguided he may have been, but he was honest in his own belief in what he was doing. Alas, the revival of the

Aryan gods had let loose passions which we hoped had been buried in Western civilisation. How deeply, I wonder?

Both Bill and Charlie came to the station at Nuremberg to see me off as I caught the night train for Paris. Poor Charlie. Everything was going his way; no wonder he became a little overwhelmed by his success. Here he was in his thirties, already a professor; his wife safely tucked away in Hamburg with her wire-haired terrier; all the girls in Berlin crazy for him; the wine plentiful and even the German champagne drinkable.

It was the German champagne that was eventually his undoing. I heard, sometime after the war started in 1939, that he had been at one of the cocktail parties for the neutrals in Berlin. He had too much to drink and spilled the beans to a neutral of the plans for the great assault on Russia, by that time supposedly Germany's ally. The word got back to Rosenberg of this unforgivable indiscretion, so Charlie was packed off as a private in the Army under orders to be sent to the Russian front when the time came. I expect he was in one of the penal battalions. Anyway, I only hope for his sake that he did not last long. Life in those battalions on the Russian front must have been absolute hell. Bill, who was in Switzerland during the war, heard all this from contacts over the border.

Chapter 21

SPY PLANE

Sitting behind his bare wooden table in the wooden hut which was his section of the French Secret Service, the Deuxième Bureau, Georges Ronin looked unhappy. The hut was too hot in August 1938, so I suggested that we might discuss our troubles with greater ease under the awning of a café across the other side of the river. He readily agreed and we strolled across the bridge.

I told him that all the evidence suggested that a complete clamp-down had been imposed on information leaving Germany and that secret agents were fearful of immediate execution. I added that I was unlikely to be able to return to Germany myself anymore. This news did not seem to surprise him; instead, he emphasised the need for caution in every aspect of our work. I asked him what he meant by this. He seemed unwilling to expand but hinted that we could not know whom to trust even in our own countries. However, he agreed that over the previous four years we had gained a fair idea of the proposed strength and composition of the new German Air Force. What we now needed to find out were the continuing production figures of the various types of aircraft and the performance of any new ones that might be developed. We also needed to know of any expansion of the aircraft factories and the sites and capacity of new aerodromes in the West.

The Chief of the French Air Force, General Joseph Vuillemin, had recently returned from a visit to Germany and Georges had produced a useful report for me about it all. As during the extraordinary detente with the RAF in 1936 and 1937, the General had been conducted around the Messerschmitt, Junkers and Heinkel factories where he had been shown all available sheds stuffed full of aircraft. He had been shown the latest aircraft coming off the assembly lines and had also seen a massed fly-past of fighters. The speed of their bombers had been remarkable; their Heinkel bomber could outstrip any fighter aircraft from other nations. All of which added up to a totally destructive offensive war. The tour had been meant to frighten Vuillemin and it did. Whether there was any more sinister reason Georges did not know, but Vuillemin had stated that the French Air Force could not last a week against what he had seen.

Until about September 1938 we had been able to get our agents to observe the numbers of aircraft parked out on the tarmac outside the aircraft factories before they were flown away to squadrons, and this gave us a reasonable idea of the production line; but without such observation reports we should now have to use other methods.

Georges told me that out of desperation he had got hold of an old aeroplane, into which he had fitted a large wooden camera, and that it was being flown up and down the Rhine by a civil pilot, an old friend of his. The camera was operated by a splendid old man with a flowing beard who was normally a portrait photographer in Paris. They managed to get a few good photographs and to keep track of some of the fortifications on the German side of the river. Couldn't this sort of exercise be profitably extended?

I have already described how I myself became a casualty escorting photographic planes in the First World War and I now told Georges how I had also been trying to find out from the Royal Air Force what progress had been made in aerial photography. But it transpired that, although technically the cameras had been enormously improved and automated, it was still impossible, some twenty years later, to take aerial photographs at all times of the year above 8000 feet because the camera lenses became fogged up with condensation from the cold air. Obviously it would not be feasible to cruise around even in a civil aeroplane in peacetime at this height taking photographs over Germany. Our purpose would very soon be discovered, with disastrous results. But it was even more disturbing to think of what might happen in time of war, and as it now seemed likely that we would soon be involved in another war with the Germans, we both agreed that, at 8000 feet, up against modern German anti-aircraft guns and ultra-modern enemy fighters, aerial photography promised sheer slaughter for the pilots and air crews. Georges also pointed out that, with the rapid movements of the Blitzkrieg, aerial photography and lots of it would probably be the only way left to us to know what the enemy was doing. Desperate remedies were now necessary. We both knew that we should fall into disfavour if intelligence about the enemy dried up at this critical juncture.

It was unlikely that we should succeed in producing something that the air forces of both our countries had not succeeded in producing. Nonetheless, we decided that if we could acquire an American executive-type aeroplane with a proper cabin for four or five people, we could at least carry out some experiments and probably take it for legitimate flights into Germany on some commercial basis or other. It might be possible to fit a hidden camera into this aircraft and, if we could produce sufficiently good cover for a pilot, take some worthwhile photographs. Meanwhile we could experiment to see if we could raise the altitude at which we took the photographs. We decided on an American Lockheed 14, a new and very handy type of twin-engined executive aircraft. It had a heated cabin with room for four or five people as well as the pilot and co-pilot. It was very up to date by European standards at that time. The next problem, of course, was how to obtain one, and George suggested that if I could manage to buy one in America he would do the same and we should then each have one with which to experiment.

Unfortunately, it was clear that, however much co-operation we might receive from our respective Air Staffs, these purchases were bound to take some time, and time was now running out. Back in London I put the proposition to the Admiral. He liked the idea but said that the Air Ministry would have to supply the aeroplane and that I had better go over to see the Chief of Air Staff, Sir Cyril Newall and talk him into it if I could. I duly explained the scheme to Sir Cyril. He was extremely sympathetic and went so far as to say that during the First World War he had been in France at the same time as I had been, where he too had been appalled at the wastage in men and planes incurred by photographic reconnaissance. He gave me permission to order a Lockheed aircraft, provided I could get it imported into the country as a civilian machine, and he suggested I should get Imperial Airways to do the job for me. I explained to him that the French also wanted one and that by buying two we might get them a bit cheaper. He asked me to let him see the plane when it was over here and ready for operation, adding that the more we could do to improve the altitude of air photography the better. I took the opportunity to ask him if we could borrow cameras and camera equipment from the RAF, and he said that he would see that we got what we wanted. I was of course delighted and let Georges know the outcome of this interview at once.

Imperial Airways proved extremely helpful. An order was placed that very week for two Lockheed 14s: Imperial Airways would order them as their own machines and the bill would be paid by the Air Ministry. Unfortunately, this sort of aircraft could not be bought off the peg, and we were informed by Lockheed that they could ship one aircraft to be erected in England within two or three weeks, but the second aircraft would not be available for several months. This was rather a blow, but I am afraid that I made up my mind there and then to obtain the first one for ourselves and I warned Georges Ronin that there would be some delay in getting his aircraft.

Now I had to find a pilot for the aircraft, and it had to be somebody who was willing to carry out experiments in high-altitude photography and indeed to take the risk of flying over Germany with a camera aboard. I mentioned to one or two of my friends, both in the Royal Aero Club and in the Royal Air Force Club, that I was looking for a pilot to do some special work. It would have to be a man entirely unconnected with the RAF and able to develop some business interest in Germany.

Before long someone put me in touch with Sydney Cotton, an adventurous type who had done a great deal of flying out in Newfoundland. I talked my proposition over with him and he seemed eager to go ahead. At least he was a good pilot with considerable knowledge of photography; moreover, he was connected with a firm which was trying to expand the development of colour photography in England and Germany, so he was not only well versed in the whole subject but also had good commercial connections which would enable him to fly into Germany without arousing suspicion. It seemed that the firm was not doing too well and that the extra sum of money I could offer him would be very welcome. So it was that Sydney Cotton came on to my payroll.

It was a shame that the Lockheed for France would be delayed, but I promised Georges that we would co-operate and that I would give him all the results that we obtained from our experiments. In the event the French aircraft only arrived in time for us to get it across to them in October 1939, just as the cold war broke out, so they had little time to make much use of it before the fall of France. To my surprise I received in return for sending it over not a cheque but a large sack full of high-value French bank notes. The French Secret Service were cautious.

Our aircraft duly arrived in large crates, and I had to rush down to the docks with a note from the Treasury to the Chief of Customs so that it was passed through without having to pay a vast amount of duty. I had arranged with my friend Nigel Norman to hire an isolated hangar at Heston aerodrome where I finally got the aircraft assembled with the aid of some of the Heston mechanics. It was an exciting moment when we wheeled it out for its first test flight.

Sydney Cotton was an aeronautical enthusiast. He flew the Lockheed around as if he had been piloting it all his life. I went up with him for the second test; it was certainly a very smooth aircraft. We tried it out for height and obtained a ceiling of about 22,000 feet. Fortunately, it was fitted with oxygen. We realised that if ever we were to get the cameras to operate at high altitude, this would be a wonderful flying laboratory. The heated cabin, too, was an absolute joy. Nigel Norman supplied me with a first-rate mechanic, who also came on my payroll and was sworn to secrecy; and once again through my friend in customs I arranged that flights of the Lockheed in and out of Heston should not be subject to customs control, although a form of customs declarations would be adhered to in order to allay suspicion that we were doing anything unlawful. It was essential to keep the whole operation secret.

Now that we had our aeroplane, our task was to see how high we could go and still obtain clear pictures. I got hold of three Leica cameras from Germany, the ones with large rolls of film normally used for bird watching. We attached them to a specially made frame, one pointing directly downwards and the other two pointing out at an angle so as to get as much coverage as possible. We then had to get a hole cut in the bottom of the fuselage. This was not an easy job because it affected the stress of the fuselage itself and the job had to be specially done by an aircraft factory in the greatest secrecy, since it was vital that as few people as possible knew of our efforts.

The plane was now ready to start experiments. It was Sydney Cotton's secretary who volunteered to lie prostrate and operate the three cameras at given intervals, which we calculated to coincide with the height and speed at which the aircraft was flying. I suggested to Cotton that he should start off at 8000 feet, take a series of pictures, and then move up about 1000 feet at a time until we had reached the ceiling of the Lockheed. We would then develop the films and find out at what height the condensation prevented us getting a clear picture. By this time, it was early in 1939, and the weather was cold. On our first day up, we were therefore not very optimistic. But when we developed the three rolls of Leica film we found that we had been taking perfectly clear pictures up to nearly 20,000 feet. Just how we had accomplished it we did not at first realise, but it was exciting, to say the least.

The next day we decided to have another go. The engines had been running for some minutes and had nicely warmed the cabin when I crawled under the belly of the aircraft just before take-off to ensure that the small flap sealing off the camera hole, which we could slide backwards and forwards from a control in the cockpit, was in proper working order. It was then I discovered that, with the engines running, warm air was emerging from the heated cabin and flowing beneath the camera lenses. Here was the explanation for the absence of condensation, and the secret of our success. It was as simple as that. It is difficult to describe my elation at this chance discovery. Both Cotton and I realised that this was something of supreme importance, not only for our own proposed operations over Germany but for the whole future of aeronautical photography; but we realised also that we had stumbled on a secret which must be kept. I decided there and then that I would tell no one until we had carried out full-scale experiments with RAF camera equipment.

Although the Leica pictures had been clear, they did not show all the small detail we really needed, so I went now to the RAF Photographic Department to ask for the loan of some of their latest cameras and equipment which the Chief of Air Staff had promised me. Group Captain Laws, who was head of the department, was extremely helpful. He supplied me with two separate cameras and several different-length lenses, and we spent a busy evening filing off all the RAF numbers and indications on this equipment in case we got caught. Better still, the RAF had produced a device for automatically timing the taking of the pictures according to the height and speed of the aircraft. This had an indicator in the cockpit to show that the cameras were working properly, and one of the cameras was duly fitted into the aircraft. The opening in the belly was camouflaged as an emergency fuel release and I had a special cover made for the cameras in the form of a spare fuel tank, so that anyone looking under the floorboards would have no reason to suspect what was going on. Now we were ready.

The results were marvellous: absolutely clear photographs taken from over 20,000 feet, overlapping so that they could be used with stereo and showing every detail. It was after these results that we decided to make a thorough test in the Mediterranean. With the aid of the Air Ministry, I had extra tanks secretly fitted in the passenger compartment and arranged with Georges in Paris that Cotton should fly directly to Malta and then across to Algiers, where he would be welcomed by the French authorities and given permission to fly up the coast to Tunis. I did not want to go as far east as Cairo as there might be too much speculation about what we were doing. The plan was to cross over from Tobruk to the north Mediterranean coast and, with the tremendous range that we now had with the extra tanks, to try to photograph the Italian bases both in the islands and on the mainland, then to turn back to Algiers. By this time, I had recruited an additional young Canadian pilot, Bob Niven. He was actually a Reservist for the RAF, but they agreed to let him come as co-pilot. We fitted out Sydney Cotton with papers saying he was a film tycoon doing a survey for possible locations for film-making. It was as good a cover as anything else. I had to warn the authorities in Malta to keep it quiet that he had flown direct from the United Kingdom; they were naturally very intrigued by the whole subject.

The result of this trip in the early spring of 1939 was fantastic. Flying almost unnoticed at 20,000 feet, Cotton photographed every Italian naval and air base on the North African coast and then did the same along the northern Mediterranean. Dockyards, harbours, aerodromes –everything was photographed in detail. I had told the Air Ministry that we were going to do some experiments, but I had not given them any idea of the scope, and it was only when we got all the photographs back and had them printed that I was able to hand over complete sets to the directors of intelligence of all three services and to Georges Ronin. At first they could not believe it, but when the explanation came the excitement was intense. Requests came pouring in from the Admiralty, the War Office and the Air Ministry for photographs of aircraft factories, dockyards, anything we could get over Germany.

Now that we had the technique, I had to organise the method. We decided to boost up the British side of Cotton's commercial film development company and increase its potential, so that those in Germany were encouraged into building up their side of the production too. Cotton started making regular trips to Berlin. The first time the hatch in the belly was kept safely closed and was without cameras. Soon the Germans got used to seeing the Lockheed coming into Berlin. They had no doubt had a good look at it the first time, and now, with the camera installed under the cabin floor, the Lockheed became operational for espionage.

Cotton had found it difficult to fly directly over the targets because one could only see out of the aircraft at an oblique angle at the side of the pilot's seat, so he invented a new form of 'tear-drop' moulded Perspex window with a bulge in it which allowed him to see straight down to the target beneath him. It was a great success. He also varied his route to Berlin, refuelling at Hamburg or Frankfurt or some other aerodrome which would give him a run over certain new aerodromes or aircraft factories we wished to photograph. So long as he kept at around 20,000 feet, the Germans did not seem to suspect that he could be using a camera.

Throughout the whole of the 1939 summer up to September, the Lockheed was in constant use. Sometimes Cotton took it over to France with some well-known people for an apparent holiday in order to keep up the pose of the wealthy tycoon with his own aircraft. Most of the summer we were concentrating on photographing aerodromes and aircraft factories, and, where possible, armament factories and dockyards as well. The German aircraft factories continued to park their newly constructed aircraft out on the tarmac and if one kept a close watch on these it was possible to judge the production of the factory concerned – information which was vital to the RAF at that time. Aerodrome construction seemed to follow a very stereotyped pattern, just as I had seen in my earlier flights over Germany.

By the summer of 1939 the RAF was studying our new technique closely. When I had dumped the 500 perfect photographs of all the Italian installations in the Mediterranean on the desk of Archie Boyle at the Air Ministry, his first remark had been, 'What am I supposed to do with these?' However, he very soon collected together all the people who knew anything about photographic interpretation, and they trained others in this highly skilled procedure. It was this nucleus of people who were able to form the great photo interpretations centre at Medmenham in Buckinghamshire after war broke out.

An over-ambitious extrovert is perhaps not the best choice for a secret operator. During the summer of 1939 Cotton had done a really great job taking photographs over Germany and his results were producing ever more requests from the service ministries. But he was impatient to cash in on his new image. Just at the end of August, apparently encouraged by his friends in Berlin, he produced a hare-brained scheme to fly Göring from Berlin to London to meet the Foreign Secretary, Lord Halifax, in an effort to avert war. In his newfound glory he took his idea over my head to Stewart Menzies, my Chief's number two and Head of the Army Section, who, in turn, was always prepared to try to get a bit of kudos from Downing Street. Presumably not understanding what it was all about, Chamberlain gave permission for the flight and, unknown to myself, Cotton set off for Berlin. Menzies himself never had the courtesy to tell me. I dared not try to contact Cotton personally, but I managed to get a signal to the Air Attaché in Berlin asking him to send Cotton back if things looked like getting too hot. Of course, nothing came of this hopeless mission.

A new RAF unit was to be set up, to be called the Photographic Reconnaissance Unit or PRU. Wanting to play a more active role, I asked if I might be given command of it. I knew that it was bound to be of great importance in the future, whereas it could be well-nigh impossible to find and operate agents in Germany once war had been declared. I was told in no uncertain terms that it was not a job for a reserve officer. However, the regular officer who took it over made a wonderful job of it, ending up as an air marshal, and I was able to make up for my disappointment when in April 1940 I was asked to organise one of the most fascinating jobs of the war, Ultra – of which more later.

When the United States came into the war and the secret of high-level photography was passed on to them, Elliott Roosevelt was put in command of the American PRU in Europe. I doubt if there was any corner of Western Europe and North Africa which was not recorded, and in due course the PRU activities were extended to the Pacific and South-East Asia; all of this with hardly a casualty.

Thus, it was, that a project, originally worked out in Paris between myself and Georges Ronin, had, by an absurdly simple discovery, become the forerunner of all spy planes. At last, I was rewarded by the knowledge that no longer would RAF fighters have to escort RAF photographic machines on suicidal missions.

Chapter 22

THE ULTRA PLAN

Nineteen-thirty-nine showed every promise of being the critical year, politically. Those who knew what France was up to despaired of any real resistance to a German Blitzkrieg. For my own part, I had established high-altitude photography and now I wanted to know if and how we could read the enemy signals, a subject that would be all-important to any chance we had of stopping the Nazi take-over of Europe.

My Chief, Admiral Sinclair, had tragically gone to hospital, and Stewart Menzies had temporarily taken over the job of Chief, and it was to him that I put the question, 'What do we know about German armed forces' signalling?' It seemed to me that a Blitzkrieg would have to have all its signals on the air. There would be no time or reason to have land lines. Stewart's answer was go and see Commander Denniston, Head of the Code Cypher Department – neither he nor anyone else had any idea what the Germans would use for encyphering their signals. I asked Menzies to send a telegram to all our representatives in the Eastern European states asking for any information on this subject.

The Poles were the only ones to reply to our telegram and it was from Warsaw that we began to get information on the whole subject of the German secret cypher traffic. The full story of how we acquired the knowledge of the Enigma cyphers did not come out until some years after the war. Our allies, the French, had acquired a spy in the German Signals Service in Berlin, back in 1934. This man had fed the French, who operated under a General Bertrand, all the details of the Enigma Machine Cypher, with instructions not only how to use it but how to construct the machines themselves. For a while the French Secret Service had operated by themselves, but when they wanted help and money they turned to the Polish Secret Service who, in turn, constructed some thirteen Enigma machines and, with the help of the agent in Berlin, devised ways of breaking the cypher.

As a result, the French General Staff had been able, over the years, to establish the size and complete organisation of the German Army. They had not told us a word. Now, in 1939, the spy had been found and shot and all ability to read the cypher signals had been lost since the Germans had added so many more possible computations to the machine.

It was now that at last the French came clean. We sent a delegation to Warsaw, including Menzies, who posed as a mathematician, and asked for their aid. A Polish model of the Enigma machine was eventually handed over to Menzies by Bertrand on Victoria station. I saw it in our office a few days later.

Thus began the story of Ultra, the greatest war-winning achievement by British brains and money. All the most brilliant mathematical brains in the country, mostly from our universities, were co-opted and brought to Bletchley Park, a country house some thirty miles from London. And here in September 1939 they declared all-out war on the problem, believing that, if man could invent a cypher machine of such complexity, he could invent another machine to solve it.

I think it must have been about the end of February 1940 that the Luftwaffe had evidently received enough Enigma machines to train their operators well enough for them to put some practice messages on the air. These signals were relatively short but must have contained the ingredients the cypher breakers had been waiting for. Menzies had ordered that any successful results were to be sent at once to him. It was in early April that the oracle of Bletchley spoke, and Menzies duly handed me four slips of paper, each bearing a short Luftwaffe message about personnel postings to units. From the intelligence point of view they were of little value, except as a small bit of administrative inventory, but to the backroom boys at Bletchley Park and to Menzies, and indeed to me, they were like the magic in the pot of gold at the end of the rainbow.

Menzies had asked me to take the precious 'first results' over to Charles Medhurst, who was Director of Air Intelligence at the Air Ministry, a post which was soon upgraded to that of Assistant Chief of Air Staff Intelligence. Charles was short, thick-set and dark, with a quick brain and a quiet voice and a very nice sense of humour. He was my Air Ministry boss, and it was with him that I had toured the Middle East in the 1930s. As I entered his office that morning, he gave me his usual smile and I handed him the bits of paper. He looked at them, and then just handed them back with the words, 'You will have to do better than that.' He had evidently taken them on their face value as rather unimportant scraps of information and not as the pieces of magic they were, even though Menzies had told him all about the Enigma and our hopes of being able to decypher some of the signals.

I had been turning over in my mind the whole subject of how best to deal with this new intelligence before I even went to see Charles. It was, I think, his lack of interest which prompted me that evening to get down to working out a plan to handle this new material, if, as I hoped, it was to develop into a vital source of information. I do not think I slept that night, but I now knew what I wanted, and the following morning I went in to see Stewart. His first question was, 'What did Charles think about it?' I told him what had happened at the Air Ministry and then I expounded all the arguments I had prepared to obtain his approval for my plan.

In normal circumstances, information from such a top-secret source as Enigma would be distributed only to the directors of intelligence of the service ministries. It would then be up to them to make whatever distribution they thought fit. This worked perfectly well where there were only a few items of intelligence in this category, but it seemed obvious that, if we were lucky enough to break the code on just one day, hundreds of signals would have to be dealt with separately by all three services, and not only might translations differ, but the number of people involved in such work, and in any subsequent distribution, would be enormous. And if, as was likely, each director wished to inform one or more commands overseas of urgent information, the same material would probably be going out on the air in several different cyphers, which was, cryptographically, an extremely risky procedure. There would be no control over its use, and, in any case, the extent of wireless traffic alone would arouse enemy suspicions. It would, in my opinion, only be a question of time before the enemy realised what was going on and the source would be blown. He might disbelieve that we were unbuttoning his cypher ourselves, but he would certainly believe that there was a leakage serious enough either to stop using the Enigma machine or complicate its operation so as to nullify our success.

I could see that Stewart agreed with what I was saying about the dangers, and that he was conscious that, although he and the Bletchley boys were primarily responsible for the breakthrough, under the present system he might well lose control of the results and weaken his own position as sitting candidate for 'C's' chair. After a few moments he asked me what I had to suggest.

I proposed that as a first step, since so far only Luftwaffe signals had been received, I should ask the Air Ministry to let me have three or four non-flying, German-speaking RAF officers whom I would install in my own intelligence hut – No. 3 at Bletchley. They would be virtually next door to Hut 6 where the signals would be decyphered in the original German. I suggested the signals should then be passed over to Hut 3 for translation, and further action as directed by me.

I should naturally have to vet the young officers for security, and I proposed to attach to them one of my own intelligence staff, who would brief them with all the known details of the German Air Force, in order to help them get names, addresses and such details as squadrons and other formations correct. Since it should only be a matter of days before the German Army started up its signalling, I could then make a similar request to the War Office.

General Davidson, the Director of Military Intelligence, was a good friend and always helpful. I felt sure that a small joint Army and Royal Air Force Intelligence Unit would appeal to him. But Admiral John Godfrey, the Director of Naval Intelligence (DNI), could be much more difficult. By tradition the Navy kept itself to itself and it would not be attracted to the idea of co-operating with members of the two junior services to produce a single translation. However, I felt that if the unit became operational, there would be more chance of the DNI joining in if, and when, naval Enigma became available, and so, as I told Stewart, I wanted to go ahead with the Army and Air Force unit for a start.

This was the first phase of the plan to get a single and correct translation of the signals. There was also another equally important angle to a combined services unit, and that was to decide the necessary priority of any given signal and who most needed to know its contents. Those of us who had worked for the three different services inside the SIS had for long hoped that one day there would be a combined intelligence department for all three service ministries. There was so much more than the bare bones of information which could be extracted by inter-service discussion. Now, if my proposals were accepted, a single translation, as well as its priority and distribution, would be agreed between a combined services unit at Bletchley.

Stewart agreed that so far I had made my case, but there still remained the security risk arising out of wide distribution of the material to commanders in the field, if it was to be used to the best advantage. This was covered by the second part of my plan, which I feared might run up against opposition from the directors of intelligence. We already had our own highly efficient Secret Service short-wave radio network and through it we could communicate direct with our organisations in most parts of the world. I suggested that, if this could be expanded to include encyphering and transmission to the main overseas commands in the field, I should then form small units of trained cypher and radio personnel and attach these to the commands in question, with the double purpose of providing an immediate link for the information and having an officer on the spot charged with seeing that all the necessary precautions were carried out for its security.

I pointed out that there would have to be very strict rules as to the number of people who could know the existence of this information and perhaps, on a more delicate footing, rules for those in receipt of the information, to ensure that they did not take any action which would either arouse enemy suspicions or confirm his fears that the Allied commander had any pre-knowledge of his plans. This one, I knew, was a hard one to put over to a commander-in-chief. In some circumstances it might be very tempting to make a quick but telltale coup. I thought that such security measures as I could devise should have behind them the Chief's full authority, with even higher backing if necessary. Special Liaison Units (SLUs) in the field would tactfully be able to ensure that no risks were taken.

In view of our own success with the Enigma machine, I proposed that all transmissions put on the air should be in what was known as 'one-time pad' cypher. It was at this time, as far as I knew, the only absolutely safe cypher in existence, although the Germans obviously thought otherwise. I also proposed that, if any of the government departments which received this material wished to put it on the air for any reason, it should be done through the Special Liaison Unit Organisation. This, I hoped, would tie up our own cypher security without too much opposition – the exception being the Admiralty, who had their own special problems and used their own cyphers. Later on, we were able to use the new RAF Type X machine cypher which had been developed with all the knowledge of our success against the German Enigma. These machines were installed at most of the main headquarters which served two or all three of the services, such as Malta, Cairo, Algiers and later Caserta and Colombo. They were never 'read' by the enemy.

This was the complete plan which I put before my Chief the day after the backroom boys' first success. No one as yet knew how many hours, or even days, would elapse between the interception of the message and the answer to the Enigma keys being found, or how many messages would have to be read, sorted for priority and distribution, translated and despatched. But the scheme did allow for expansion and, above all, for security. Copies of all signals would, of course, still be sent to the directors of intelligence whose responsibility it would be to keep their Chiefs of Staff fully informed and to co-ordinate the logistical information of the various enemy units, which we call the order of battle. I suppose it had taken me the best part of an hour to put the whole plan forward, it took another five minutes of careful weighing up by Stewart before I got my answer. 'All right,' he said, 'if you can get the approval of the directors of intelligence.' I saw his point; it would not look such a major decision on his part if I made the arrangements. If it came off, it would leave the power of this almost unbelievable triumph in his own hands.

When I went to see Charles Medhurst, he was in an excellent mood and took the whole thing in his stride. 'It seems a good way of getting the translations done,' he said, but he still did not seem to grasp the immense potential of the source. The next day three junior German-speaking flying officers reported to me. Charles had kept his word, a search had been made through the Air Ministry Intelligence Branch, so that they had already been screened for security. They were all young men who had recently joined up and were obviously the right type and keen. I myself took them up to Bletchley and installed them in Hut 3, together with one of my own intelligence officers, armed with maps and the Luftwaffe order of battle with as many details of the various units and their commanders as we could get together.

As luck would have it, the next signals to be caught and unbuttoned were from the German Army, once again unimportant and probably practice ones, so the next morning I went to the War Office and explained my proposals to General Davidson, the DMI. I told him that they had the approval of Stewart and that I had already got my RAF officers, and I hoped he would give me his co-operation. Two Army officers and a sergeant arrived at Bletchley the next day, bringing with them all they knew about the German Army.

I spent the next few days with them, getting them settled into suitable billets and initiating them into the work that I wanted them to do, together with all the priority and security angles of the whole business, though until I got my Special Liaison Units operational, obviously the messages would go only to the directors of intelligence and myself in London. Fortunately, they were able to settle themselves in slowly; there was no rush of signals being broken. Sometimes it was taking as much as twenty-four hours to get a result; later on, with some luck, we got the answer in three or four. Prime Minister Chamberlain had been told of the success so far, also the Chiefs of Staff, who had now given Menzies backing for additional money.

After several weeks of rather slow and relatively unimportant progress, Charles Medhurst telephoned me one day and told me that he had got a very good German-speaking officer who had just joined up – would I like him? Wing Commander Humphreys, 'Humph' as he was called, was a godsend. A former commercial salesman in Germany, he knew the country like his clean-shaven chin. I do not think there was a dialect that he could not speak perfectly. He was a bundle of energy, and it was all the more to his credit that he stuck the desk job I gave him and worked all hours of the day and night. He was a good talker – I suppose it stemmed from his sales job – but when required he could put his ideas in a nutshell. He seemed to me the obvious leader for Hut 3. I made him a wing commander and put him in charge. He quickly won the confidence of the team, which was destined to grow from six to sixty.

It was only a little while after I had got the Army and RAF components operational that the German naval Enigma was broken. I knew it would not have been any good trying to get John Godfrey, the DNI, to come in earlier. Now, however, he did supply my Hut 3 with a naval commander. At last, I had achieved a full inter-service unit. Alas, it was not to last. I was surprised one day to find John coming out of my Hut 3. I had had no notice of his visit. Now I learned that he had personally put his naval commander (because he outranked Humphreys) in charge of my hut, and he instructed me that all naval Enigmas dealing with submarines should not be sent to Coastal Command because it gave the RAF too much advantage in getting to the enemy. I felt that his maverick assistant, Ian Fleming of James Bond fame, had a lot to do with all this. However, that evening, I promoted Humphreys to a group captain and again put him in charge of Hut 3. The request about submarine intelligence I referred to Menzies, who had by then been appointed 'C'. I gather there was a pretty acrid discussion with the Chief of Naval Staff which ended in the latter taking all naval signals away from Bletchley control. Instead, there was to be a daily three-way telephone conference between the Admiralty, Coastal Command, and Western Approaches, to decide who should go after any located U boat.

I suppose there is ever a price to pay for efficiency. The naval Commander in charge of the cypher-breaking at Bletchley eventually decided he wanted my Hut 3. Alas, Stewart was too weak to say no. He did not want another showdown with the Navy. My own time, however, became fully occupied as the signals increased to hundreds a day. I also had to set up a WAAF unit in the London office which received all signals from Bletchley which might interest Churchill (who succeeded Chamberlain in May 1940) and it was my job to sort out the important ones for the Prime Minister each day, and often phone them to him at weekends or late at night. Churchill used to spend some time in bed in the mornings and liked to have his overnight Ultra early.

It was at this point that I got the agreement of the three directors of intelligence to give the Enigma material a special name. There were various sorts of security such as 'secret' and 'most secret', but I wanted something only for the Enigma. This was the birth of the word 'Ultra'.

Chapter 23

THE BATTLES OF FRANCE AND BRITAIN

I do not intend to recapitulate the history of the build-up to the Battle of France, but to recite how at the beginning of the Second World War my job was to keep those few commanders who were allowed to see and act on Ultra as fully informed as possible. Ultra's effect was in this case remarkably small, because the battle itself was not only short and sharp but had been carefully planned and needed little in the way of signals.

The speed of the Blitzkrieg advance by the German Army through Holland and Belgium caused little astonishment to those who knew the strategy. I had supplied a Special Liaison Unit of signallers and cypher sergeants to the Commander of the Air Component at Maux while Humphrey Plowden, a colleague from the office, had been sent out to Landforce HQ in France.

Chamberlain had resigned, a very disillusioned man, and Churchill had taken his place, but his arrival could make no difference to events on the Continent. From the moment the German attack began it became evident not only that Holland and Belgium could play no part in the war, but that France was not prepared to stand up either. The rest is history, except that it was Hitler himself who gave the command to his Army not to close in on the British as they evacuated from Dunkirk but to let them go back to England minus their arms. Ultra showed us that Rommel was fuming with his tanks on the hills behind Dunkirk at not being allowed to attack the British.

The Post Office had given us a direct line to our Paris office, and when the French collapse became inevitable, Georges Ronin rang me up. He had left his job and gone back to his squadron, where he had flown until there were no more bombs to drop and no petrol left.

He wanted to know if he should come to England or stay in France. I suggested he stay. He joined the Vichy government as aide to the new Air Minister and with the help of a wireless transmitter, which I supplied, kept us informed of events behind the closed doors at Vichy, until the Germans took over the whole of France at the end of 1942. Georges and his old boss then flew over to Algiers, where we all met once again. He was a very gallant Frenchman.

Tubby Long, in charge of evacuating my SLU equipment from France, made off towards Brest with some SLU personnel. He tells a good story of the crowded roads going west, all lights out due to the German bombers, when a car load of Frenchmen came roaring along, headlights on, trying to get past the convoy. Tubby and his men stopped it, put their boots through the headlights and then threw the car over a bridge into a river. Luckily, Tubby had his revolver, which stopped any arguments.

It was, I suppose, one of Hitler's most human but worst mistakes to allow the British Expeditionary Force to return virtually unharmed from Dunkirk. It was no doubt thought that we would automatically, our army defeated, ask for an armistice, leading to peace. It did not work that way and now the German Army and Air Force called for an invasion of Britain, codenamed Operation *Sea Lion*. It was now that Ultra really started to play a leading role. There was a pompous Order of the Day put out by Göring: the Luftwaffe was to destroy the Royal Air Force. Back in the 1930s I had learned from Rosenberg that Hitler mistrusted the sea. Maybe his astrologer had warned him, but he had obviously made it plain to his Army and to Göring that he was not going to risk an invasion of England unless all air resistance was removed.

Kesselring had got his Air Fleet and was to be one of the leading sources of attack against England. I remembered his impatience to get his command. Peter Portal had taken over the job of Chief of Air Staff. Ultra was now in full swing, giving us all the details of the barges and their engines being collected at the Channel ports to transport the invading troops. There were all-important air-loading points in Holland, where supply aircraft could be turned round with a minimum of delay. These would be vital to sustain an invasion force across the water.

On our side, thanks to the 1935 decision to go ahead with the Spitfires, we had an ace up our sleeves. Moreover, our radar detection was far ahead of the Germans', thanks to Sir Robert Watson-Watts's efforts. It had been a great encouragement to him when we found out how far behind us the Germans were.

Now, once again, in August 1940 the wailing of the banshee was heard in the land, as the air-raid warnings signalled the approach of German bombers. But the German losses in their daylight raids on RAF airfields were surprising them. The Spitfire and our wizard pilots were making it too hot for them. Air Chief Marshal Sir Hugh Dowding, Commander-in-Chief of Fighter Command – forewarned by Ultra of the time and the target of many of the Luftwaffe raids, of how many planes there were and where they were flying from – was able to send up small numbers of Spitfires to attack the raiders. By using small numbers, Dowding not only spared his aircraft but also encouraged Göring to send over larger and larger formations to force the commitment of greater numbers of Spitfires. But these unwieldy formations only presented easier targets. When later, the night bombing came, it was not nearly so accurate. I took to sleeping in our office and we mostly used the underground cubicles where we could also now feed.

In September, Dowding still met the daylight raids with small numbers of Spitfires. The Luftwaffe could not imagine where they all came from. Those of us who had worked out the German timetable knew that the invasion of Britain must take place before the end of the month, so that the whole war effort of Germany could be moved to the Russian front, and yet the Spitfires kept coming up. While they did so, Hitler would not invade.

Göring was getting very cross and on 5 September he ordered a final death blow to England in the form of an all-out raid, not on the aerodromes, but on the London docks. Three hundred bombers took part in the attack and, by sheer weight of numbers, inflicted severe damage on their target. But the switch of bombing to the docks had saved the remaining RAF fighters from being grounded: Göring had made a fatal strategic mistake.

It is characteristic of the British that when a situation grows really serious, deadly calm prevails. That is what was happening now. My head WAAF officer, Mrs Owen, who kept her small flock of cypher officers in faultless order in my teleprinter room, took on a more formal and purposeful entrance when she brought me the urgent signals in the middle of the night. She was one of those completely capable women, whose only apparent weakness was for Siamese cats. Later her quiet efficiency led me to send her as part of Churchill's staff when he went on his visits across the Atlantic to meet Roosevelt. She looked after all the Ultra for him.

Despite the fact that Göring had not achieved complete air superiority, it was feared that he still might feel that he had been sufficiently successful to give Hitler the green light for Operation *Sea Lion*, for the German invasion fleet appeared to be as ready as it was ever likely to be. The nests of barges along the Belgian and French coasts were becoming small armadas according to the daily count kept by the photographers of the spy-plane unit. The standby alert for everyone in Britain was codenamed *Cromwell*, and the hitherto silent bells of all the churches in Britain would tell the people when the invasion began.

On 7 September Invasion Alert No. 1 was sent out, which meant that the Germans might be expected within twelve hours, and troops and Home Guard were brought to immediate readiness. That night, once again, our bombers, such as they were, struck back at the massed barges, but that night, too, the German bombers struck again at London itself, the first of the real night Blitzes, purely against the civilian population. On 9 September we got Göring's orders at 11 a.m. for an early-evening raid by 200-plus bombers, again on London itself, but this time our fighters were able to meet them further south and few got through to the city. That night, however, they came again. On 10 September came blessed rain and clouds; it lasted for four days.

Those of us who were scrutinising every signal of the German armed forces, had formed the impression ever since Göring's switch of attack away from our aerodromes, that time had run out for *Sea Lion*. Churchill, I know, felt this although he could not relax the mood of the nation in any way. That Hitler and his generals would not risk *Sea Lion* while the RAF still lived was evident, and Göring's last-minute efforts to break the morale of the civil population with bombs was having the opposite effect. The odds against invasion lengthened.

A month had now passed since the first of the mass attacks, a month of taut-strung nerves, of hopes that someone, perhaps Göring would put the invasion plans on the air via Enigma, though from the position of the barges and the air-loading installations, the areas were not hard to guess. It was obvious too that it must be now or, we hoped, never. On the 14th the rains lessened but the weather was not good enough for any major effort. But, Sunday, 15 September dawned, alas, an ideal day for the German planes, cloudy but with sufficient gaps for them to find their way. Once again the hand of Göring was guiding what he hoped would be the final knockout. By midday, wave upon wave of bombers were heading for London.

Dowding, correctly judging his moment, the low morale of the German bomber crews, the lack of adequate fighter protection due to the size of their fuel tanks, the desperate state of the RAF and the knowledge that it was now or never for Operation *Sea Lion*, threw in everything we had. The unexpected strength of our fighters was too much for the Luftwaffe; they had been told we had none left. They turned and fled. Göring must have been getting frantic by this time. He promptly ordered a second raid, and this time it was to be pressed home. His signal was duly picked up and this was an occasion when the speed of the Ultra operation and the direct line to Dowding made history. The fighters were refuelled, rearmed and ready again to meet the second wave, and once again the raiders dropped their bombs wherever they could and fled. It was a tremendous day. There was an unconfirmed rumour that the admirals were prepared to guard Nelson's Column in Trafalgar Square in case the statue on top should be replaced by one of Dowding. He has never yet received the credit that, not least in his understanding of Ultra, is his due.

We did not, of course, know at that time when or whether the mass air attacks would start again or whether the invasion was still a serious threat. But one of the main features of the German invasion plans had been the vast preparations that had been made on the Belgian and Dutch aerodromes for loading and quick turn-round of the supply and troop-carrying aircraft, which were by this time supposed to have an unopposed flight to England. On the morning of the 17th the officer-in-charge of these operations in Holland received a signal from the German General Staff to say that Hitler had authorised the dismantling of the air-loading equipment at the Dutch aerodromes. It was quite a short signal, but its significance was so great that 'Humph' had telephoned it down to me the moment it had been decyphered. If the loading equipment was being dismantled, the invasion could not take place, and I sent it over to the Prime Minister's underground war room at Storey's Gate in its yellow box with a note to Churchill's Principal Secretary, John Martin, asking him to see that the Prime Minister had it at once. I also explained the signal to Menzies, just in time, because the Prime Minister phoned Stewart immediately, asking him to go to a Chiefs of Staff meeting he had called for 7.30 p.m. and to take me along with him. I also phoned Charles Medhurst, to ensure that the Chief of Air Staff was properly briefed.

Göring was hard to convince and was still determined to go on trying to bring Britain to her knees by bombing her cities, and that evening the banshee wails of sirens heralded the now nightly air raids soon after dusk. There was already intermittent bombing and anti-aircraft fire as we left in Stewart's car for Storey's Gate; it was drizzling, and ghostly forms moved about in the darkening streets. Underground, in Churchill's war room, General Ismay was already welcoming the Chiefs of Staff and setting the conference in place. They had been briefed by their directors of intelligence. Winston arrived. I was struck by the extraordinary change that had come over these men in the last few hours. Now there were controlled smiles on their faces. Churchill read out the signal, his face beaming, then he rightly asked the Chief of the Air Staff to explain its significance. The CAS had been well briefed; he gave it as his considered opinion that this marked the end of *Sea Lion*, at least for this year. Churchill asked Menzies if there were anything further to confirm the signal. Stewart turned to me; I confirmed that in my opinion it ended the threat of invasion. The conference now accepted that the dismantling of the air-loading equipment meant the end of the threat. There was a very broad smile on Churchill's face as he lit up his massive cigar and suggested that we should all take a little fresh air. An air raid was going on at the time, but Churchill insisted on going outside the concrete screen at the door. I shall ever remember him in his boiler suit and steel helmet, cigar in his mouth, looking across the park to the now blazing buildings beyond, all his Chiefs of Staff, together with Menzies and myself, behind him. His hands holding his long walking stick, he turned to us and growled, 'We will get them for this.' Ismay managed to get him to go inside again as some bombs were getting closer.

It has I think been rightly said that, if we had lost the Battle of Britain, we should have had to surrender, just as later we should have had to do so had we lost the Battle of the Atlantic. To many it was a comforting thought that we had Dowding at the controls during that critical period.

Chapter 24

THE MEDITERRANEAN

So now came the time to consolidate the Ultra flow, after our jamboree with Göring's signals. I began to build up the Special Liaison Units, which consisted of three Army signallers, six RAF cypher sergeants and an RAF officer. They had to be chosen with great care, and I even went to their school teachers and local police before accepting them. They were the vital link between Hut 3 and those commanders of armies and air forces allowed to see this wonderful material. I had put Tubby Long in charge of their training. We used a disused school-house in North London. When I had finally vetted a batch of thirty or forty RAF sergeants, they were told to report to the school. In the entrance hall stood Tubby, a large revolver in his hand. When he had checked each man he told them solemnly, pointing his empty gun at them, 'If ever you let drop one word of what you are going to learn today, I shall personally shoot you.' It was a good start. Not one gave any trouble.

Admiralty now offered Bletchley some two hundred WRNS to operate the cypher-breaking machines, and as, for security reasons, they could not establish an HMS Bletchley, I was asked to take them on my own establishment. I agreed provided I was not made responsible for their matrimonial affairs. I need not have done this, for those splendid girls were put in purdah with their machines in a number of houses around Bletchley and I doubt they ever met any young men during the whole war. They were a splendid team and seemed tireless at their highly important jobs.

In February 1941, Ultra told us that Rommel himself had arrived in Tripoli; later, in reply to a note from Churchill, I was able to confirm to him that Rommel's Blitzkrieg Army had come to Africa.

Now it was Montgomery's turn to be briefed on the dos and don'ts of Ultra. The Prime Minister had decided to do this himself with my aid, but Stewart Menzies wisely suggested that he go instead of me as Montgomery did not like the RAF uniform or being told what he could not do. The result according to Stewart was frosty. After he had explained just what the General would receive and how it must be handled, Montgomery turned to Churchill and asked, 'Presumably, Prime Minister, I shall be the only person to receive this information?' Churchill replied, 'Certainly not, other people will also be entitled to receive it.' Whereupon the General turned on his heel and walked out of the room, closing the door sharply behind him – as Stewart said, rather like a proverbially insulted housemaid.

The story of Alamein is in reality the story of how Ultra gave Admiral Sir Andrew Cunningham's Mediterranean Fleet the chance to sink practically every convoy of supplies sailing from Naples to Rommel's army. So desperate did Rommel become that he complained to the German security service, the Abwehr, alleging that we must be reading the cyphers. I took swift action to prevent any investigation by the Abwehr; by sending a signal in a cypher I knew the Germans could read, congratulating 'Giuseppe' on his work at Naples and raising his salary. Giuseppe did not exist, but the unfortunate Italian Admiral at Naples was arrested and put in gaol. There, alas, he died, but the sinking went on.

When I was in Malta at a party given by Lord Gort, the Governor, I noticed a young naval officer well covered with medals. I congratulated him, and in reply he told me of his extraordinary luck: he had commanded a submarine in the Mediterranean and each time he had received an order to surface there was a convoy of ships with supplies for Rommel right in front of him. I hope no one ever disillusioned him about his luck.

Just before Alamein, we read in Ultra that Rommel was to make a last desperate effort to drive a squadron of tanks round the south of Montgomery's army in a dash for Cairo. The 'deception' boys led by Dudley Clark, who had been at Oxford with me, borrowed a German spy who had just been caught in Cairo. They drove him out to Eighth Army headquarters, where for a minute they left him in the jeep. He wisely made off across the desert. In the back of the jeep was a map of the Southern Desert but unluckily for Rommel the soft sand had been marked as hard, and vice versa. Eighth Army were able to deal with the tanks stuck in the sand.

After Alamein, Hitler had sent a personal signal to Rommel ordering him to fight to the last man. Rommel wisely did not receive it until he and his Afrika Korps were well on their way to Tunisia.

American and British forces were now ready to make a landing in North Africa. General Eisenhower, who had been put in the Ultra picture by Churchill, introduced me to his principal commanders for their indoctrination in the new USA headquarters at Norfolk House in London in August 1942. It was at this point that Stewart Menzies confirmed me in the job as his deputy with full responsibility for ensuring the vital security of Ultra in the field and also for the complete service of Ultra to the Prime Minister, adding that the job would take all my time and tact. For this reason, I had to relinquish control over Hut 3 to the General Administration at Bletchley.

In early 1942 Colonel Palmer Dixon, a US Army Air Force officer, had been attached to the Intelligence Department at the Air Ministry, and at Charles Medhurst's request I had put Palmer in the Ultra picture with the usual security briefing. With the prospect of large numbers of US Army Air Force units coming to Europe, Palmer had asked me whether I could let him have Humphreys from Hut 3 to join the staff of the US Army Air Force Commander in order that he might have the best possible advice on the interpretation and use of Ultra intelligence in operation. It was obviously going to be a highly responsible job, and I was personally all in favour. It would, I felt, add tremendously to the full, yet secure, use of the intelligence by the American air generals. Over the past two and a half years, Humphreys had organised the output of Hut 3 so well that, in his opinion, it now only required a good administrator to keep it running. I therefore made arrangements for his transfer on loan to the American Air Force, where his first job would be to go to North Africa with Major-General Carl Spaatz, Commanding General Eighth Air Force.

Stewart Menzies had also stressed the point that in future I would have to travel to all the theatres of operations and make sure that Ultra, the greatest secret of the war, remained as such. He assured me that I would not only have this authority as his deputy, but that the Prime Minister himself would make it plain to all commanders-in-chief that I was acting with his authority also. This was a clear indication of the Prime Minister's view of the place this information occupied in the war effort. I felt that the time had come to codify security instructions and to get them fully agreed with Washington. The Americans had already agreed to the general outline of both the physical and operational security precautions in the Pacific, but I thought it better to have a US Joint Chiefs of Staff instruction sent to Eisenhower to back up our SLUs which would be attached to the commanders of the American forces. The sheet anchor was to be absolute ruthlessness in keeping to a minimum the number of people who were allowed to receive and be aware of Ultra in the commands at home and overseas. This now included Operation *Torch,* the landing of US and British troops in North Africa. I briefed the British General Sir Kenneth Anderson and also Air Marshal Sir William 'Sinbad' Welch, who was in command of the British air forces component. I had gone to Gibraltar to be with Eisenhower during the crucial landing of the American troops in Algeria. On the day of the landing Eisenhower was standing on the rocks outside the entrance to the underground rooms where I was receiving Ultra. He was naturally impatient to know how the landing was going. Then I got a signal from Kesselring ordering an airlift of 15,000 men to Tunis. I showed it to Eisenhower. He remarked, 'He can't do this to me.' I assured him that Kesselring would do the airlift. He did.

Eisenhower arrived in Algeria on 13 November; I had managed to get over there on the 10th on a submarine-hunting aircraft. Halfway across we suddenly started to dive as the pilot pointed to a black object moving in the sea below, and an inoffensive porpoise nearly had the shock of its life. The warmth of Algiers was very welcome after the cold of London; the purple bougainvillaea's, the bright blue plumbago and the pink oleanders were still in full bloom. I found Anderson in an isolated farmhouse among the bracken-covered hills some thirty miles east of Algiers. It looked much like his native Scotland. He explained with a wry smile that he had chosen a spot where he could keep his eye on the single railway line which had to carry the supplies up to the front. Due to the news on Ultra of Kesselring's rapid moves into Tunis (Kesselring, after the failure of Operation *Sea Lion*, had abandoned the Luftwaffe and become an Army General), he was doing his best to get the armies on the move eastwards before the Germans could seize too much ground.

Later on that evening, we received Kesselring's orders signalled to the Air Command at Tunis for a parachute battalion to seize the coastal aerodrome at Bône which lay in the path of the advancing Allies. It was essential that the Allies should have this aerodrome, because airfields were few and far between. Kesselring's orders were for the Germans to seize it on 12 November, the following day. It was a busy evening at HQ. A small section of British parachute troops who had had very little training, but at least were keen and available in Algiers, were ordered to seize the Bône aerodrome on the morning of the 12th before the Germans got there and a number of American Dakota aeroplanes had to be gathered together in order to transport them. Despite the late hour, the operation was duly laid on. I shared a restless night on a camp bed with Anderson's RAF liaison officer.

We rose before dawn to await news of the race against the Germans. At least we had the edge on them since they did not know that we should be doing the same job as them. Fortunately, they left Tunis later than we left Algiers. The German aircraft arrived just as the last British parachutist landed and the Germans had to turn back to base. We had a rather joyful, if late, breakfast of orange juice, bacon and eggs at the old farmhouse. The incident, I think, convinced both Anderson and his staff that Ultra could be of tactical as well as strategical use and that this was a classic case where Kesselring could not suspect we had read the signals.

Back in Algiers I saw Admiral Cunningham, who was, in addition to his purely naval Ultra, being given the general situation reports by the SLU. I did not discuss the naval Ultra with him, but I had learned from the Air Officer Commanding at Gibraltar, who incidentally had been my first flight commander in France in 1917, that Ultra had got the German submarine position in the Mediterranean well buttoned up.

I hitchhiked in one of those remarkable war-horses, the Douglas Dakotas, back to Gibraltar, then on a flying-boat back to Plymouth, having arranged to return to Algiers in six weeks' time. Meanwhile, I should have to watch the operation from the German point of view in London with Kesselring's help. I found that the arrangements I had made for headlining the signals going over to the Prime Minister had worked smoothly during my absence. I also found that the urgency which had characterised his demands for Ultra had eased a little. Now that Eisenhower was accepted as Supreme Commander of *Torch*, Churchill was able to sit back and relax his direction of the war in North Africa, which hitherto had been his main preoccupation.

Meantime, Montgomery was following up Rommel with considerable skill and, knowing where and when Rommel intended to make a stand, gave him no chance of success, despite Hitler's orders that Rommel should fight to the last man.

By Christmas I was already getting requests for more SLUs for the forward areas in Tunisia, so I decided to see the position for myself before extending Ultra distribution. It would mean a greater security risk which would have to be justified. I found some changes at headquarters; Air Chief Marshal Sir Arthur Tedder had come from Cairo and taken over command of all the Allied Air Forces and was generally helping Eisenhower to get co-operation from everybody. Arthur Tedder was an old friend with whom I had worked during the 1930s, and I felt I now had a good ally right at the top who would watch security. These two men were of much the same temperament; they understood each other and it was no surprise when Tedder was chosen by Eisenhower to be his Deputy Chief for the great events of 1944.

Tedder wanted to see me as soon as I arrived. He had Spaatz with him in his office, and now came a request from Spaatz for Ultra to go to his forward operational headquarters. Humphreys, who was Spaatz's adviser, had given the project his support and Tedder wanted it done. We at once organised a SLU from the spare staff I had sent out for emergencies. Spaatz was delighted. He was using Ultra to the utmost advantage, bombing endless targets such as newly arrived German aircraft on the outlying airfields, and any other targets which Ultra identified.

Tedder also told me that Major-General George Patton was now in Algiers and would like to be briefed. He had sailed direct from the United States with his landing force to Casablanca, so I had had no opportunity to brief him before. Hearing so many stories of his gold-plated tin hat and his personal armament, I was a little nervous as I knocked on his office door. I need not have worried; he greeted me with a broad smile and a cheery welcome and a 'Now, young sir, what's it all about?' He was delighted at the idea of reading the enemy's signals, but when I got on to the security angle he stopped me after a few minutes. 'You know, young man, I think you had better tell all this to my intelligence staff, I don't go much on this sort of thing myself. You see I just like fighting.' He had summed himself up pretty accurately. One point he did not like was the rule which referred to personal safety, requiring recipients of Ultra not to put themselves in positions where they might fall into enemy hands. I was to meet him often in the next few years; he always smiled but never would submit to any restraint. I just had to rely on Tedder to keep an eye on him, and on his very excellent intelligence staff to keep him 'wised'.

General Alexander came over to Tunisia from Egypt and in February was given overall command of the British First Army and the American forces, together with the Eighth Army on the other side of Tunisia, to form the Eighteenth Army Group. By February too, the Americans began to threaten the Afrika Korps from both the flank and the rear as the Allied armies came closer together. The two German armies, the Afrika Korps and the army commanded by General Jürgen von Arnim, had joined together with the First Italian Army under General Giovanni Messe to form Army Group Afrika commanded by Rommel.

At the beginning of May I was able once again to get out to Algiers. The fall of Tunis was now imminent, and I wanted to sort out what SLUs would be available for the next step to Sicily. I went up to Constantine to see the large SLU which was now operating there. Since my visit in December 1942, we had been able to switch a large part of the traffic on to the Typex cypher machine. This SLU served principally the US North-West African Air Forces and the Mediterranean Tactical Air Force, as well as the Eighteenth Army Group. I found a busy team. I also learned a good deal about the ingenuity and ability to improvise that the SLUs had had to employ. Supplies were always a problem; Sergeant Reynolds told me that they had had to adapt their Typex machines, first of all to work off the French 120 volts and then the American power plants of 110 volts and finally they had had to use some old German equipment. There was an interesting example, too, of how little things can prove dangerous to security. The SLU had at one time received prior information of an enemy air raid on Constantine and quite naturally they took their tin hats with them when they went on duty. When the air raid arrived other people at headquarters became suspicious, so after that it was no tin hats even if there was a warning on Ultra.

Kesselring, on Ultra, was now preparing the OKW (the German High Command) for the surrender of Tunisia. He was getting both dirty ends of the stick, from Berlin and Tunis, but already he was asking the OKW for help and instructions as to what he should do against the next Allied move, whatever it would be. The end came quickly after the final Allied assault on 6 May. Ultra was able to give all the North African Air Forces the movement orders for the fleet of German Ju-52 transport aircraft and their Me-323 gliders which were to be used in the evacuation of German troops from Tunisia. The SLU told me they had a job to restrain the Allied Air Forces from taking too quick action; however, in the event, most of the enemy aircraft were shot down. The same fate was suffered by the *Hermes*, the last German destroyer in the Mediterranean, and also the Belino evacuation convoy, although some senior German officers managed to escape in a hospital ship. Ultra became silent until Kesselring, on 13 May, repeated to Berlin, quite shortly, the total loss of Tunisia and of the Army Group Afrika.

When I visited General Alexander's small camp near Carthage he suggested that we should take a walk among the sand-dunes where we could talk. He was fascinated with the Ultra story, and I gave it to him in detail. Hitherto, he had not been able to understand how we managed to get it to him so accurately and quickly. He wanted to know the prospects for its continuance for the Italian campaign, and I told him that unless there was a serious mistake by anyone, I could not see the Germans changing Ultra now and, barring accidents, there was every hope for good results in view of the fact that Hitler and the OKW were a long way from Rome, and all signals would go on the air.

He seemed very satisfied with the whole outfit. He was fascinated, too, by my picture of the tough character of his opponent, which I was able to draw from my personal knowledge of Kesselring. He also wanted to know just who in his new command was in the Ultra picture. He told me that he had known from his first meeting with Churchill in Egypt before Alamein that the Prime Minister was well informed from Ultra, but he had had no idea, until I had told him, that he received direct signals annotated by me. Alexander was a little thoughtful on this subject. He must have realised that Churchill would be following the campaign closely. I did, however, take pains to assure Alexander that I annotated the signals only from the German point of view since I was unaware of any orders or actions on the part of the Allies.

Before I left Tunis, Kesselring thought it wise to inform the OKW by Ultra of the complete set-up of the Italian and German forces in Sicily and continued to fill the air with Enigma signals. The British and American commanders were happy and confident. Meanwhile the much-battered Rommel had gone back to Germany pleading sick leave.

Chapter 25

ITALY

In May 1943 I toured Algiers, Cairo, Alexandria and Malta, checking that all was in order at my various SLUs so that they were ready to give maximum help and information for the invasion of Sicily, codenamed *Husky*. In Algiers Tedder gave me the command set-up for *Husky*. He himself was taking over command of all the air forces in the Mediterranean and suggested that I wait until the principal commanders had assembled at La Marsa near Carthage in about two weeks' time, when it would be easier for me to contact anyone I wanted to see.

During my tour, I found that at all the main SLU stations a great deal of high-level traffic was being sent over the SLU channels by the Chiefs of Staff in London to Eisenhower and Alexander, and also between the various commanders-in-chief in the Mediterranean area. This was primarily because so much of the planning for Sicily and Italy was based on Ultra information and any discussion or change of plan based on this intelligence had rightly to be sent over our own channel; added to which the top brass as well as Winston Churchill found our channel quicker than the normal signals organisation, and its maximum secrecy was useful when personalities had to be discussed. The SLUs were, in consequence, working flat out.

The climax in the Sicilian Campaign came when George Patton, taking full advantage of the move of the panzers to hold Montgomery's army at Catania, and knowing from Ultra that there was nothing to stop him, was already making his famous high-speed left hook towards Palermo and Messina. By 8 August Kesselring reported to the OKW his withdrawal from Catania, followed shortly after by his decision to withdraw all units to the Italian mainland. The conquest of Sicily ended on 17 August. Ultra had played a vital part.

Churchill had always been convinced that if the Allies invaded Italy the Italians would throw in the towel. Latterly Roosevelt had been brought round to the same view. Mussolini was now facing the collapse of his regime after the success of Operation *Husky*. He was an extremely worried man, and Hitler had no illusions about the difficulties he might have in keeping his Axis partner in the war. Mussolini's ebullience at their meeting on 17 July had not deceived him, but he probably had not bargained for the rapid chain of events which followed. Only one week later Mussolini's Fascist Grand Council told him to quit; the next day he was arrested by the King. Marshal Badoglio took over the government and assured Kesselring that Italy would stay in the war. Kesselring repeated this assurance in a signal back to Hitler, who rightly did not believe a word of it; within a week the Italians started secret negotiations for an armistice with the Allies, and before long had declared war on Germany.

In September 1943, the Allies invaded Italy, the main force making an opposed landing at Salerno, thirty miles south of Naples. We had learned from Ultra that Kesselring had no idea where the landings would be made, so he had started to withdraw northwards, expecting the main assault to take place nearer Rome. The Allies duly consolidated their positions and began to move north.

In due course, an important signal from Kesselring advised the OKW that he expected an all-out attempt by the Allies to break the mountainous Cassino line which he had established, as soon as the flooded rivers and the countryside permitted. So far, this airman turned soldier had done a remarkable job stopping the Allied drive to Rome and overcoming the defection of his Italian allies.

It was about midday on Sunday, 13 May, that I had a telephone call from the Prime Minister at Chequers. He asked that I meet him at his flat at Storey's Gate that evening at 9 p.m. and would I bring round all signals dealing with the Cassino front. I wondered what it was all about. His Private Secretary rang a few minutes later and put me wise. Apparently Winston had returned to Chequers on Saturday night from a secret visit to Alexander's headquarters in Caserta; I knew the Prime Minister had been getting more than worried at the inability of the Allies to make progress in Italy. He desperately wanted Rome before he started on Operation *Overlord*, the codename for the invasion of France, which was already being planned under Eisenhower and Montgomery.

At midnight on 12 May 1944, Alexander's offensive at Cassino had begun and Kesselring reported that the main attack on Monte Cassino itself had been repulsed, but that some ground had been lost south of

Cassino town. In a signal on 13 May he told the OKW that all available German reserves had now been committed.

The Anzio fiasco (where troops landed for a drive on Rome had got bogged down on the coast), though no fault of Alexander's, had boosted German morale, and now, before we landed in France, we needed to stir things up a bit. It was obvious that Churchill had been briefed by Alexander, but I had only two or three signals reporting small advances by the Eighth Army around Cassino, and Kesselring's claim to have beaten off the attack on Monte Cassino. They were not a particularly encouraging selection to present to Churchill. It was a cold evening for May and the Prime Minister was sitting in his boiler suit deep in his green leather chair in front of a fire. He looked tired. As he asked me to sit down and tell him my news, he was puffing gently at a large cigar. I had the uncomfortable feeling that he took my normal matter-of-fact opening to the conversation as my own way of telling him something exciting. I had given him the various small details of the fighting which had come in during the afternoon. When he said, 'Is that all?' I had to say that I was afraid that was so. We went across to the map room where the few alterations I had brought over were flagged up, but Churchill was obviously puzzled and disappointed. In his usual courteous manner, he thanked me for coming over and then, with a broad smile, he said, 'See that I get anything more first thing in the morning. I think you will find there will be something of interest.'

It was now late but I phoned the watch at Bletchley and warned them to keep their eyes skinned. It came through about 3 a.m. with Mrs Owen's knock on my office door and a welcome cup of coffee. The French Moroccan troops had scaled the mountains south of Cassino. Kesselring was calm, but obviously dismayed at the feat; he reported to Hitler that 'the whole Cassino line is now in danger'. I sent the signal over to Storey's Gate before seven-thirty in the morning. That day Kesselring reported to Berlin that now both the British and the Americans were gaining some ground. He was a worried man; he was also not being properly kept in the picture by General Vietinghoff, who commanded the German Tenth Army on the Cassino line. For, early on the 14th, he sent a snorter to Vietinghoff telling him to report to him by midday exactly what was happening.

On the 15th Kesselring sent a signal to Hitler reporting a breakthrough by a strong French force over the massive Monti Aurunci which dominated the whole Liri valley and the supply routes to the Cassino line. On the 16th came reports from Kesselring of the successes of the British and Polish forces around Cassino, and then on the 17th came the one we had been waiting for: Kesselring ordered the evacuation of the entire Cassino front, since, as he said, the Allies had penetrated twenty-five miles behind the German lines. His signal was repeated to the OKW. Bletchley was in good form and Churchill, Alexander and the US Chiefs of Staff in Washington had it within a few minutes of its despatch by Kesselring.

The attack by the Moroccan troops across the mountains was, according to Kesselring's report to Berlin, entirely unexpected. By the 19th it was hard, even from the Ultra signals, to sort out just what was happening. The German Tenth Army signalled desperately for reinforcements, having lost most of two divisions. That communications were extremely bad, was evident from a further signal by Kesselring demanding to be told what was going on. Vietinghoff seemed to be out of touch with his divisions. He did not reply. Kesselring ordered withdrawal from the Liri valley on the 22nd, and the Allies started their break-out attack from Anzio the next day. Kesselring signalled to Berlin that his Tenth and Fifteenth Armies had been divided by the Allies, and he asked Hitler's permission to abandon the Adolf Hitler line, some ten miles behind the now abandoned Cassino line, and withdraw to the Caesar line, which was some twenty miles south of Rome. In another signal he ordered his last reserve divisions from Northern Italy into the battle. Hitler signalled his permission to withdraw to the Caesar line on 24 May.

Stewart Menzies told me that on his visit to Italy Winston Churchill had agreed with Alexander's plan to try to trap and destroy the German armies south of Rome rather than try to drive them northwards. The plan, if successful, would obviously dent the morale of the whole German army at this critical moment before *Overlord*.

General Mark Clark had been fully briefed on Alexander's plan and had received his instructions to use the forces now ready to break out from Anzio to move rapidly eastwards to trap the retreating Tenth and Fifteenth Armies from the rear. (Ultra had given him the weak point.) Instead, he chose to ignore them, and while sending a small token force to the east, decided himself to try and make a dash up the west coast to Rome. The result was that neither objective was attained. Clark neither unlocked the door to Rome, nor trapped the Germans. By this time Hitler had sent one of his death-or-glory signals to the troops in Italy, which Kesselring duly passed on to Vietinghoff.

It was on 2 June that Kesselring asked Hitler for permission to evacuate Rome without fighting. Hitler agreed on 3 June, by which time Kesselring's forces were already slipping away to the north, and now General Clark finally took some notice of Ultra. He knew from Kesselring's signals that Rome was undefended. He organised two flying columns and made a triumphal personal entry into the Eternal City, ahead of anyone else.

It is, I think, greatly to Kesselring's credit that he did not defend Rome; perhaps he did not want his name linked with Nero, but I believe that under the rough, tough, thrusting exterior, there must have been some sensitivity to history and the arts which induced him to save Rome and, later on, Florence. Churchill had got his Rome just two days before Operation *Overlord* broke the quiet of the English Channel.

I suppose, looking back on it, the Italian campaign had given us almost as complete a picture of the German side as could have been found in Kesselring's files in his office in Rome. It had obviously been necessary to put all signals between Kesselring and the OKW and Hitler on the air, a point I had previously made with Alexander. In my London office, it was as if I were sitting at Kesselring's right hand watching the campaign entirely from his point of view.

Chapter 26

OVERTURE

If it appears that the names of Hitler, Rommel and Kesselring appear almost exclusively in this part of my narrative, it is not just because I knew two of them personally, but because it was through them that we really got the vital information to win the war. The volatile Hitler who thought his mandate from the devil gave him a military authority over his generals, the tough Kesselring, whose personal charm I had known, who was more diplomatic in his handling of his Führer, and Rommel, the firebrand, blaming his unsuccess on others, little knowing how much Ultra owed to him. To me these were the principals in the melodrama and opposite them now the quiet almost studious Eisenhower and the totally unflappable Arthur Tedder. And behind it all, just down the road, the Big White Chief, Winston Churchill. It was a pretty good cast and maybe the gods at Bletchley and their winged messenger, who saw that no one blabbed, played a secret part also.

The fall of Italy and the removal of Mussolini are now history. It was now Albert Kesselring's turn to get the dirty end of the stick. Mark Clark's triumphal entry into Rome instead of obeying orders to cut off part of the German Army in Italy was not popular; nor was Rommel's re-entry on the scene in north Italy welcomed by Kesselring. However, the Italian campaign was folding up and all attention in Britain was now focused on the Allied invasion of France, Operation *Overlord*.

Lieutenant-General Freddie Morgan had been appointed COSSAC, or Chief of Staff to the Supreme Allied Commander, and his task was to set up a planning organisation for invasion by the Allies. As early as March 1943 he took over Norfolk House, where Eisenhower had previously established his headquarters before Operation *Torch* in North Africa.

I had discussed with him the provision of Ultra for his planning operations, and we agreed that he could find all the information he required already digested and co-ordinated at the War Office and Air Ministry. However, I told him I would bring round any item of urgent or special interest, should it arise.

It was at this time that the VI (doodlebug) became a threat. By ingenious work on the part of my scientific assistant, R.V. Jones, and the help of both Ultra and high-altitude photo reconnaissance, we knew what to expect, but as the launching pads were mobile and set up in France and Belgium, where Ultra told us at the end of May that fifty sites were ready for launching, it was difficult to counter this new menace. These flying bombs could do considerable damage once again to London. This finally determined Churchill to press for the start of *Overlord* in June at all costs. Time was obviously going to be very precious. It was on D-Day, 6 June that the German officer-in-charge received a signal ordering him to prepare for an immediate all-out offensive to start on 12 June. In the event, it was not until the 13th that the first VI landed.

But to go back to 1943. In November there was a piece of important information for Morgan; it was a signal from the OKW to all units in the West, notifying them of the arrival of Rommel to undertake a general inspection of the coast defences of France and Belgium – Hitler's Atlantic Wall.

Since 1942 there had been a fair stability in the number of German troops in the west – some sixty divisions. It was part of the job of General Karl von Rundstedt (the German Commander in France) to rest and re-equip the tired and depleted divisions from Eastern Europe. The new divisions thus reorganised only amounted to about half the original numbers. This was, of course, vital news for the planners. On the few occasions when Rundstedt went on the air to the OKW in Berlin, it was usually to complain about the state of inadequacy, as regards both manpower and the general condition of the defences in the West. One subject, however, which came over with great clarity, and was of extreme importance to Morgan in late 1943, was Rundstedt's own appreciation of where he considered the Allied invasion would take place. True to orthodox German military thinking, he gave it as his opinion that the Allies would surely take the shortest sea route and attack in the Pas de Calais area. I think it is true to say that it was this signal that sowed the seed of the elaborate deception plan to install a phantom army in Kent, opposite the Pas de Calais, in order to bolster up Rundstedt's views.

Back in July, in Tunisia, Tedder had told me that he hoped to get a job with Eisenhower, and now I discovered that he was to be Deputy Supreme Commander under 'Ike'. This was excellent news.

In February 1944 Eisenhower set up his headquarters of SHAEF – Supreme Headquarters Allied Expeditionary Force. I now began to make my own plans for the provision of a new network of SLUs and made it my business to get to know all the commanders and their staffs personally. This was a very special sort of intelligence and required a special relationship if the best was to be got out of Ultra. I did not share the view which seemed to be held by Montgomery that all intelligence must be impersonal and under no circumstances must there be any contact, or acknowledgement, of the source by the commander. Ultra's broad coverage provided those who continually handled it with a large amount of background information, in addition to that culled from reading so many of the signals of the German High Command; I found it was this that the majority of commanders were always interested to know about.

When the principal commanders had settled in I therefore got to know each one. There were long green wooden huts making up a little American township in Bushey Park. Here the Stars and Stripes flew at the masthead and received the full ceremonial to which it was entitled. Around the tidy square were the huts of the Supreme Commander and principal staff officers, and I usually made for Tedder's hut to find out if there were any particular aspects which SHAEF wanted watched.

General Omar Bradley had been aware of Ultra in Tunisia, but now I was able to give him a full briefing, together with those members of his staff that he had asked me to put on the Ultra list. As the war progressed I became great friends with Bradley's intelligence officer, Colonel Monk Dickson. I would meet him in his working caravan, situated in some corner of a field or wood, and find him always the same quietly efficient soldier.

I first met General Sir Miles Dempsey – commanding the British Second Army – when he invited me round to his flat in London one evening to brief him about Ultra. I spent a long time with him, going over aspects of the intelligence that he was to receive. As we drank our scotch and sodas he sometimes laughed outright at the idea of reading Hitler's own signals. When I eventually left his flat at midnight, I was confident that he would use Ultra to the full and be scrupulously careful of this precious source.

Another newcomer to Ultra was Lieutenant-General Henry Crerar, commanding the Canadian Army, who had set up his headquarters at Lord Beaverbrook's house near Leatherhead in Surrey. At Crerar's request, I also put General G.C. Simonds, one of his corps commanders, in the picture; he was to prove not only a brilliant commander, but an enthusiastic Ultra customer.

General Spaatz had returned to England from Tunisia to command the Strategic Bomber Force, and I found him at General Jimmy Doolittle's new headquarters in Wycombe Abbey girls' school at High Wycombe. He was not directly responsible to *Overlord*, but his force was, when necessary, to be at Eisenhower's disposal. So, he was very much involved. He was always a keen user of Ultra, especially grateful for the German secret weather reports for Europe.

Now that we had so many Ultra customers and could expect many more as further operational units got under way in *Overlord*, I had to establish a large programme for the training of SLUs. I required about sixty RAF cypher sergeants and a dozen officers. They were an exceptional and highly intelligent selection of men and became absolutely dedicated to the job. The SLUs were ready by the beginning of May to be attached to their commands, where they began taking Ultra direct from Hut 3.

During March we noticed no increase in the signals of importance to *Overlord*, but by April we learned from an OKW signal that Rommel had been given command of Army Group B, which was responsible for the defence of the coast from Holland right round Normandy and Brittany, as far south as Nantes. Very soon he started sending urgent requests for materials and labour to strengthen Hitler's much-vaunted Atlantic Wall. He clearly thought it inadequate, but no matter how often he signalled, for cement, steel, timber and guns, nothing much appeared to happen. Before long, Rommel told the OKW that the reinforcing of the coastal defences was being carried out by the troops themselves, which meant that their state of readiness was severely affected.

In the course of spring 1944 the Germans took what was probably the most important decision of all those affecting Operation *Overlord*. The decision arose from a clash of views between Hitler, Rundstedt, Rommel, General Heinz Guderian and General Geyr von Schweppenburg, who commanded a group of four panzer divisions which made up the panzer reserve stationed near Paris. Rundstedt, as I have said, had taken the view that the Allies would invade across the Pas de Calais. Rommel was convinced that the invasion would be made on the Normandy beaches; he therefore wanted the panzers to be positioned just behind the Normandy defences, so that they could be brought down to the beaches at short notice to wreak havoc among the invading forces. Guderian and Schweppenburg preferred to keep the tanks safely in reserve, so that they could be sent to meet any new threat as events unfolded. Back and forth went the signals, and Hitler gradually abandoned Rommel's view, seemingly infected by Rundstedt's.

The brilliant deception plan of Patton's phantom army in Kent, opposite the Pas de Calais, must have reinforced Rundstedt's views and added to Hitler's doubts. German intelligence no doubt picked up and analysed the huge quantity of bogus wireless traffic that went on in the phantom-army area. General Patton himself was constantly in evidence, along with his white bull-terrier, in and around the area of the hutted encampment, which was manned by a skeleton staff of US soldiers.

Finally, in May, we caught a signal to Rundstedt from Hitler which ordered that the four panzer divisions should be held where they were, as an assault force, under the direct control of the OKW. There were still no signs of a move by any of the infantry divisions of the Fifteenth Army from the Pas de Calais area.

Events towards the end of May once again showed Ultra's value in a negative role. Every signal was scrutinised for hints of any change in the strength and location of the German formations, or any sign that the enemy knew the timing or the exact location of our landing beaches. There was nothing. Yet those first few days of June 1944 were about the tensest I have ever known.

Chapter 27

OVERLORD

I suppose that Operation *Overlord,* which was finally to win the war in the West was one of the most exciting times of my life. Here was the culmination of the strange story of the Enigma; born in 1939 and now come of age, wielding its victorious power over the war in a way that few people could have imagined.

The dreadful weather in those first days of June put everybody's nerves on edge; we knew that the ships and the men had already put to sea, and the risk of detection must increase with every hour's delay.

Around 2 a.m., on D-Day, 6 June, the first signal came through from the German naval headquarters in Paris. It was addressed both to the Commander-in-Chief West and to Hitler at his headquarters at Rastenburg in East Prussia. It stated simply that the invasion had commenced. Rundstedt's response was merely to alert the Fifteenth Army in the Pas de Calais. His signal was an absolute godsend to us all at that moment, especially as he evidently did not think it worthwhile alerting the Seventh Army in Normandy. He seemed convinced that the parachute troops, now being reported back to him by the Seventh Army, were a bluff. Not until dawn did his Chief of Staff, General Günther Blumentritt, send a signal direct to the OKW advising them of the urgency of the situation and at the same time asking Hitler's permission to employ the OKW panzer reserve.

During these critical hours it was vital to watch every move by Rundstedt and Rommel and to analyse the thinking behind the orders they were sending out. It was these signals which I sent over to the Prime Minister on D-Day morning. There was, as yet, nothing from Hitler.

One reason, as we now know, was that Hitler was asleep and the generals on his staff had not dared to wake him up until well into the afternoon. So, it is not surprising that it was not until the evening of the 6th that we picked up a signal from Hitler agreeing to release to Rundstedt the 12th Panzer Division from the OKW reserve. But it was already too late. Rommel's plan to defeat the landings had been to meet them with tanks at the water's edge. By evening the Allies were well ashore and, in any case, with the sky full of Allied aircraft, the 12th Panzer Division did not dare move until dusk. This was the first indication that Hitler was taking the invasion seriously. Late that night Rommel signalled in his situation report to the OKW that 'the British advance on Caen has been halted and that the 21st and 12th SS Panzer Divisions are in position west of the town from the north round to a point some seven miles to the south-west.'

Fierce resistance by the enemy in defence of the town of Caen succeeded on 7 June in holding the British to the west of this important objective. This was confirmed in a signal from Rommel in which he also informed the OKW that he had ordered the withdrawal from Brittany of a motorised and an infantry division together with the XI Parachute Corps to try and hold the Americans on the Cotentin peninsula.

It seems that Rundstedt gave a generous interpretation to Hitler's orders releasing the 12th SS Panzer Division because we caught a signal from him ordering another of the reserve panzer divisions –the Panzer Lehr – to move to the Caen area in addition to the 12th SS Division. He then signalled to Rommel on 9 June to counter-attack. But the armoured reserve about which so much argument had raged must have been caught napping, because in a signal back to Rundstedt and the OKW, on the 9th, Rommel objected, 'The 12th SS Panzer Division has arrived short of fuel and the Panzer Lehr Division is quite unready for action. Under the circumstances no immediate dislodgement of the enemy is possible and a return to the defensive on the Vire-Orne front is necessary until preparations for a counter-attack are complete.' This was an important signal which gave Miles Dempsey of the British Second Army a short and welcome breather.

On the 10th Monty went over to Normandy, and he soon realised that it was unlikely that the British and Canadians would be able to take Caen in face of the mounting German panzer forces revealed by Ultra, so instead of trying to capture Caen, as originally planned, he decided to pin down as many of the main enemy armoured forces as possible, in order to give Bradley's First Army a chance to try and break out to the south against less heavily armed resistance. A British thrust by the 7th Armoured Division towards Caen on the 10th drew the German armour into the open and the Panzer Lehr Division was reported by Rommel on the night of the 13th as having 'lost 100 tanks and now unable to thrust towards the sea'. So, Montgomery's strategy was working.

Meantime, on the 13th, Bradley's forces had taken the important little town of Carentan at the eastern base of the Cherbourg peninsula, with its main road and railway connections. Rommel signalled the loss to the OKW on the 14th, but at the same time he reported: 'I am satisfied at the moment that the American landing at the east of Vierville (Omaha beach) is only making slow progress and the Caen front is now held.' Next day Hitler signalled his orders to Rundstedt to attack Bayeux and also signalled the garrison commander at Cherbourg that 'the port must be held at all costs'. But the American VIII Corps drove right across the peninsula to the western coast, cutting off Cherbourg and the northern half of the Cotentin. Rommel had to signal the news to the OKW on the 18th and to admit the almost total loss of his 91st and 77th Divisions.

We now knew from Ultra that Hitler himself was directing main strategy. As the Americans closed in on Cherbourg, he sent a personal signal to General Carl Wilhelm von Schlieben, commanding the garrison, saying: 'Even if the worst comes to the worst, it is your duty to defend the last bunker and leave the enemy not a harbour but a heap of ruins. German people and the whole world are watching your fight; on it depends the conduct and result of operations to smash the Allied beachhead and the honour of the German Army and of your own name.'

The unfortunate Schlieben could only signal to Hitler: 'In view of the great superiority of the enemy in aircraft, tanks, and artillery and now finally the naval bombardment, I must state in the line of duty that further sacrifices can alter nothing.' Rommel's reply cannot have cheered him: 'You will continue to fight to the last cartridge in accordance with the orders of the Führer.'

We soon learned from Ultra that the three German armoured divisions around Caen were in full working order, and that two more armoured divisions, the 9th and 10th were on their way from the Russian front to the Caen area. Hitler's decision to bring armour from the hard-pressed Eastern Front to Normandy showed that he was now determined to prevent us from making a break-out in the West. It was bad news, but it was soon to be followed by a further signal from OKW to Rundstedt and Rommel, stating that the 1st SS Panzer Division was coming across from Belgium, and the 2nd SS Panzer Division was coming up from Toulouse to the St Lo area on the American sector.

Fearing that these moves might seriously affect Bradley's chances of a break-out, Montgomery decided to act. Dempsey attacked to such effect that General Paul Hausser, commanding the German Seventh Army, relayed a signal to Rommel from General Sepp Dietrich, who commanded the I Panzer SS Corps, saying that unless reinforcements were sent to him that night there would be an Allied breakthrough. Clearly we had unsettled them more than we had thought. Rommel, already having difficulty in collecting a force to carry out Hitler's orders for an attack on Bayeux, with some reluctance signalled Seventh Army to use the 9th and 10th and the 1st SS Panzer Division to help Dietrich. More importantly, he was to 'bring back part of the 2nd SS Panzer Division', then opposing Bradley at St Lo. Ultra had worked again, showing Dempsey precisely the weak spot to go for.

By 22 June the British Second Army had made further gains. Both Rundstedt and Rommel were in Berchtesgaden, so the Commander of Seventh Army sent his situation report to them there that night. He proposed a counter-attack at 7 a.m. on the 29th on the salient created by the British thrust. This signal reached all commanders in good time for the 2nd Tactical Air Force to be alerted, and just before 7 a.m. they acted so effectively that Hausser later reported to Rommel that 'as soon as the tanks had assembled they were attacked by fighter bombers and were so disrupted that the attack had to be put off for some seven hours'. Here was Ultra at its best in actual battle.

We learned after the war that Rundstedt and Rommel had gone to Berchtesgaden, with the full support of Hausser and Schweppenburg, to ask Hitler's permission for a phased withdrawal from Caen. The day after Rundstedt returned from Berchtesgaden with Rommel, Hitler sent a signal to Rundstedt: 'Present positions are to be held.' It was Ultra's first indication that Rundstedt and Rommel had seen the red light and wanted to withdraw.

Another drama we knew nothing about until after the war was how Rundstedt had phoned General Wilhelm Keitel, Chief of Staff to the OKW, and told him that it would be impossible to carry out Hitler's orders to attack Bayeux. Keitel is reported to have said: 'What shall we do?' 'What shall we do?' Rundstedt replied. 'Make peace, you fools! What else can you do!' The following day Rundstedt was relieved of his command. The first indication we had over Ultra that Rundstedt had been replaced was a signal by Field Marshal Günther von Kluge as Commander-in-Chief West. His first signal had promptly repeated Hitler's 'Present positions to be held' order to all commands.

It was just at this time, three weeks after D-Day, as the German command fell into momentary disarray, that I decided to go over and see if all was well with the SLU system and security. I made first for Bradley's HQ, where Monk Dickson, Bradley's intelligence officer, warned me that his Chief was depressed by the First Army's inability to make headway through the difficult *bocage* country. Nevertheless, when I entered the office in his caravan, the General greeted me with his usual courtesy. He paid tribute to Ultra, which was good to hear. 'Never,' he said, 'did I expect to get such concise information about my opponents; the only trouble is that there seems to be too many of them.'

I spent the evening with the SLU under the apple trees. They were on top of their form enjoying every minute of their job.

The next afternoon I sought out Major-General Elwood R. Quesada, commanding the Ninth US Tactical Air Force. I had put an American officer in charge of the SLU here, with the usual complement of RAF cypher sergeants and wireless traffic (W/T) personnel. Quesada himself was tickled to death with Ultra, especially the movement orders which gave him ready-made targets without having to search for them, and woe betide any German tank or transport that put its nose out from under a hedge or wood in daylight. Quesada had worked out a brilliant system of communication between his aircraft and the US tanks which worked in practice much the same way as the dive-bombers had done for the German tanks in the Battle of France in 1940.

Near Bayeux the following afternoon I called in on Montgomery's headquarters, a huge tent covered all over by an even larger camouflage net, pitched on a small hill. The SLU, on instructions from the Commander-in-Chief himself, had been banished to a solitary spot in a little quarry some half a mile away. It meant a long walk at night. Montgomery's excuse was that he feared that the enemy might get a bearing on the W/T. As we used very short-wave transmissions and the acknowledgement signals from the SLU were equally short and at different times each day, and since no enemy, either in North Africa or Italy, for the past two years had shown any interest in the whereabouts of our SLUs, I was forced to the conclusion that it was the presence of RAF personnel concerned with intelligence which for some reason the General did not like.

As I stood outside my tent on the top of that little hill in Normandy the next afternoon, I watched 450 Lancaster bombers, black against the evening sky, their deep drone rising to a roar as they swept overhead. Then came the thunder of their bombs on the dug-in tanks of the defences of Caen. The earth trembled, even though we were some miles away.

Dempsey's tent at his Second Army headquarters was a much smaller affair than Montgomery's, nor had it got a camouflage net. Here the SLU was only some fifty yards away and they were well looked after on Dempsey's own orders. He welcomed me warmly and said he was much taken with Ultra, having had no idea that he would be so well informed about German intentions.

Back in England I soon found reason to be grateful that Kluge was a methodical general. After taking over from Rundstedt he had a good look at the various formations under his command; listed them carefully and sent the inventory back to the OKW and the Army HQ in Berlin. His signal, which we were able to pick up, was especially useful since it provided up-to-date information about the actual strength of the various units, and also indicated the extent of the German losses. No doubt he had been warned by Rommel that Hitler had a habit of ordering attacks by non-existent or non-operational units, so it was as well to start off on the right foot. Moreover, his signal revealed that the Fifth Panzer Army had even fewer serviceable tanks than we had estimated.

Bradley finally captured St Lo on 17 July. Hausser then signalled to Rommel for permission to retire II Parachute Corps and we were puzzled when there was no reply. We had been expecting the usual uncompromising 'no withdrawal' order from Rommel. The Parachute Corps, however, did withdraw. It transpired that Rommel's car had been shot up by an Allied aircraft, and his Chief of Staff had telephoned Hausser instructing him to take whatever action he considered best. For me it was like abruptly losing a pen pal, since I had been reading his signals ever since May 1940, and his direct access to Hitler had been of supreme value to us. The story of his implication in the 20 July bomb plot and his subsequent forced suicide are too well known to need retelling.

Now that Bradley was moving into St Lo, Montgomery was once more required to bring pressure on Caen to keep the Panzers away from the Americans, for at last the planned break-out by the United States First Army was possible. Attacks by the British and Canadians were so successful that by 18 July the whole of Caen was cleared of the enemy. The success of Montgomery's strategy was amply confirmed by signals revealing that the two SS Panzer Divisions, the 11th and the 12th, which had been sent from Poland to join the Seventh Army facing Bradley, were now ordered to be kept at Caen. So there remained nine armoured divisions facing the British and Canadians. They were not up to strength, but it was a formidable force of armour.

Chapter 28

VICTORY

On 20 July 1944 the attempt on Hitler's life at Rastenburg was announced over the ordinary wireless. That the majority of German generals wanted Hitler dead was hardly surprising: they had been able to see the approaching end of the Third Reich for some time. Hitler's escape from the Rastenburg bomb seemed to restore his belief in his ability to perform his own miracles of strategy, for which his hard-pressed armies in Normandy had been waiting.

Operation *Cobra*, the codename for Bradley's break-out, struck on 25 July. That evening Kluge signalled to the OKW: 'As from this moment the front has burst.' I phoned the signal over to the Prime Minister, who I knew would be waiting anxiously for news. He took the call himself, and I heard a quiet grunt of satisfaction. On 27 July German resistance in the lower part of the Cherbourg peninsula was rapidly weakening, so much so that Bradley was able to report to Eisenhower, 'That we are riding high tonight is putting it mildly.' Operation *Cobra* was turning into a rout.

As the Americans advanced, a large pocket of German troops on the left of the German line had been cut off and surrounded. General Hausser ordered them to break out to the south-east. His signal, which we did not pick up was evidently intercepted by Kluge, who, anxious about his already disintegrating left flank, at once signalled orders countermanding Hausser's order for the break-out of the surrounded troops. This signal revealed not only that Kluge was completely out of touch with the battle, but that at last we had got the German command off balance. Thanks to this Ultra signal, General Quesada's fighter bombers had a field day, and only a few of the enemy who escaped the pocket were to get back to their comrades, with all their transport and equipment destroyed.

We soon realised that Kluge was unable to find out what was going on – he was not getting any replies to his signals to Hausser's Seventh Army demanding information. Not until 31 July did Kluge signal to Hitler at OKW that the Americans had occupied Avranches; in fact, they had arrived the day before. Kluge went on to admit that the situation was completely unclear, that the Allied air activities were unprecedented, and that the Americans had ripped open the whole Western Front.

Kluge's admissions were music to our ears. The German line had shattered, Brittany was at the mercy of the Americans, and the road to Paris looked wide open. At last George Patton could abandon his empty camp in Kent, and he was soon leading his Third Army through Avranches. Originally Patton's army had been destined for Brittany, but as he now turned east towards the Seine, he was scenting the open country and speed.

Hitler chose this moment to signal Kluge that he had assumed command of the whole western theatre. We had learned in North Africa and Italy to regard this as excellent news. He next signalled the Todt organisation who were building VI and V2 launching fortresses in the Pas de Calais area, ordering them to move their activities to defensive positions further inland. He then signalled orders to all the units in the west that 'if withdrawal is ordered, all railways, locomotives, bridges and workshops are to be destroyed, and the commanders of the fortress ports are to fight to the last man to deny the ports to the Allies'. It looked as though he was really getting down to business.

On 2 August in an extremely long signal, Hitler instructed Kluge 'not to pay any attention to the American break-out, which will be dealt with later'; he followed this with orders to collect together four of the armoured divisions from the Caen front with sufficient supporting infantry divisions and make a decisive counter-attack to retake Avranches and thus to divide the American forces at the base of the Cherbourg peninsula. Kluge was then to drive the American forces to the north of his armoured thrust back to the sea. Here then was the Führer's master-plan: a repetition of his successful strategy in the 1940 Battle of France. I knew Churchill would want to see Hitler's signal right away and I sent it over to him with a note to say I would let him have any follow-up material as it came in.

Bradley, for whom everything was now going well, was placed in command of the Twelfth Army Group. SHAEF was still down at Portsmouth, and Tedder rang me up to ask if I was certain that Hitler's signal was not a bluff; it was of such importance, he said, that Eisenhower did not want to take any chances. I phoned Hut 3 to check that the original German version was in Hitler's own distinctive style and language. They told me that the signal had without doubt come from Führer headquarters. Tedder was satisfied.

Kluge immediately saw the tremendous risks in Hitler's miracle strategy. The next day, we found that he had had the temerity to reply to his Führer in an equally long signal setting out all the possible consequences of such a move: 'Apart from withdrawing the essential defensive armoured divisions from Caen, such an attack, if not immediately successful, would lay open the whole attacking force to be cut off in the west.' That was just what Eisenhower was thinking, and he had already warned Bradley to be ready to push Patton's Third Army swiftly eastwards so as to be able to move north behind the attacking force; only one corps was to be left behind to clear up in Brittany.

Who was going to win the argument, Hitler or Kluge? Excitement was mounting, not only in London, but in Washington too. Hitler did not keep us waiting long. Next day another long signal came from him in which he had the courtesy to acknowledge Kluge's arguments, but now he said, 'The situation demands bold action. The attack to split the American forces must be carried out.' Kluge must take the risk of temporarily withdrawing the panzer divisions from Caen. Thanks to Kluge's objections, we had already been given three days' warning and Eisenhower now decided to change the whole plan of the broad frontal advance eastward across France, and instead seize the chance to encircle and destroy the bulk of the German armies in the west.

Churchill was elated especially on one occasion when I had to enlarge on a point in one of the signals on the telephone. He was receiving Hitler's signals in London within an hour of Hitler despatching them. Hut 3 at Bletchley had risen to the occasion and, with a supreme effort, had provided the answers for several days running at record speed.

But Kluge was stubborn, and on 5 August he made one more attempt to dissuade Hitler. Churchill had travelled down to Chequers on 4 August which meant I would have a busy weekend on the telephone. Everybody, from Bletchley to the Prime Minister, was deeply involved in the Hitler-Kluge drama and I certainly would not leave the office while it was being played out.

Kluge staked his whole career on trying to stop this attack. In his last signal he pulled no punches and boldly stated that it could only end in disaster. It was not hard to imagine the feelings of this courageous man; one could get a glimmer of his utter hopelessness from his signals.

He must have known it was the end for him anyway. Back now, without even a comment, came the order from the Führer to proceed. Kluge had now no alternative; Eisenhower, too, knew what to do.

When I was reading these last signals over the telephone to Churchill, I sensed his controlled excitement. I think we all felt that this might well be the beginning of the end of the war.

Ultra's security was greatly threatened by all the Allied manoeuvres made in response to Hitler's signals. I therefore sent an instruction to all the SLUs concerned warning them to watch out for commanders whose orders might give away their prior knowledge. In the event, security was excellent.

At first light on 7 August the 4th Panzer Division roared through the forward American road blocks and into the little town of Mortain. Their tremendous momentum took them seven miles beyond the town and then the Allied aircraft started on them. They next ran into Bradley's massed artillery. The panzers were brought to a halt, their commanders bewildered; their tank losses were mounting so rapidly that the panzers began to dig in feverishly around midday. The devastating American artillery fire must have aroused some suspicion that their attack was no surprise, but no evidence of this ever appeared in their signals.

That evening, Kluge sent his situation-report signal to OKW: 'The attack has been brought to a standstill with the loss of over half the tanks.' He went on to say that he proposed to disengage his remaining forces at Mortain to cover the British strike towards Falaise. Hitler signalled straight back: 'I command the attack to be prosecuted daringly and recklessly to the sea, regardless of the risk.' He then instructed Kluge that far from reinforcing General Heinrich Eberbach's remaining panzer group at Falaise he was to 'remove forces from Eberbach and commit them to the Avranches attack, in order to bring about the collapse of the enemy's Normandy front by a thrust into the deep flank and rear of the enemy facing the Seventh Army'. There then followed some rather hysterical rhetoric: 'The greatest daring, determination and imagination must give wings to all echelons of command. Each and every man must believe in victory. Cleaning up in rear areas and in Brittany can wait until later.' If Kluge complied with this order, we might get the lot in the bag.

Winston Churchill must have enjoyed that last signal. Now it was Hitler's turn to rally his nation, and he was giving a rather poor imitation of Churchill's inimitable style.

Kluge duly sent a signal to Eberbach early that evening ordering him to send three of his precious panzer divisions to Mortain. At the same time, General Simonds began the famous Canadian onslaught to try and cut through the German armour guarding the way to Falaise. When the attack began one of Eberbach's panzer divisions had just set out for Mortain, and Kluge immediately cancelled the movement westward of the two others. In the middle of the night, he sent a signal to Hitler informing him that the attacks could not now take place.

Hitler replied to Kluge's signal: 'The front attack has been launched too early and was too weak; a new attack must be launched on 11 August.' (He was now specifying the actual date.) 'A massive attack by several corps to be commanded by Eberbach himself.' Eberbach replied that there could be no attack before 20 August, and on 10 August Kluge signalled OKW that the Americans were moving north to Argentan. For the first time he warned the OKW that he was threatened with envelopment. This was one of the signals that brought home to me the enormous difference that Ultra was making to our operations. We had all known what was happening for the past four days, but Kluge had only just discovered that his worst fears were becoming a reality.

That evening, 10 August, Kluge sent another signal to OKW recommending to Hitler that the Seventh Army should be withdrawn from Mortain and switched against the American thrust from the south. The OKW replied that, although the American thrust required a quick response, Hitler still wanted another attack on Avranches. We noted he did not reply himself. He had obviously got himself out on a limb and did not know how to get back. Now, despite the OKW signal, Hausser began to withdraw his Seventh Army from Mortain. The Hitler myth was not working any more.

With the Americans attacking at Argentan and the Canadians at Falaise, the pocket containing the German armies was being slowly closed. Demonstrating once more his loosening grip on reality, Hitler on the 14th sent a signal to the effect that 'the present situation in the rear of the Army Group is the result of the failure of the attack at Avranches. A further attack is to be launched.' Perhaps the OKW had been too frightened to tell Hitler the truth, as regards both the perilous position of Kluge's Army Group and the state of their armament.

We now know that on the next day, 15 August, Kluge went into the pocket to talk to Hausser and Eberbach and he got lost. We only guessed that something had happened when signals from the Seventh Army were unanswered, and when a little later Kluge's own headquarters were asking the Seventh Army where he was. Already the Allied armies were squeezing the bag to death, as the trapped German armies came to a standstill on the roads crowded and littered with wrecked vehicles and dying men.

A signal was sent to Hitler telling him of Kluge's disappearance, and in the evening Hitler signalled back appointing Hausser temporary Commander in the west and ordering him to destroy the American forces near Argentan which threatened all three armies with encirclement. So, the penny had dropped at last. On the 16th Kluge had evidently turned up, for he soon came on the air again. Later we learned he had spent the day in a ditch with a broken radio; now he signalled OKW, recommending an immediate withdrawal of all forces through the Argentan-Falaise gap. He added that 'hesitation in accepting this recommendation would result in unforeseeable developments'.

As the Führer could not be wrong, he laid the blame on Kluge, and a signal sent to Kluge on the 16th informed him that General Walther Model would take over the armies in the west. Kluge must have known this was the inevitable end of Hitler's mad strategy. That day the Canadians had captured Falaise, and by midnight on 20 August the exit from the bag was finally sealed.

It had been an epic story. Catching signals between Hitler and Kluge which led up to the Battle of Falaise and the destruction of a large part of the German Army in the west were probably Ultra's greatest triumph. The backroom boys at Bletchley had been superb. It was the beginning of the end of the war in the west for Hitler, despite the fact that it was estimated that between twenty and thirty thousand men had escaped east, many of them veteran panzer troops. For Kluge it was the end. He wrote a letter to Hitler which we found after the war. In it he told Hitler the true facts and declared that the grand and daring operational concept ordered by him was impractical to exercise – a moderation of expression worthy of his officer-corps background. On the night of 18 August, the Field Marshal who had dared to question the Führer's orders set off for Germany. He never arrived; he committed suicide on the way.

Chapter 29

THE END OF THE WAR AND AFTER

In the summer of 1944, I had been invited to dine with some friends who lived just off Park Lane. There I sat next to a very lovely girl called Petrea. She was in the WAAF, one of those girls who plotted the enemy raids down in the underground war room at Fighter Command HQ. I made it my business to call in there not long afterwards and arranged to meet her after her watch. Before long I found I had fallen in love with her. By then she had told me that she had had one of those early wartime marriages which had come unstuck, and her husband had gone off to India. I told her of my own marriage break-up.

By December 1944, after the defeat of the German armies in France, I was scheduled to go to India and Australia on Ultra business. We decided that Petrea should write to her estranged husband in India asking for a divorce and that I would visit him out there so that he knew that I was real. It had been a long hot journey from Delhi out to Lucknow where he was stationed, but I was surprised at the cordiality with which I was received. We decided to dine together that night, but to my discomfort I found that he had never received Petrea's letter, so I had to explain the whole thing to him. I suppose this was a civilised way of doing it, but it was difficult.

I saw a great deal of northern India in the short time that I was there, and the memories are vivid. In Delhi my accommodation was a tent in the grounds of a large hotel, where I was looked after by a magnificent Sikh sergeant-major, his breast covered in medals. His pride in looking after my own uniform and keeping it as immaculate as his own was a potent reminder of earlier days of the British Raj. The city was crowded, even the great open spaces of the new Delhi. After a few days I moved to a comfortable hotel in old Delhi and had a car and chauffeur allotted to me. The chauffeur was a Moslem who capitalised on the fact he was driving a senior British officer and took every opportunity to bump into the sacred cows that roamed around, which was not popular with the Hindu population.

Back in London in 1945 there was every hope of ending the war within months. The Tartar hordes of Russia, now equipped with tanks instead of Mongolian ponies, were fulfilling Hitler's horoscope. He had not been able to conquer the Russian Army within his allotted time of two years and I like to believe that this was partly due to the Russians at last taking some note of the Ultra information we were able to send them, though they would never admit it. I heard through Bill de Ropp in Switzerland that General von Reichenau had committed suicide when his plans started to go wrong. After the war it was officially said that he had had a stroke and had died in a Berlin hospital. No doubt the historians will record this as correct. The European war was rapidly drawing to a close and the end came quickly. Hitler was dead and, with him, Ultra.

Petrea and I joined a vast crowd outside Buckingham Palace – everyone was hoarse from cheering and singing. I had missed this wonderful demonstration after the First World War as I did not return from the prison camp until some months later. It was a stirring sight, and we were strangely silent as we walked back across Green Park to lunch at my club in Piccadilly.

Just before the end of the war I had circulated to one or two of my friends a short paper which I had written concerning the post-war civil aviation position in Britain, asserting the point that when Churchill had arranged the lend-lease deal with Roosevelt, the US President had made it a condition that Britain should not build large civil aeroplanes until the war was over. This of course gave the Americans a tremendous lead in the civil aviation business, and I was very anxious that some people at the top, like Lord Beaverbrook and Lord Reith, who was now head of post-war reconstruction, should bend their minds to the subject. Lord Reith had got quite excited about the paper, and I had talked to him a good deal about it. Now with the end of the war I thought that if I could get into the civil aviation business myself, my experience with the government might be of some use. Luckily my good friend Oliver Stanley knew Lord Knollys, who was Chairman of the post-war British Overseas Airways Corporation; I also knew some of the members of the Board. An interview resulted in my being offered a job as an executive of the Corporation.

Another point which had made me determined to leave the Secret Service was that at the end of the war the Air Ministry civil service, who had paid part of my salary but knew nothing of what I had been doing, decided to get me cheap when peace came along. I was informed that I had been made a permanent civil servant at a pretty low grade which would have just about kept me in tobacco. I went to see Arthur Street, the chief civil servant at the Air Ministry and he admitted that even if I worked two further years in the civil service, I should at the end of it have a pension of about £250 a year. I told him that I was going to leave and go to British Overseas Airways. He replied that I could not do that as I was a civil servant; however, I persuaded him that I was determined to do it, and he let me go.

I spent three years as an executive with BOAC, assisting Lord Knollys in his dealings with the government, since BOAC was one of the first nationalised industries, and also helping in the starting up of our flying-boat routes to Australia, South Africa and the USA. Later I spent two years with the Colonial Development Corporation, again assisting the Chairman (first Lord Trefgarne, later Lord Reith) in dealings with the government.

By 1952 both the air travelling and the daily commuting to London from Effingham in Surrey, where we had bought a small house, became too much and my wife reminded me that she would prefer me to live away in the country again.

We bought a small farm looking out over the sea near Kingsbridge in Devon, Petrea's home county. It was about eighty acres, with woodland close by, and it was here that our greatest joy, a baby girl called Sally, completed our happiness.

Farming was now a different proposition from my experiences in the 'hungry twenties' in Gloucestershire. Now, after the war, farm produce was really needed. I bred and fattened endless small pigs on skimmed milk from a nearby creamery and grew corn and young cattle. Petrea learned to milk our one cow, who from time to time made off across the railway level-crossing to her favourite bull on a farm the other side; a phone call from the crossing-keeper helped us to get her back. When Sally was two, a lovely farm near the sea at Stokenham came on the market. It had more acreage and a part of the freshwater lake near the sea at Slapton. The good red Devon soil would grow anything, and it was here that Sally grew up among the sheep and young cattle.

One day in 1972, a man came knocking on our farmhouse door. He told me that he was a journalist and had just come back from America where a friend had told him that I could inform him all about a story called Ultra, the breaking of the German cyphers in the war. I trust I did not bat an eyelid, but invited him in, where I quizzed him on how much he knew about this great secret, which I had never expected to hear about again after the war. He knew virtually nothing but wanted the story for a book he had agreed to write in America.

I felt very strongly that if the story of Ultra was to be made public, then it should be done properly and officially, and I promptly got in touch with Admiral Denning, the head of the D Notice people at the Ministry of Defence. They asked me to meet them in London and after weighing up the whole problem, they agreed that a proper account of the Ultra secret should be published as soon as possible and suggested that as I knew the whole of the distribution and security side (no details of the actual code-breaking side were to be given) I was probably the best person to write it. It was fortunate that the head of the American publishing firm which was to publish the journalist's book was an old Oxford friend, who at once got in touch with me when he heard of the contact the journalist had made with me. He later asked me to let his firm publish my own book. Now the race was on to get the proper version out first. I had the advantage of having the whole story still fresh in my mind, while my writer-friend would have to spend a lot of time trying to get the facts, if he could ever do so.

I bought a tape machine and started talking. I have always been lucky to have a good memory and, when I had dictated the story, I enlisted the help of Robin Denniston, the son of the original head of Bletchley Park, who was now himself an editor at a London publisher, to transcribe the tapes. The completed book was readily accepted by the American publishers in 1974, and was later published not only in Britain, but in every major language in the world – except Chinese.

The sudden change from farmer to author was more than just exciting. For years, up to now, Petrea and I had made ends meet with few extras. Suddenly, there were new motorcars, both for us and our newly grown-up daughter, there were horses, and holidays abroad. There was joy and untold happiness.

Before long Sally decided to move up to Gloucestershire, where she could get more eventing and hunting with her horses. Later she went on to Dorset. However, Petrea and I missed her badly, so in order to be together we moved up to Dorset from our Devon farm. I was getting a bit old for tractor-driving anyway. Kelloways Mill, a lovely old mill-house with the river running through the old mill and around the garden seemed an ideal spot. It had eighteen acres of paddocks for Sally's horses. We built a swimming pool, widened the river to make a trout lake near the house and built a flat for Sally. The family antiques felt they were in the right place at last. The green sandy soil on the clay grew anything one planted. So, with a greenhouse, I was able to grow our own vegetables. At last, in 1982, we felt we had found the ideal house.

By 1985 Sally had met her future husband. But Petrea was not well and then came the terrible news that she had cancer. My darling wife died soon after Christmas in 1986.

Sally duly married and, as I write, her year-old baby girl, despite her big blue eyes and blonde hair, is the image of her lovely grandmother Petrea.

I have always believed that, when it is possible, a story should have a happy ending.

When in 1929, I came home from my fact-finding trip to Africa, I found that my marriage had broken down in my absence. Later, I fell in love with a Gloucestershire girl, but it was all impossible at the time, as I was determined to keep my very young family together for as long as I could. Kathleen was a good deal younger than I; she was very popular and soon married.

Nevertheless, we kept in touch over the years. Now I was alone, and she too had been widowed. We decided to get married.

INDEX